# EVOLVE

## STUDENT'S BOOK

with Digital Pack

Leslie Anne Hendra, Mark Ibbotson,
and Kathryn O'Dell

# 1

CAMBRIDGE
UNIVERSITY PRESS

CAMBRIDGE
UNIVERSITY PRESS & ASSESSMENT

Shaftesbury Road, Cambridge CB2 8EA, United Kingdom

One Liberty Plaza, 20th Floor, New York, NY 10006, USA

477 Williamstown Road, Port Melbourne, VIC 3207, Australia

314–321, 3rd Floor, Plot 3, Splendor Forum, Jasola District Centre, New Delhi – 110025, India

103 Penang Road, #05-06/07, Visioncrest Commercial, Singapore 238467

Cambridge University Press & Assessment is a department of the University of Cambridge.

It furthers the University's mission by disseminating knowledge in the pursuit of education, learning and research at the highest international levels of excellence.

www.cambridge.org
Information on this title: www.cambridge.org/9781009231763



First published with Digital Pack 2022

20 19 18 17 16 15

Printed in Italy by L.E.G.O. S.p.A.

*A catalogue record for this publication is available from the British Library*

ISBN 978-1-009-23167-1 Student's Book with eBook
ISBN 978-1-009-23176-3 Student's Book with Digital Pack
ISBN 978-1-009-23177-0 Student's Book with Digital Pack A
ISBN 978-1-009-23178-7 Student's Book with Digital Pack B
ISBN 978-1-108-40894-3 Workbook with Audio
ISBN 978-1-108-40859-2 Workbook with Audio A
ISBN 978-1-108-41191-2 Workbook with Audio B
ISBN 978-1-108-40512-6 Teacher's Edition with Test Generator
ISBN 978-1-108-41062-5 Presentation Plus
ISBN 978-1-108-41201-8 Class Audio CDs
ISBN 978-1-108-40791-5 Video Resource Book with DVD
ISBN 978-1-009-23149-7 Full Contact with Digital Pack

Additional resources for this publication at www.cambridge.org/evolve

# ACKNOWLEDGMENTS

**The *Evolve* publishers would like to thank the following individuals and institutions who have contributed their time and insights into the development of the course:**

Ivanova Monteros A., **Universidad Tecnológica Equinoccial (UTE)**, Ecuador; Monica Frenzel, **Universidad Andrés Bello**, Chile; Antonio Machuca Montalvo, **Organización The Institute TITUELS, Veracruz**, Mexico; Daniel Martin, **CELLEP**, Brazil, Roberta Freitas, **IBEU**, Brazil; Verónica Nolivos Arellano, Language Coordinator, Quito, Ecuador; Daniel Lowe, **Lowe English Services**, Panama; Maria Araceli Hernández Tovar, **Instituto Tecnológico Superior de San Luis Potosí**, Capital, Mexico; Lenise Butler, **Laureate**, Mexico; Gloria González Meza, **Instituto Politecnico Nacional, ESCA (University)**, Mexico; Miguel Ángel López, **Universidad Europea de Madrid**, Spain; Diego Ribeiro Santos, **Universidade Anhembi Morumbi**, São Paulo, Brazil; Esther Carolina Euceda Garcia, **UNITEC (Universidad Tecnologica Centroamericana)**, Honduras.

**To our student cast, who have contributed their ideas and their time, and who appear throughout this book:**

Anderson Batista, Brazil; Carolina Nascimento Negrão, Brazil; Felipe Martinez Lopez, Mexico; Jee-Hyo Moon, South Korea ; Jinny Lara, Honduras; Josue Lozano, Honduras; Julieth C. Moreno Delgado, Colombia; Larissa Castro, Honduras.

And special thanks to Katy Simpson, teacher and writer at *myenglishvoice.com*; and Raquel Ribeiro dos Santos, EFL teacher, EdTech researcher, blogger, and lecturer.

**Authors' Acknowledgments:**

The authors would like to extend their warmest thanks to all of the team at Cambridge University Press who were involved in creating this course. In particular, they would like to thank Ruby Davies and Robert Williams for their kindness, enthusiasm, and encouragement throughout the writing of the A1 level. They would also like to express their appreciation to Caroline Thiriau, whose understanding and support have been of great value. And they would like to thank Katie La Storia for her dedication and enthusiasm throughout the project.

Kathryn O'Dell would like to thank her parents (and grandparents) for passing down a love for words and stories. She also thanks her husband, Kevin Hurdman, for his loving support.

Leslie Anne Hendra would like to thank Michael Stuart Clark, her *sine qua non*, for his support and encouragement during this and other projects.

Mark Ibbotson would like to thank Aimy and Tom for their patience and understanding as family life was bent and squeezed around the project, and – especially – Nathalie, whose energy and creative solutions made it all possible.

**The authors and publishers acknowledge the following sources of copyright material and are grateful for the permissions granted. While every effort has been made, it has not always been possible to identify the sources of all the material used, or to trace all copyright holders. If any omissions are brought to our notice, we will be happy to include the appropriate acknowledgements on reprinting and in the next update to the digital edition, as applicable.**

**Photo:**

Key: B = Below, BG = Background, BL = Below Left, BR = Below Right, C = Centre, CL = Centre Left, CR = Centre Right, L = Left, R = Right, TC = Top Centre, TL = Top Left, TR = Top Right.

All images are sourced from Getty Images.

p. xvi (listen): Tara Moore/DigitalVision; p. xvi (say): Tara Moore/The Image Bank; p. xvi (write): Kohei Hara/DigitalVision; p. xvi (watch): Felbert+Eickenberg/Stock4B; p. xvi (students), p. 124: Klaus Vedfelt/DigitalVision; p. 1, p. 2 (Gabi), p. 8 (CR), p. 14 (L), p. 36 (email), p. 106 (C): Hero Images; p. 2 (Karina): oscarhdez/iStock/Getty Images Plus; p. 2 (Antonio): Vladimir Godnik; p. 2 (Max): DMEPhotography/iStock/Getty Images Plus; p. 2 (map): Colormos/The Image Bank; p. 2 (network): OktalStudio/DigitalVision Vectors; p. 2 (globe): Image by Catherine MacBride/Moment; p. 4: Tara Moore/Taxi; p. 4, p. 6, p. 22 (living room), p. 24 (lamp), p. 52 (CR), p. 66 (photo 5), p. 68 (2d, 2f, 2i), p. 82 (TC), p. 88, p. 117, p. 120 (fish), p. xvi (read): Westend61; p. 7: ATGImages/iStock Editorial/Getty Images Plus; p. 8 (1.1a): .shock/iStock/Getty Images Plus; p. 8 (1.1b): Carl Olsson/Folio Images; p. 8 (1.1c): Phil Boorman/Cultura; p. 8 (1.1d), p. 54 (college), p. 62 (photo h), p. 74: Caiaimage/Sam Edwards; p. 8 (1.1e): Mark Edward Atkinson/Blend Images; p. 8 (1.1f): Thomas Northcut/DigitalVision; p. 8 (1.1g), p. 36 (man), p. 37, p. 49 (CR): Sam Edwards/Caiaimage; p. 8 (1.1h): Glow Images, Inc/Glow; p. 8 (BR), p. 98 (walk): Alistair Berg/DigitalVision; p. 9 (L): ajr_images/iStock/Getty Images Plus; p. 9 (R): Ivan Evgenyev/Blend Images; pp. 10, 20, 30, 42, 52, 62, 74, 84, 94, 106, 116, 126: Tom Merton/Caiaimage; p. 10 (photo a): Georges De Keerle/Hulton Archive; p. 10 (photo b): Monica Schipper/FilmMagic; p. 10 (photo c): DEA/D. DAGLI ORTI/De Agostini; p. 10 (photo d): Scott Gries/Getty Images Entertainment; p. 10 (photo e, i): Bettmann; p. 10 (photo f): Sgranitz/WireImage; p. 10 (photo g): Christopher Furlong/Getty Images News; p. 10 (photo h): Dan Kitwood/Getty Images Entertainment; p. 10 (photo j): ALFREDO ESTRELLA/AFP; p. 11: Thomas Barwick/Stone; p. 13: Paco Navarro/Blend Images; p. 14 (couple), p. 20: Ronnie Kaufman/Larry Hirshowitz/Blend Images; p. 14 (Erika): Tony Anderson/DigitalVision; p. 14 (boy): Flashpop/Stone; p. 14 (woman): aldomurillo/E+; p. 16: Alyson Aliano/Image Source; p. 17: Richard Jung/Photodisc; p. 18: powerofforever/E+; p. 19: Steve Prezant/Image Source; p. 21, p. 30 (chair): Johner Images; p. 22 (bedroom): svetikd/E+; p. 22 (bathroom): JohnnyGreig/E+; p. 24 (bed): Diane Auckland/ArcaidImages; p. 24 (chair): Daniel Grill; p. 24 (table): Steve Gorton/Dorling Kindersley; p. 24 (desk): pbombaert/Moment; p. 24 (bookcase): Andreas von Einsiedel/Corbis Documentary; p. 24 (couch): Fotosearch; p. 24 (shower): RollingEarth/E+; p. 24 (refrigerator): Karen Moskowitz/The Image Bank; p. 24 (TV), p. 80, p. 114 (woman): Tetra Images; p. 24 (sink): Mark Griffin/EyeEm; p. 24 (rug): Art-Y/E+; p. 25: Hinterhaus Productions/Taxi;p. 26 (coffee): Dobroslav Hadzhiev/iStock/Getty Images Plus; p. 26 (tea): a-poselenov/iStock/Getty Images Plus; p. 26 (sugar): Maximilian Stock Ltd./Photographer's Choice; p. 26 (milk): YelenaYemchuk/iStock/Getty Images Plus; p. 26 (cookie): SvetlanaKoryakova/iStock/Getty Images Plus; p. 27: Shestock/Blend Images; p. 28 (TL), p. 84 (soccer): Hinterhaus Productions/DigitalVision; p. 29 (TR): Lilly Bloom/Cultura; p. 30 (TL), p. 108 (book): PeopleImages/DigitalVision; p. 30 (sofa): jakkapan21/iStock/Getty Images Plus; p. 30 (bookcase): Hany Rizk/EyeEm; p. 30 (couch): Nicholas Eveleigh/Photodisc; p. 30 (bed): Artem Perevozchikov/iStock/Getty Images Plus; p. 30 (desk): tifonimages/iStock/Getty Images Plus; p. 30 (chair): SKrow/iStock/Getty Images Plus; p. 30 (refrigerator): Customdesigner/iStock/Getty Images Plus; p. 30 (TV1): Dovapi/iStock/Getty Images Plus; p.30 (TV2): Jorg Greuel/Photographer's Choice RF; p. 30 (dining), p. 34 (CR): s-cphoto/E+; p. 30 (frame): Matthias Clamer/Stone; p.30 (rug): Chaloner Woods/Hulton Archive; p. 30 (lamp): xxmmxx/E+; p. 30 (plant), p. 61 (BG), p.66 (photo 2), p. 72 (cat), p. 118 (bread): Dorling Kindersley; p. 33: VCG/Getty Images News; p. 34 (tablet): daboost/iStock/Getty Images Plus; p. 34 (earphone), p. 72 (cat), p. 118 (tomato): Dave King/Dorling Kindersleyl; p. 34 (phone): Lonely_/iStock/Getty Images Plus; p. 34 (laptop): scanrail/iStock/Getty Images Plus; p. 34 (smartwatch): Nerthuz/iStock/Getty Images Plus; p. 35: Images By Tang Ming Tung/DigitalVision; p. 36 (cellphone): hocus-focus/iStock/Getty Images Plus; p. 36 (chat): David Malan/The Image Bank; p. 36 (tab, text): ymgerman/iStock Editorial/Getty Images Plus; p. 36 (game): Keith Bell/Hemera/Getty Images Plus; p. 36 (phone): Bloomberg; p. 36 (symbol): jaroszpilewski/iStock/Getty Images Plus; p. 38: ferrantraite/E+; p. 39: John Fedele/Blend Images; p. 41 (C): Adrin Gmez/EyeEm; p. 41 (CR): Tim Hawley/Photographer's Choice RF; p. 42 (TR): Lilly Roadstones/Taxi; p. 42 (BR): Caiaimage/Tom Merton; p. 43: Digital Vision./Photodisc; p. 44 (walk): Inti St Clair/Blend Images; p. 44 (run): JGI/Tom Grill/Blend Images; p. 44 (work): Squaredpixels/E+; p. 44 (study): Geber86/E+; p. 44 (soccer): Thomas Barwick/ Taxi; p. 47: David Stuart/Stockbyte; p. 48: Christopher Malcolm/The Image Bank; p. 49 (B): Wavebreakmedia/iStock/Getty Images Plus; p. 51: Juanmonino/E+; p. 52 (man): Jacqueline Veissid/Blend Images; p. 52 (commuters): Ovidio Ferreira/EyeEm; p. 53: David Nunuk/All Canada Photos; p. 54 (mall), p. 62 (photo c): Henglein And Steets/Photolibrary; p. 54 (store): m-imagephotography/iStock/Getty Images Plus; p. 54 (hotel): John Warburton-Lee/AWL Images; p. 54 (school): Robert Daly/Caiaimage; p. 54 (restaurant): Tom Merton/OJO Images; p. 54 (supermarket): David Nevala/Aurora; p. 54 (museum): Eric VANDEVILLE/Gamma-Rapho; p. 54 (hospital), p. 62 (photo g): Steven Frame/Hemera/Getty Images Plus; p. 54 (café): Klaus Vedfelt/Taxi; p. 54 (bookstore): M_a_y_a/E+; p. 54 (thetre), p. 62 (photo e): Clara Li/EyeEm; p. 54 (park), p. 62 (photo a): Eric You/EyeEm; p. 54 (zoo): John Hart/EyeEm; p.55: fotoVoyager/E+; p. 56 (1a): Aimin Tang/Photographer's Choice; p. 56 (1b): Barry Kusuma/Stockbyte; p. 56 (1c): Alan_Lagadu/iStock/Getty Images Plus; p. 56 (1d): swedewah/E+; p. 56 (1e): Witold Skrypczak/Lonely Planet Images; p. 56 (statue): Jeremy Walker/Photographer's Choice; p. 57: cinoby/E+; p. 58: JGI/Jamie Grill/Blend Images; p. 59: Julia Davila-Lampe/Moment Open; p. 60 (BG): Macduff Everton/Iconica; p. 60 (CR): Cesar Okada/E+; p. 60 (TL): Neil Beckerman/The Image Bank; p. 61 (waterfall): Kimie Shimabukuro/Moment Open; p. 61 (Christ): joSon/The Image Bank; p. 61 (flower): SambaPhoto/Cristiano Burmester/SambaPhotol; p. 61 (monkey): Kryssia Campos/Moment; p. 62 (BG): Planet Observer/UIG/Universal Images Group; p. 62 (photo b): Bernard Jaubert/Canopy; p. 62 (photo d): Caiaimage/Robert Daly/OJO+; p. 62 (photo f): Gary Yeowell/The Image Bank; p. 65: jameslee999/Vetta; p. 66 (photo 1): Phil Boorman/The Image Bank; p. 66 (photo 3): Vincent Besnault/The Image Bank; p. 66 (photo 4): David Zach/Stone; p. 66 (photo 6): LM Productions/Photodisc; p. 67: Jonathan Knowles/The Image Bank; p. 68 (2a, 2b): alvarez/E+; p. 68 (2c): Samuelsson, Kristofer; p. 68 (2e): Plume Creative/DigitalVision; p. 68 (2g): Jordan Siemens/Taxi; p. 68 (2h): Ezra Bailey/Taxi; p. 69: Lorentz Gullachsen/The Image Bank; p. 70 (BL): Robert Kneschke/EyeEm; p. 70 (BG), p. 108 (beautiful): Dougal Waters/DigitalVision; p. 71: Flavio Edreira/EyeEm; p. 72: Lane Oatey/Blue Jean Images; p. 73: Dave Nagel/Taxi; p. 75: Mint Images RF; p. 76 (surf): Christian Kober/AWL Images; p. 76 (skateboard): yanik88/iStock/Getty Images Plus; p. 76 (snowboarding): Maximilian Groß/EyeEm; p. 76 (draw): Ruth Jenkinson/Dorling Kindersley; p. 76 (boys): Resolution Productions/Blend Images; p. 76 (paint): Glowimages; p. 76 (sing): Kyle Monk/Blend Images; p. 76 9(dance): catalinere/iStock/Getty Images Plus; p. 76 (guitar): Justin Case/Taxi; p. 76 (swim): pixdeluxe/E+; p. 76 (wheel): Philip Gatward/Dorling Kindersley; p. 76 (CR), p. 121: Jose Luis Pelaez Inc/Blend Images; p. 77: Lilly Roadstones/The Image Bank; p. 78: Reza Estakhrian/Iconica; p. 79: PeopleImages/E+; p. 81: Allison Michael Orenstein/The Image Bank; p. 82 (TL): Kristy-Anne Glubish; p. 82 (TR): PhonlamaiPhoto/iStock/Getty Images Plus; p. 84 (photo 1): ibrahimaslann/iStock Editorial/Getty Images Plus; p. 84 (photo 2), p. xvi (teacher): Marc Romanelli/Blend Images; p. 84 (photo 3): Yew! Images/Image Source; p. 84 (photo 4): PaulBiryukov/iStock/Getty Images Plus; p. 85: Johannes Spahn/EyeEm; p. 86 (airplane): Jan Stromme/The Image Bank; p. 86 (woman): Caroline Schiff/Taxi; p. 86 (girl): Peathegee Inc/Blend Images; p. 86 (country): Instants/E+; p. 86 (parrot): Busakorn Pongparnit/Moment; p. 86 (boat): Richard Cummins/Lonely Planet Images; p. 86 (park): Lidija Kamansky/Moment Open; p. 87 (C): Waring Abbott/Michael Ochs Archives; p. 87 (hikers): Debra Brash/Perspectives; p. 87 (Lake): Jeff Greenberg/Universal Images Group; p. 89: Cláudio Policarpo/EyeEm; p. 90: Image Source; p. 92: Anna Gorin/Moment; p. 93: hadynyah/E+; p. 94 (Jim): John Lund/Marc Romanelli/Blend Images; p. 93 (Flo): Blend Images - Erik Isakson/Brand X Pictures; p. 94 (Carter): Alexander Robinson/Blend Images; p. 97: Darryl Leniuk/DigitalVision; p. 98 (TL): Chan Srithaweeporn/Moment; p. 98 (art): Randy Faris/Corbis/VCG; p. 98 (dinner, shopping): Cultura RM Exclusive/Frank and Helena; p. 98 (airport): Maskot; p. 98 (picnic): Uwe Krejci/DigitalVision; p. 99: Billy Hustace/Corbis Documentary; p. 100 (fall): Shobeir Ansari/Moment; p. 100 (summer): AL Hedderly/Moment; p. 100 (spring): Lelia Valduga; p. 100 (rainy): Chalabala/iStock/Getty Images Plus; p. 100 (dry): skodonnell/E+; p. 101: Julia Davila-Lampe/Moment; p. 102: Caiaimage/Chris Ryan; p. 103: filadendron/E+; p. 104: Rudimencial/iStock/Getty Images Plus; p. 105: ©Leonardo Muniz/Moment; 106 (TL): Toshi Sasaki/Photodisc; p. 106 (TC): skynesher/iStock/Getty Images Plus; p. 106 (TR): AJ_Watt/E+; p. 106 (CL): Luke Stettner/Photonica; p. 106 (CR): Mike Kemp/Blend Images; p. 107: Shanina/iStock/Getty Images Plus; p. 107 (TR): Simon Winnall/Taxi; p. 108 (kart): Images Of Our Lives/Archive Photos; p.108 (awful): PM Images/Stone; p. 108 (dog): Kevin Kozicki/Image Source; p. 108 (baby, quiet baby): Emma Kim/Cultura; p. 108 (fast car): Martin Barraud/Caiaimage; p. 108 (slow car): Michael Mrozek/EyeEm; p. 108 (shoe): Jeffrey Coolidge/The Image Bank; p. 108 (vacation): swissmediavision/E+; p. 109: Satoshi Yamada/EyeEm; p. 110: NexTser/iStock/Getty Images Plus; p. 111: real444/E+; p. 112: Mark Cuthbert/UK Press; p. 113: Mike Powell/Stone; p. 114 (toy car): Peter Zander/Photolibrary; p. 114 (shoe): Willer Amorim/EyeEm; 114 (comic): Bernd Vogel/Corbis; p. 115: George Steinmetz/Corbis Documentary; p. 116: Shan Shui/DigitalVision; p. 118 (chicken): Floortje/E+; p. 118 (coconut): RedHelga/E+; p. 118 (pineapple): Moodboard Stock Photography Ltd./Canopy; p. 118 (apple): t_kimura/E+; p. 118 (soup): David Marsden/Photolibrary; p. 118 (butter): SvetlanaK/iStock/Getty Images Plus; p. 118 (banana): Andy Crawford/Dorling Kindersley; p. 118 (cheese): Steven Mark Needham/Corbis Documentary; p. 118 (potato): jerryhat/E+; p. 114 (beef): Frank Bean/UpperCut Images; p. 118 (sandwich), p. 125: LauriPatterson/E+; p. 118 (orange): julichka/E+; p. 118 (lamb): pmphoto/iStock/Getty Images Plus; p. 118 (crackers): Bernard Prost/StockFood Creative; p. 118 (CR): Stephanie Leong/EyeEm; p. 119: Lumina Images/Blend Images; p. 120 (steak): Joy Skipper/Photolibrary; p. 120 (pizza): Nomadsoul1/iStock/Getty Images Plus; p. 120 (beans): Angela Bragato/EyeEm; p. 120 (chocolate): Angela Bragato/EyeEm; p. 120 (cookies): DigiPub/Moment; p. 120 (water): Retno Ayu Adiati/EyeEm; p. 122: Justin Case/The Image Bank; p. 123: Maarten De Beer/EyeEm; p.124 (Chinese): Naltik/iStock/Getty Images Plus; p. 124 (Mexican): rez-art/iStock/Getty Images Plus; p. 124 (Italian): Jon Spaull/Perspectives; p. 126: andresr/E+; p. 143 (living room): imagenavi; p. 143 (kitchen): Glasshouse Images/Corbis.

The following images are sourced from other libraries:

p. 76 (music): otnaydur/Shutterstock; p. 84 (CR): AlanHaynes.com/Alamy Stock Photo.

Front cover photography by Arctic-Images/The Image Bank/Getty Images.

Illustrations by: Ana Djordevic (Astound US) p. 5; Alejandro Mila (Sylvie Poggio Artists Agency) pp. 23, 30; Joanna Kerr (New Division) pp. 44, 50, 100; Dusan Lakicevic (Beehive Illustration) pp. 24, 46, 88, 90, 91.

Audio production by CityVox, New York.

# EVOLVE

## SPEAKING MATTERS

EVOLVE is a six-level American English course for adults and young adults, taking students from beginner to advanced levels (CEFR A1 to C1).

Drawing on insights from language teaching experts and real students, EVOLVE is a general English course that gets students speaking with confidence.

This student-centered course covers all skills and focuses on the most effective and efficient ways to make progress in English.

**Confidence in teaching.**
**Joy in learning.**

### Better Learning WITH EVOLVE

Better Learning is our simple approach where insights we've gained from research have helped shape content that drives results. Language evolves, and so does the way we learn. This course takes a flexible, student-centered approach to English language teaching.

# Meet our student contributors

Videos and ideas from real students feature throughout the Student's Book.

Our student contributors describe themselves in three words.

**LARISSA CASTRO**
*Friendly, honest, happy*
Centro Universitario Tecnológico, Honduras

**JINNY LARA**
*Free your mind*
Centro Universitario Tecnológico, Honduras

**CAROLINA NASCIMENTO NEGRÃO**
*Nice, determined, hard-working*
Universidade Anhembi Morumbi, Brazil

**JOSUE LOZANO**
*Enthusiastic, cheerful, decisive*
Centro Universitario Tecnológico, Honduras

**JULIETH C. MORENO DELGADO**
*Decisive, reliable, creative*
Fundación Universitaria Monserrate, Colombia

**ANDERSON BATISTA**
*Resilient, happy, dreamer*
Universidade Anhembi Morumbi, Brazil

**FELIPE MARTINEZ LOPEZ**
*Reliable, intrepid, sensitive*
Universidad del Valle de México, Mexico

**JEE-HYO MOON (JUNE)**
*Organized, passionate, diligent*
Mission College, USA

# Student-generated content

EVOLVE is the first course of its kind to feature real student-generated content. We spoke to over 2,000 students from all over the world about the topics they would like to discuss in English and in what situations they would like to be able to speak more confidently.

The ideas are included throughout the Student's Book and the students appear in short videos responding to discussion questions.

### INSIGHT

Research shows that achievable speaking role models can be a powerful motivator.

### CONTENT

Bite-sized videos feature students talking about topics in the Student's Book.

### RESULT

Students are motivated to speak and share their ideas.

# "It's important to provide learners with interesting or stimulating topics."

Teacher, Mexico (Global Teacher Survey, 2017)

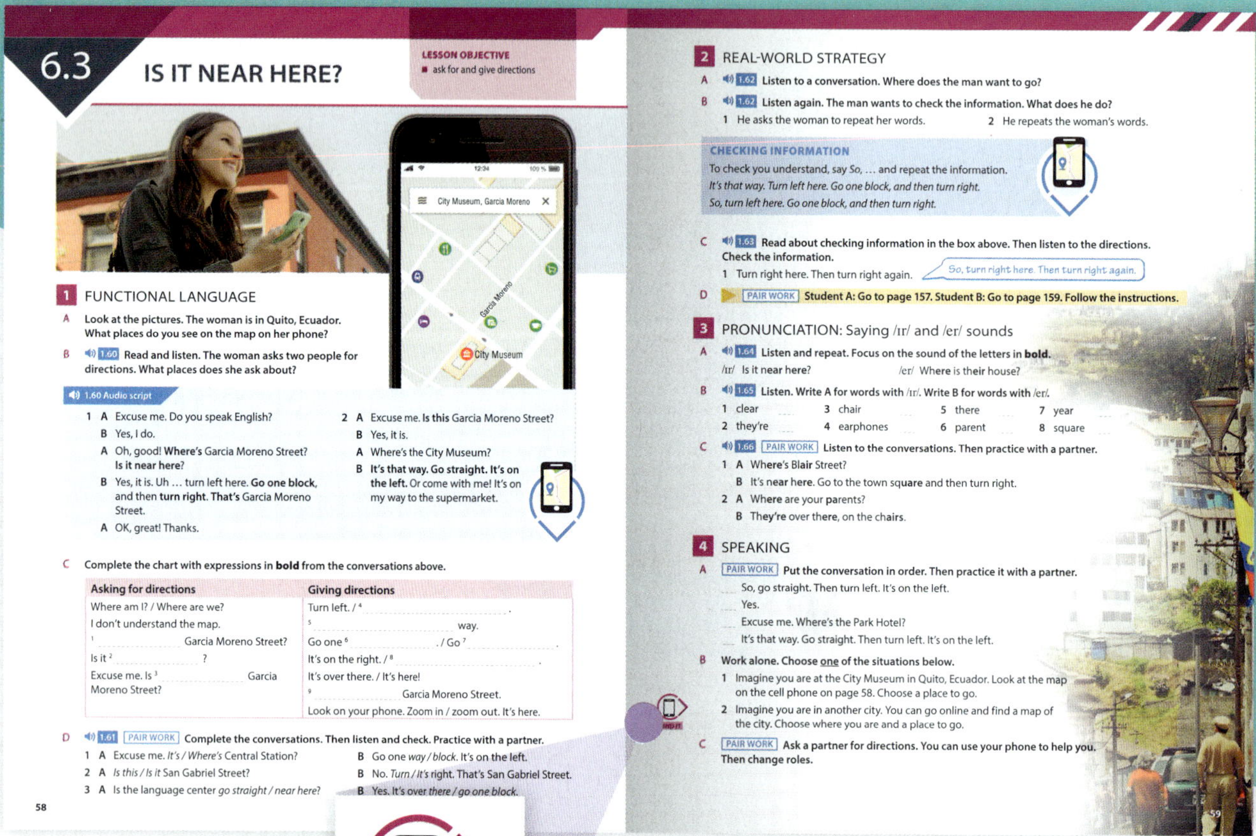

6.3 IS IT NEAR HERE?

LESSON OBJECTIVE
- ask for and give directions

1 FUNCTIONAL LANGUAGE

A Look at the pictures. The woman is in Quito, Ecuador. What places do you see on the map on her phone?

B 1.60 Read and listen. The woman asks two people for directions. What places does she ask about?

1.60 Audio script

1 A Excuse me. Do you speak English?
B Yes, I do.
A Oh, good! **Where's** Garcia Moreno Street? **Is it near here?**
B Yes, it is. Uh … turn left here. **Go one block**, and then **turn right**. **That's** Garcia Moreno Street.
A OK, great! Thanks.

2 A Excuse me. **Is this** Garcia Moreno Street?
B Yes, it is.
A Where's the City Museum?
B **It's that way. Go straight. It's on the left.** Or come with me! It's on my way to the supermarket.

C Complete the chart with expressions in **bold** from the conversations above.

| Asking for directions | Giving directions |
|---|---|
| Where am I? / Where are we? | Turn left. / [4] ______. |
| I don't understand the map. | [5] ______ way. |
| [1] ______ Garcia Moreno Street? | Go one [6] ______. / Go [7] ______. |
| Is it [2] ______? | It's on the right. / [8] ______. |
| Excuse me. Is [3] ______ Garcia Moreno Street? | It's over there. / It's here! |
| | [9] ______ Garcia Moreno Street. |
| | Look on your phone. Zoom in / zoom out. It's here. |

D 1.61 PAIR WORK Complete the conversations. Then listen and check. Practice with a partner.

1 A Excuse me. *It's / Where's* Central Station? B Go one *way / block*. It's on the left.
2 A *Is this / Is it* San Gabriel Street? B No. *Turn / It's* right. That's San Gabriel Street.
3 A Is the language center *go straight / near here*? B Yes. It's over *there / go one block*.

58

2 REAL-WORLD STRATEGY

A 1.62 Listen to a conversation. Where does the man want to go?

B 1.62 Listen again. The man wants to check the information. What does he do?
1 He asks the woman to repeat her words. 2 He repeats the woman's words.

CHECKING INFORMATION
To check you understand, say *So, …* and repeat the information.
*It's that way. Turn left here. Go one block, and then turn right.*
*So, turn left here. Go one block, and then turn right.*

C 1.63 Read about checking information in the box above. Then listen to the directions. Check the information.
1 Turn right here. Then turn right again. *So, turn right here. Then turn right again.*

D PAIR WORK Student A: Go to page 157. Student B: Go to page 159. Follow the instructions.

3 PRONUNCIATION: Saying /ɪr/ and /er/ sounds

A 1.64 Listen and repeat. Focus on the sound of the letters in **bold**.
/ɪr/ Is it near here? /er/ Where is their house?

B 1.65 Listen. Write A for words with /ɪr/. Write B for words with /er/.
1 clear ___ 3 chair ___ 5 there ___ 7 year ___
2 they're ___ 4 earphones ___ 6 parent ___ 8 square ___

C 1.66 PAIR WORK Listen to the conversations. Then practice with a partner.
1 A Where's Blair Street?
B It's near here. Go to the town square and then turn right.
2 A Where are your parents?
B They're over there, on the chairs.

4 SPEAKING

A PAIR WORK Put the conversation in order. Then practice it with a partner.
___ So, go straight. Then turn left. It's on the left.
___ Yes.
___ Excuse me. Where's the Park Hotel?
___ It's that way. Go straight. Then turn left. It's on the left.

B Work alone. Choose one of the situations below.
1 Imagine you are at the City Museum in Quito, Ecuador. Look at the map on the cell phone on page 58. Choose a place to go.
2 Imagine you are in another city. You can go online and find a map of the city. Choose where you are and a place to go.

C PAIR WORK Ask a partner for directions. You can use your phone to help you. Then change roles.

59

FIND IT

# Find it

## INSIGHT

Research with hundreds of teachers and students across the globe revealed a desire to expand the classroom and bring the real world in.

## CONTENT

*Find it* are smartphone activities that allow students to bring live content into the class and personalize the learning experience with research and group activities.

## RESULT

Students engage in the lesson because it is meaningful to them.

# Designed for success

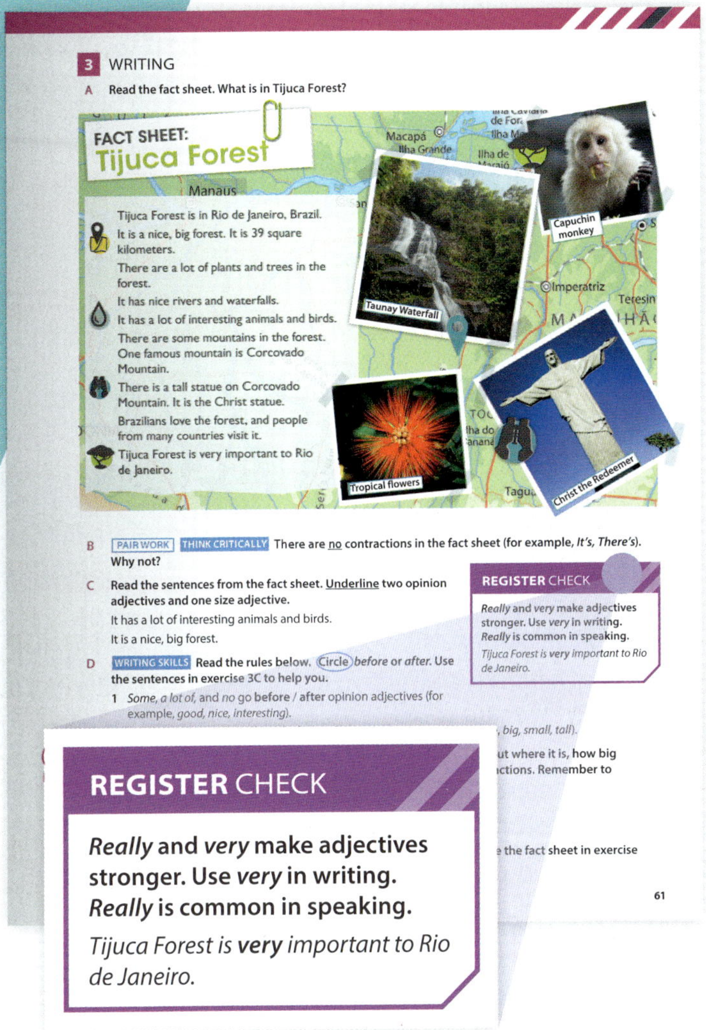


## Pronunciation

### INSIGHT

Research shows that only certain aspects of pronunciation actually affect comprehensibility and inhibit communication.

### CONTENT

EVOLVE focuses on the aspects of pronunciation that most affect communication.

### RESULT

Students understand more when listening and can be clearly understood when they speak.

## Register check

### INSIGHT

Teachers report that their students often struggle to master the differences between written and spoken English.

### CONTENT

*Register check* draws on research into the Cambridge English Corpus and highlights potential problem areas for learners.

### RESULT

Students transition confidently between written and spoken English and recognize different levels of formality as well as when to use them appropriately.

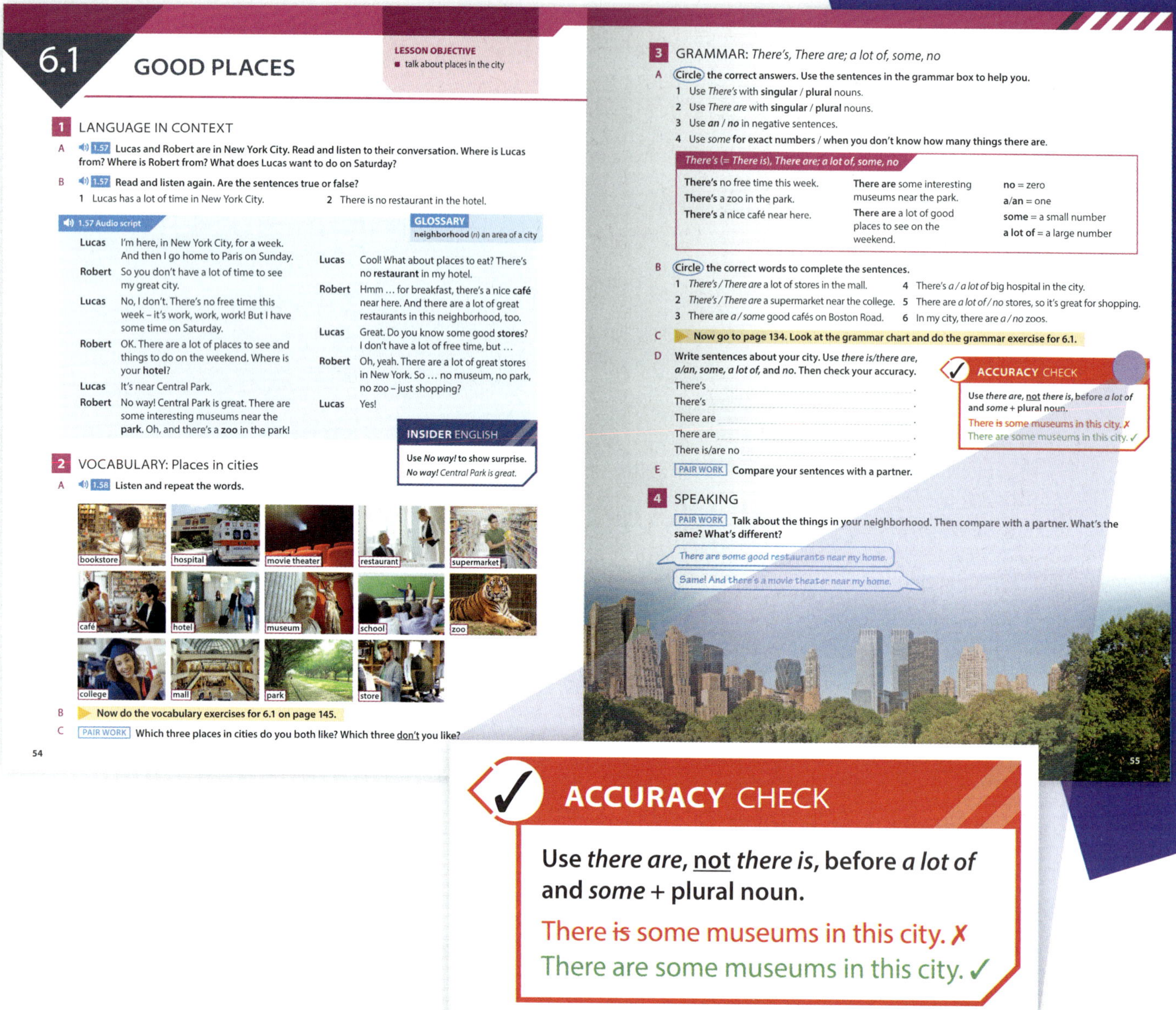

6.1 GOOD PLACES

LESSON OBJECTIVE
- talk about places in the city

1 LANGUAGE IN CONTEXT

A 1.57 Lucas and Robert are in New York City. Read and listen to their conversation. Where is Lucas from? Where is Robert from? What does Lucas want to do on Saturday?

B 1.57 Read and listen again. Are the sentences true or false?

1 Lucas has a lot of time in New York City.
2 There is no restaurant in the hotel.

1.57 Audio script

GLOSSARY
**neighborhood** (*n*) an area of a city

**Lucas** I'm here, in New York City, for a week. And then I go home to Paris on Sunday.
**Robert** So you don't have a lot of time to see my great city.
**Lucas** No, I don't. There's no free time this week – it's work, work, work! But I have some time on Saturday.
**Robert** OK. There are a lot of places to see and things to do on the weekend. Where is your **hotel**?
**Lucas** It's near Central Park.
**Robert** No way! Central Park is great. There are some interesting museums near the **park**. Oh, and there's a **zoo** in the park!
**Lucas** Cool! What about places to eat? There's no **restaurant** in my hotel.
**Robert** Hmm … for breakfast, there's a nice **café** near here. And there are a lot of great restaurants in this neighborhood, too.
**Lucas** Great. Do you know some good **stores**? I don't have a lot of free time, but …
**Robert** Oh, yeah. There are a lot of great stores in New York. So … no museum, no park, no zoo – just shopping?
**Lucas** Yes!

INSIDER ENGLISH
Use *No way!* to show surprise.
*No way! Central Park is great.*

2 VOCABULARY: Places in cities

A 1.58 Listen and repeat the words.

bookstore, hospital, movie theater, restaurant, supermarket, café, hotel, museum, school, zoo, college, mall, park, store

B Now do the vocabulary exercises for 6.1 on page 145.

C PAIR WORK Which three places in cities do you both like? Which three don't you like?

54

3 GRAMMAR: *There's, There are; a lot of, some, no*

A Circle the correct answers. Use the sentences in the grammar box to help you.

1 Use *There's* with **singular / plural** nouns.
2 Use *There are* with **singular / plural** nouns.
3 Use ***an / no*** in negative sentences.
4 Use *some* **for exact numbers / when you don't know how many things there are.**

*There's (= There is), There are; a lot of, some, no*

| | | |
|---|---|---|
| **There's** no free time this week. | **There are** some interesting museums near the park. | **no** = zero |
| **There's** a zoo in the park. | **There are** a lot of good places to see on the weekend. | **a/an** = one |
| **There's** a nice café near here. | | **some** = a small number |
| | | **a lot of** = a large number |

B Circle the correct words to complete the sentences.

1 *There's / There are* a lot of stores in the mall.
2 *There's / There are* a supermarket near the college.
3 There are *a / some* good cafés on Boston Road.
4 There's *a / a lot of* big hospital in the city.
5 There are *a lot of / no* stores, so it's great for shopping.
6 In my city, there are *a / no* zoos.

C Now go to page 134. Look at the grammar chart and do the grammar exercise for 6.1.

D Write sentences about your city. Use *there is/there are, a/an, some, a lot of,* and *no*. Then check your accuracy.

There's ______.
There's ______.
There are ______.
There are ______.
There is/are no ______.

ACCURACY CHECK
Use *there are*, not *there is*, before *a lot of* and *some* + plural noun.
There ~~is~~ some museums in this city. ✗
There are some museums in this city. ✓

E PAIR WORK Compare your sentences with a partner.

4 SPEAKING

PAIR WORK Talk about the things in your neighborhood. Then compare with a partner. What's the same? What's different?

There are some good restaurants near my home.
Same! And there's a movie theater near my home.

55

## ✓ ACCURACY CHECK

Use *there are*, not *there is*, before *a lot of* and *some* + plural noun.

There ~~is~~ some museums in this city. ✗

There are some museums in this city. ✓

# Accuracy check

## INSIGHT

Some common errors can become fossilized if not addressed early on in the learning process.

## CONTENT

*Accuracy check* highlights common learner errors (based on unique research into the Cambridge Learner Corpus) and can be used for self-editing.

## RESULT

Students avoid common errors in their written and spoken English.

"The presentation is very clear and there are plenty of opportunities for student practice and production."

Jason Williams, Teacher, Notre Dame Seishin University, Japan

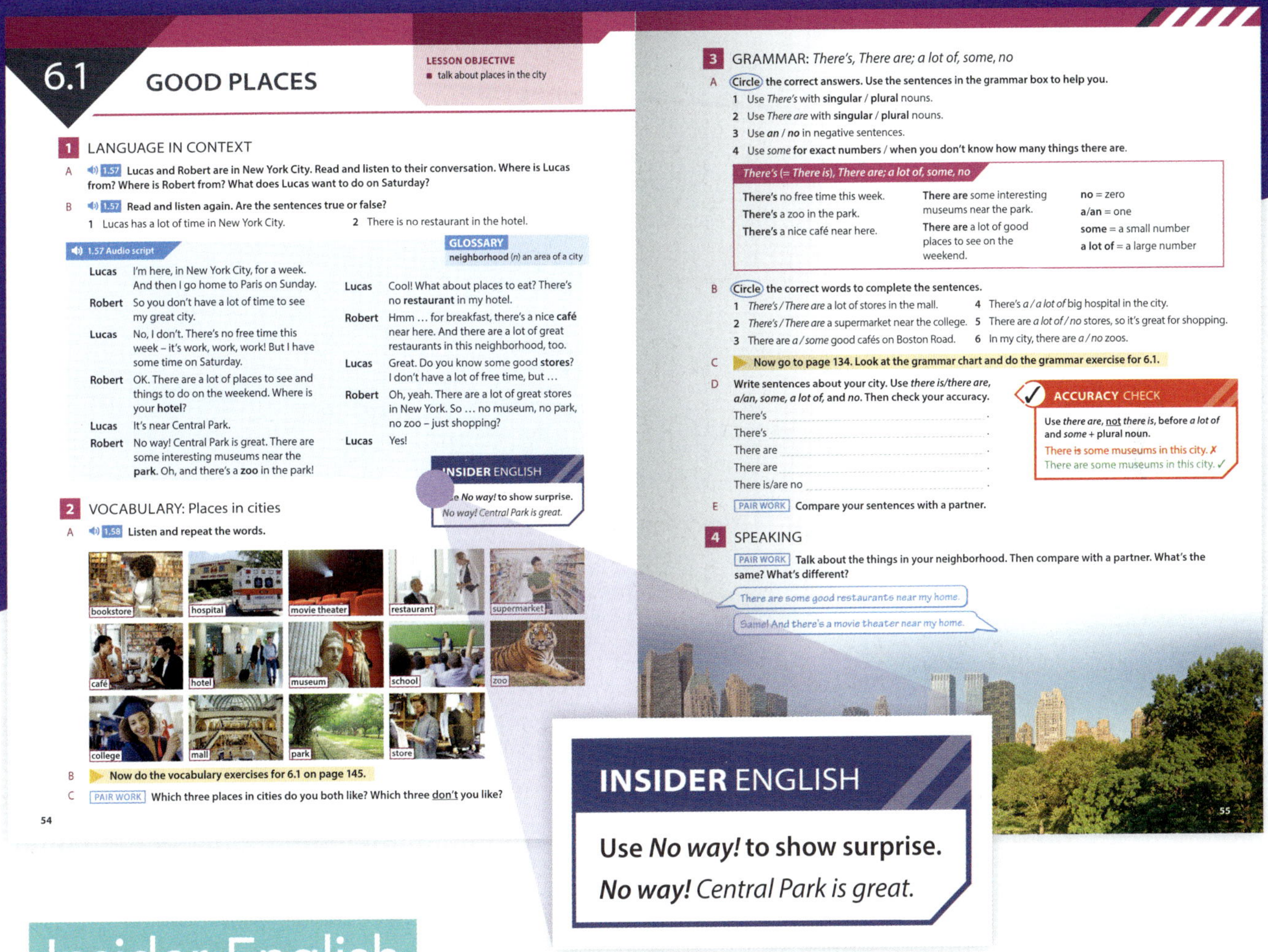


## Insider English

### INSIGHT

Even in a short exchange, idiomatic language can inhibit understanding.

### CONTENT

*Insider English* focuses on the informal language and colloquial expressions frequently found in everyday situations.

### RESULT

Students are confident in the real world.

# You spoke. We listened.

Students told us that speaking is the most important skill for them to master, while teachers told us that finding speaking activities which engage their students and work in the classroom can be challenging.

That's why EVOLVE has a whole lesson dedicated to speaking: Lesson 5, *Time to speak*.

# Time to speak

## INSIGHT

Speaking ability is how students most commonly measure their own progress, but is also the area where they feel most insecure. To be able to fully exploit speaking opportunities in the classroom, students need a safe speaking environment where they can feel confident, supported, and able to experiment with language.

## CONTENT

*Time to Speak* is a unique lesson dedicated to developing speaking skills and is based around immersive tasks which involve information sharing and decision making.

## RESULT

*Time to speak* lessons create a buzz in the classroom where speaking can really thrive, evolve, and take off, resulting in more confident speakers of English.

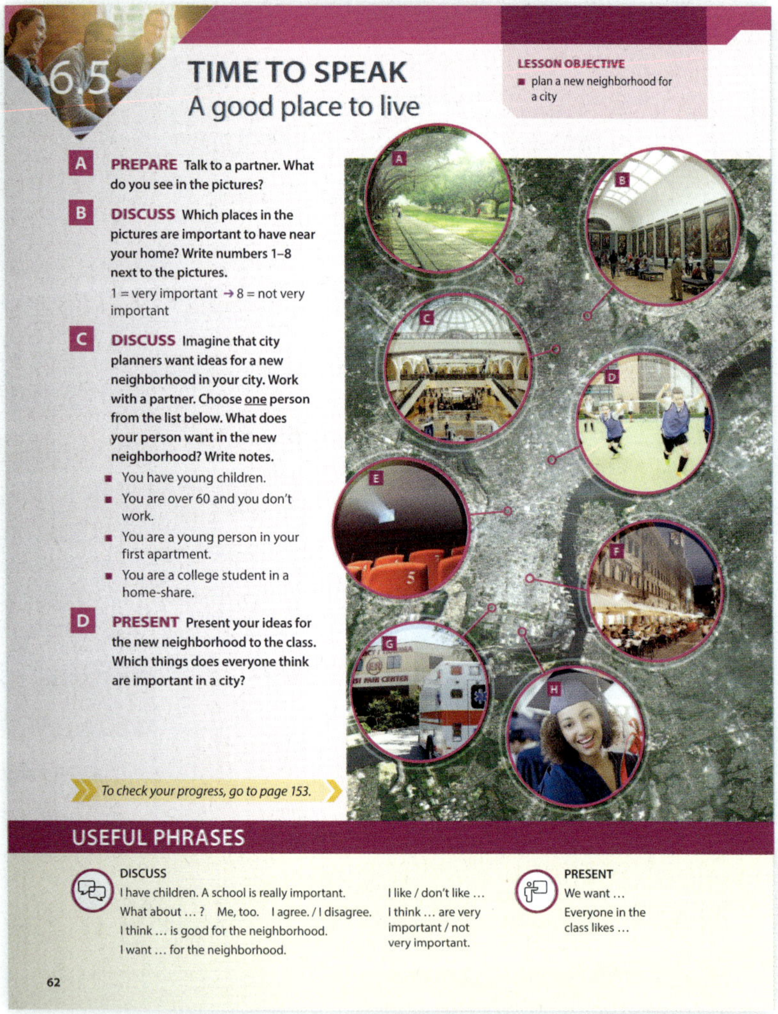

6.5 **TIME TO SPEAK**
A good place to live

**LESSON OBJECTIVE**
- plan a new neighborhood for a city

**A PREPARE** Talk to a partner. What do you see in the pictures?

**B DISCUSS** Which places in the pictures are important to have near your home? Write numbers 1–8 next to the pictures.
1 = very important → 8 = not very important

**C DISCUSS** Imagine that city planners want ideas for a new neighborhood in your city. Work with a partner. Choose one person from the list below. What does your person want in the new neighborhood? Write notes.
- You have young children.
- You are over 60 and you don't work.
- You are a young person in your first apartment.
- You are a college student in a home-share.

**D PRESENT** Present your ideas for the new neighborhood to the class. Which things does everyone think are important in a city?

*To check your progress, go to page 153.*

**USEFUL PHRASES**

**DISCUSS**
I have children. A school is really important.
What about … ? Me, too. I agree. / I disagree.
I think … is good for the neighborhood.
I want … for the neighborhood.
I like / don't like …
I think … are very important / not very important.

**PRESENT**
We want …
Everyone in the class likes …

62

Experience Better Learning with EVOLVE: a course that helps both teachers and students on every step of the language learning journey.

Speaking matters. Find out more about creating safe speaking environments in the classroom.

# EVOLVE unit structure

## Unit opening page

Each unit opening page activates prior knowledge and vocabulary and immediately gets students speaking.

## Lessons 1 and 2

These lessons present and practice the unit vocabulary and grammar in context, helping students discover language rules for themselves. Students then have the opportunity to use this language in well-scaffolded, personalized speaking tasks.

## Lesson 3

This lesson is built around a functional language dialogue that models and contextualizes useful fixed expressions for managing a particular situation. This is a real world strategy to help students handle unexpected conversational turns.

## Lesson 4

This is a combined skills lesson based around an engaging reading or listening text. Each lesson asks students to think critically and ends with a practical writing task.

## Lesson 5

*Time to speak* is an entire lesson dedicated to developing speaking skills. Students work on collaborative, immersive tasks which involve information sharing and decision making.

# CONTENTS

| Functional language | Listening | Reading | Writing | Speaking |
|---|---|---|---|---|
| ■ Check in to a hotel<br>**Real-world strategy**<br>■ Check spelling | | **Meet the artists**<br>■ Profiles of two artists | **A profile**<br>■ A personal or work profile<br>■ Capital letters and periods | ■ Introduce yourself<br>■ Say where you're from<br>■ Say and spell personal information<br>■ Arrive at a hotel and check in<br>**Time to speak**<br>■ Talk to people at a party |
| ■ Ask about and say people's ages and birthdays; give birthday wishes<br>**Real-world strategy**<br>■ Correct yourself | **Here's my band**<br>■ A conversation between friends | | **A post**<br>■ A post about friends in a photo<br>■ *and* to join words and sentences | ■ Describe the people in a picture<br>■ Talk about your family<br>■ Describe your friends and family<br>■ Talk about ages and birthdays<br>**Time to speak**<br>■ Talk about things in common |
| ■ Make and reply to offers<br>**Real-world strategy**<br>■ Ask about words you don't understand | | **A home-share in Burnaby**<br>■ Emails about a home-share | **An email**<br>■ An email about a home-share<br>■ Question marks | ■ Describe a house in a picture<br>■ Talk about rooms in your home<br>■ Talk about unusual furniture<br>■ Offer a drink or snack<br>**Time to speak**<br>■ Discuss what furniture to buy for a new home |
| ■ Ask about a new topic; ask for a response<br>**Real-world strategy**<br>■ Show you are listening | **Product reviews**<br>■ A radio program about product reviews | | **A review**<br>■ A product review<br>■ *but* and *because* | ■ Talk about things that you love or like<br>■ Talk about your favorite technology<br>■ Discuss what phone plan is good for you<br>■ Talk about how you communicate with people<br>**Time to speak**<br>■ Talk about your favorite music |
| ■ Show you agree or have things in common<br>**Real-world strategy**<br>■ Short answers with adverbs of frequency | | **Work, rest and play**<br>■ An article about work-life balance | **A report**<br>■ A report about your activities<br>■ Headings and numbered lists | ■ Talk about your fun days<br>■ Say when and how often you do things<br>■ Talk about your daily routine<br>■ Compare information about your activities<br>**Time to speak**<br>■ Talk about the best week for your body clock |
| ■ Ask for and give directions<br>**Real-world strategy**<br>■ Check information | **Walk with Yasmin**<br>■ A podcast about a place in nature | | **A fact sheet**<br>■ A fact sheet<br>■ Order size and opinion adjectives | ■ Describe a picture of a city<br>■ Talk about good places in your neighborhood<br>■ Talk about nature in your area<br>■ Give directions to a visitor<br>**Time to speak**<br>■ Talk about a good place to live |

| | Learning objectives | Grammar | Vocabulary | Pronunciation |
|---|---|---|---|---|
| **Unit 7 Now is good** | ■ Talk about activities around the house<br>■ Ask and answer questions about travel<br>■ Share news on the phone<br>■ Write a blog about things happening now<br>■ Ask what people are doing these days | ■ Present continuous statements<br>■ Present continuous questions | ■ Activities around the house<br>■ Transportation | ■ *–ing* at the end of the word |
| **Unit 8 You're good!** | ■ Talk about your skills and abilities<br>■ Say what you can and can't do at work or school<br>■ Say why you're the right person for a job<br>■ Write an online comment with your opinion<br>■ Talk about what people in your country are good at | ■ *can* and *can't* for ability; *well*<br>■ *can* and *can't* for possibility | ■ Verbs to describe skills<br>■ Work | ■ Saying groups of words<br>■ Listening for *can* and *can't* |
| **Unit 9 Places to go** | ■ Talk about travel and vacations<br>■ Make travel plans<br>■ Ask for information in a store<br>■ Write a description of a place<br>■ Plan a vacation for someone | ■ *this* and *these*<br>■ *like to, want to, need to, have to* | ■ Travel<br>■ Travel arrangements | ■ Saying prices |
| | **Review 3 (Review of Units 7–9)** | | | |
| **Unit 10 Get ready** | ■ Make outdoor plans for the weekend<br>■ Discuss what clothes to wear for different trips<br>■ Suggest plans for evening activities<br>■ Write an online invitation<br>■ Plan and present a fun weekend in your city | ■ Statements with *be going to*<br>■ Questions with *be going to* | ■ Going out<br>■ Clothes<br>■ Seasons | ■ The letter *s*<br>■ Listening for *going to* |
| **Unit 11 Colorful memories** | ■ Describe people, places, and things in the past<br>■ Talk about colors and memories<br>■ Talk about movies and actors<br>■ Write an email about things you keep from your past<br>■ Talk about TV shows from your childhood | ■ Statements with *was* and *were*<br>■ Questions with *was* and *were* | ■ Adjectives to describe people, places, and things<br>■ Colors | ■ /oʊ/ and /ɑː/ vowel sounds |
| **Unit 12 Stop, eat, go** | ■ Talk about snacks and small meals<br>■ Talk about meals in restaurants<br>■ Offer and accept food and drink<br>■ Write a restaurant review<br>■ Create a menu for a restaurant | ■ Simple past statements<br>■ Simple past questions; *any* | ■ Snacks and small meals<br>■ Food, drinks, and desserts | ■ /h/ and /r/ sounds<br>■ Listening for *Do you want to… ?* |
| | **Review 4 (Review of Units 10–12)** | | | |
| | **Grammar charts and practice, pages 129–140** | **Vocabulary exercises, pages 141–151** | | |

| Functional language | Listening | Reading | Writing | Speaking |
|---|---|---|---|---|
| ■ Answer the phone and greet people; ask how things are going<br>**Real-world strategy**<br>■ React to news | | **Jamie's blog**<br>■ A blog about a difficult place | **A blog post**<br>■ A blog about a busy place<br>■ *and, also,* and *too* | ■ Talk about the lives of people in a picture<br>■ Talk about good and bad times to call someone<br>■ Tell a friend what you are doing right now<br>■ Talk about your news<br>**Time to speak**<br>■ Talk about your life these days |
| ■ Ask for and give for opinions<br>**Real-world strategy**<br>■ Explain and say more about an idea | **Technology Talks**<br>■ A podcast about computers | | **A comment**<br>■ Comments about an online post<br>■ Quotations | ■ Discuss activities you do<br>■ Talk about skills you have<br>■ Talk about what you can and can't do at work<br>■ Ask and answer questions in a job interview<br>**Time to speak**<br>■ Discuss national skills |
| ■ Ask for and give information<br>**Real-world strategy**<br>■ Ask someone to repeat something | | **Places to go near Puno**<br>■ A travel guide | **A description**<br>■ A description of a place<br>■ Imperatives to give advice | ■ Talk about a place you like<br>■ Describe people and places in a picture<br>■ Talk about organizing a trip<br>■ Ask for information at an airport store<br>**Time to speak**<br>■ Talk about planning a vacation |
| ■ Make, accept, and refuse suggestions<br>**Real-world strategy**<br>■ Say why you can't do something | **Montevideo**<br>■ A TV travel show | | **An invitation**<br>■ An event invitation<br>■ Contractions | ■ Talk about your plans for the future<br>■ Talk about outdoor activities in your city<br>■ Talk about clothes to take for a trip<br>■ Talk about where to go out for dinner<br>**Time to speak**<br>■ Plan a fun weekend in your home city |
| ■ Express uncertainty<br>**Real-world strategy**<br>■ Take time to think | | **Picturing memories**<br>■ An article about things people keep | **An email**<br>■ An email to a friend<br>■ Paragraphs and topic sentences | ■ Describe a happy time in your life<br>■ Talk about things you remember<br>■ Talk about colors you remember from when you were a child<br>■ Talk about people in a movie<br>**Time to speak**<br>■ Present your memories of a TV show from your past |
| ■ Offer, request and accept food and drink<br>**Real-world strategy**<br>■ Use *so* and *really* to make words stronger | **Where do you want to eat?**<br>■ A conversation about restaurants on a food app | | **A review**<br>■ A restaurant review<br>■ Commas in lists | ■ Describe a good meal you had<br>■ Talk about snacks and small meals you like<br>■ Talk about a meal you had in a restaurant<br>■ Ask for food in a restaurant or at a friend's house<br>**Time to speak**<br>■ Design a menu for a new restaurant |

# CLASSROOM LANGUAGE

### 1.02 Get started

Hi. / Hello.

What's your name?

My name is ______________.

This is my class.

This is my partner.

This is my teacher.

### Ask for help

I don't understand.

I have a question.

How do you say ______________ in English?

What does ______________ mean?

How do you spell ______________?

Can you repeat that, please?

Sorry, what page?

### Your teacher

I'm your teacher.

Open your book.

Close your book.

Go to page ______________.

Do you have any questions?

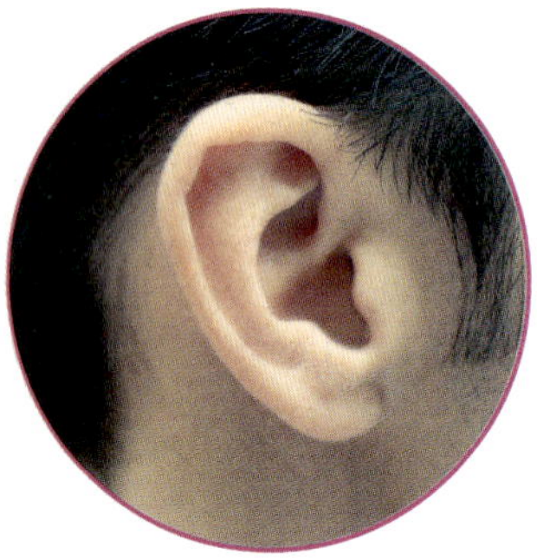

Listen.

Say.

Read.

Write.

Watch.

Work in pairs.

Work in groups.

UNIT OBJECTIVES

- say where you're from
- ask for and give personal information
- check into a hotel
- write a profile
- meet new people

# I AM ...

# 1

## START SPEAKING

CLASS WORK **Say your name. Watch Josue for an example.**

I am Marco.

I am Anya.

REAL STUDENT

*Where is Josue from?*

# 1.1 I'M BRAZILIAN. AND YOU?

**LESSON OBJECTIVE**
- say where you're from

## 1 VOCABULARY: Countries and nationalities

A 1.03 **Complete the chart. Then listen and check.**

| Capital city | Country | Nationality |
|---|---|---|
| Brasília | Brazil | 1 ______ |
| Santiago | Chile | Chilean |
| Beijing | China | Chinese |
| Bogotá | 2 ______ | Colombian |
| Quito | Ecuador | Ecuadorian |
| Paris | France | French |
| Tegucigalpa | Honduras | Honduran |
| Tokyo | Japan | Japanese |
| Mexico City | 3 ______ | Mexican |
| Lima | Peru | Peruvian |
| Moscow | Russia | 4 ______ |
| Seoul | South Korea | South Korean |
| Madrid | Spain | Spanish |
| Washington, D.C. | the United States | American |

B **Now do the vocabulary exercises for 1.1 on page 141.**

C PAIR WORK **Talk to a partner. Say your name, nationality, and city.**

*Hi! I'm Yessica. I'm Peruvian, and I'm from Callao.*

*Hello! I'm Daniel. I'm from Madrid, in Spain.*

## 2 LANGUAGE IN CONTEXT

A **Read the messages from students and teachers. What cities are they from? Who is a teacher?**

**International school project**

Hi!

Hi, I'm Gabi. I'm **Brazilian**. I'm from **São Paulo**.

You're from **Brazil**! Wow! My name is Karina, and I'm from **Colombia**.

Are you from **Bogotá**?

No, I'm not. I'm from **Medellín**.

Write a message ...

**International school project**

My name is Antonio. I'm from **Mexico City** – in **Mexico**!

Hi, I'm Max. I'm **Russian**. I'm from **Moscow**.

Hi, Max. Are you a teacher?

Yes, I am. And you?

No, I'm not a teacher! I'm a student.

Write a message ...

## 3 GRAMMAR: *I am, you are*

A Circle the correct answers. Use the sentences in the grammar box to help you.

1 For questions (?), say ***Are you … ?*** / ***You are … ?***
2 For affirmative (+) answers, say ***Yes, I am.*** / ***Yes, I'm.***
3 For negative (-) answers, say ***No, I am not.*** / ***No, I'm not.***

***I am (= I'm), you are (= you're)***

**I'm** Brazilian.
**You're** from Mexico City.

**I'm not** from Lima.
**You're not** from Bogotá.

**Am I** in room 6B?
Yes, **you are.** / No, **you're not.**
**Are you** from Tokyo?
Yes, **I am.** / No, **I'm not.**

B **Complete the sentences.**

1 ______________ 'm Ecuadorian.
2 Wow! ______________ 're from Rio!
3 ______________ you from Quito?
4 A Are you American?
B Yes, I ______________ .

C **Now go to page 129. Look at the grammar chart and do the grammar exercise for 1.1.**

D **Look at the chart. You are Alex. Write four sentences. Then read the information in the Accuracy check box and check your work.**

| Name | City | Nationality | Country |
|---|---|---|---|
| Alex | Orlando | American | the United States |

1 ______________
2 ______________
3 ______________
4 ______________

**ACCURACY CHECK**

**Use *I* with *am*.**
~~Am~~ Spanish. ✗
I'm Spanish. ✓

E PAIR WORK **Choose a name. Don't tell your partner. Ask and answer questions to find the person.**

**Harry,** student, New York, American
**Barbara,** student, New York, Brazilian
**Mike,** student, Chicago, American
**Victor,** student, Chicago, Brazilian
**Kristy,** teacher, New York, American
**Nayara,** teacher, New York, Brazilian
**Robert,** teacher, Chicago, American
**Juliano,** teacher, Chicago, Brazilian

Are you a student?
Yes, I am.
Are you from New York?
No, I'm not. I'm from ….

## 4 SPEAKING

GROUP WORK **Imagine you're a different person. Choose a new name, city, nationality, and country. Talk to other people. Ask questions. For ideas, watch Anderson.**

REAL STUDENT

*What's Anderson's city, nationality, and country?*

# 1.2 WHAT'S YOUR LAST NAME?

**LESSON OBJECTIVE**
- ask for and give personal information

## 1 LANGUAGE IN CONTEXT

A 1.04 **Rudy and Juana are at a conference. Listen to the conversation. Check (✓) the information they say.**

- [ ] college name
- [ ] company name
- [ ] email address
- [ ] first name
- [ ] last name (= family name)

**INSIDER ENGLISH**

**Say *Uh-huh* to show you are listening.**
*My last name is Garcia. G-A-R-C-I-A.*
***Uh-huh**. What's your email address?*

B 1.04 **Read and listen again. What information do they spell?**

**1.04 Audio script**

| | |
|---|---|
| **Rudy** | So, your **first name** is Juana. H-U- … |
| **Juana** | No. J-U-A-N-A. My **last name** is Garcia. G-A-R-C-I-A. |
| **Rudy** | **Uh-huh**. What's your **email address**? |
| **Juana** | It's juanagarcia@bestmail.com. |
| **Rudy** | And what's the name of your **college**? |
| **Juana** | It's Garcia College. I'm Juana Garcia from Garcia College! |
| **Rudy** | Great! OK, my last name is Jones. |
| **Juana** | OK. What's your email address? |
| **Rudy** | It's rudythejones@kmail.com. |
| **Juana** | Rudy*the*jones! The? T-H-E? |
| **Rudy** | Yes. R-U-D-Y-T-H-E-J-O-N-E-S. |
| **Juana** | From Jones College? |
| **Rudy** | No! From Miami Dade College. |

## 2 VOCABULARY: The alphabet; personal information

A 1.05 **Read and listen. Then listen again and repeat.**

Aa Bb Cc Dd Ee Ff Gg Hh Ii Jj Kk Ll Mm
Nn Oo Pp Qq Rr Ss Tt Uu Vv Ww Xx Yy Zz

B 1.06 **Listen and circle the spelling you hear.**

| | | | |
|---|---|---|---|
| 1 **first name:** | a Raymund | b Raimund | c Raymond |
| 2 **last name:** | a Cummings | b Cummins | c Comyns |
| 3 **email address:** | a cb_smith@kmail.com | b cg_smith@kmail.com | c cd_smith@kmail.com |
| 4 **college:** | a Wallice | b Wallis | c Wallace |
| 5 **company:** | a Jeferson | b Jefferson | c Jeffersen |

C **Now do the vocabulary exercises for 1.2 on page 141.**

D PAIR WORK **Talk to a partner. Say your first name, last name, email address, and college or company name.**

> **!** **In email addresses:**
> - "." is "dot"
> - "@" is "at"
> - "_" is "underscore"

## 3 GRAMMAR: *What's … ?, It's …*

A **Circle the correct answers. Use the sentences in the grammar box to help you.**

1 For questions, say ***What's … ? / It's …***

2 For answers, say ***What's … ? / It's …***

***What's …? (= What is), It's … (= It is)***

| | |
|---|---|
| **What's** your first name? | **It's** Juana. |
| **What's** the name of your college? | **It's** Garcia College. |

> **ACCURACY CHECK**
>
> **Use the apostrophe (').**
>
> ~~Whats~~ your first name? ✗
> What's your first name? ✓
>
> ~~Its~~ Juana. ✗
> It's Juana. ✓

B **Write *What's* or *It's* in the spaces. Match the questions (1–3) with the answers (a–c). Then check your accuracy.**

1 ________ the name of your company? ___

2 ________ your last name? ___

3 ________ your email address? ___

a ________ luzmendes@xyz.com.

b ________ Mendes.

c ________ Warton Homes.

C **Now go to page 129. Look at the grammar chart and do the grammar exercise for 1.2.**

## 4 SPEAKING

A **Look at the information in the box. Circle three things to talk about.**

| | | | | |
|---|---|---|---|---|
| college name | company name | email address | first name | last name |

B CLASS WORK **Talk to other people. Ask questions about the information in the box.**

*What's the name of your college?*

*It's Wallace College.*

# 1.3 THIS IS THE KEY

**LESSON OBJECTIVE**
- check in to a hotel

## 1 VOCABULARY: Numbers

A 1.07 **Listen and repeat the numbers.**

| | | | |
|---|---|---|---|
| 0 zero | 3 three | 6 six | 9 nine |
| 1 one | 4 four | 7 seven | 10 ten |
| 2 two | 5 five | 8 eight | |

B PAIR WORK **Say a number from exercise 1A. Your partner points to the number. Then change roles.**

**INSIDER ENGLISH**

For **0**, say ***zero*** or ***oh***.
*Your room number is two-**zero**-one.*
*My address is seven-**oh**-nine …*

## 2 FUNCTIONAL LANGUAGE

A 1.08 **Paulo is at a hotel. Read and listen. Check (✓) the information the hotel clerk asks for.**

- ☐ cell phone number
- ☐ city
- ☐ company
- ☐ email address
- ☐ name
- ☐ room number

**1.08 Audio script**

**Clerk** Welcome to New York! What's your name?
**Paulo** I'm Paulo Vasques. **I'm here for three nights.**
**Clerk** Ah, yes. **What's your cell phone number?**
**Paulo** **It's (593) 555-2192.**
**Clerk** Thanks. And what's your email address?
**Paulo** It's pvasques89@travelmail.org.
**Clerk** Thanks. One moment. **Please sign here. Here's a pen.**
**Paulo** OK.
**Clerk** Thank you. **This is the key.** It's room 6B.
**Paulo** 6D. Thanks.
**Clerk** No, you're not in 6D. **You're in room 6B.**
**Paulo** Oh, OK. Thank you.
**Clerk** You're welcome.

B **Complete the chart with expressions in bold from the conversation above.**

| Checking in (clerk) | | Checking in (Paulo) |
|---|---|---|
| What's your [1] ______ number?<br>Please [2] ______ here. | Here's a [3] ______.<br>This is the [4] ______.<br>It's room 6B.<br>[5] ______ room 6B. | [6] ______ (593) 555-2192.<br>I'm here for three [7] ______. |

C 1.09 **Complete the conversations. Then listen and check. Practice with a partner.**

1 A What's your *email / cell phone number*? B *I'm / It's* (593) 555-3194.
2 A Please *sign / write* here. B OK.
3 A Hello. Welcome to the Garden Hotel. B Thanks. I'm here for two *mornings / nights*.
4 A *This is / It's* the key. You're in room 4D. B OK. Thanks.
5 A *Here's a / You're* pen. B Thank you.

## 3 REAL-WORLD STRATEGY

A 1.10 **Listen to a conversation. Circle the correct answers.**

1 The woman is at *a hotel / home.*

2 She says her *room number / cell phone number.*

B 1.10 **Read about checking spelling in the box below. Listen to the conversation again. What does the man ask the woman to spell?**

**CHECKING SPELLING**

To check spelling, ask *How do you spell your first name / your last name / it?*

*My name is Paulo Vasques.*

*How do you spell your last name?*

*V-A-S-Q-U-E-S.*

C 1.11 **Listen to the questions. Answer the questions and spell words.**

1 How do you spell your last name? R-I-V-E-R-A.

## 4 PRONUNCIATION: Saying /ɪ/ and /i/ vowel sounds

A 1.12 **Listen and repeat the two different vowel sounds.**

/ɪ/ six You're in room **6**A. /i/ three You're in room **3**A.

B 1.13 **Look at the underlined letters below. Then listen and repeat. What vowel sounds do you hear? Write A for words with /ɪ/, for example *six*. Write B for words with /i/, for example *three*.**

1 ___ email
2 ___ is
3 ___ information
4 ___ please
5 ___ key
6 ___ company

C 1.14 PAIR WORK **Listen to the conversations. Underline words with the vowel sounds /ɪ/ and /i/. Then practice with a partner.**

1 **A** Is this your key? **B** No, it's the key for room three.

2 **A** What's your company email address? **B** It's c.b.smith@wallis.com.

3 **A** What's your Instagram name? **B** It's SusieSix.

## 5 SPEAKING

A PAIR WORK **Put the conversation in the correct order. Then practice with a partner.**

[7] **A** Thanks. One moment. Please sign here.

[5] **A** Great. Thank you. And what's your email address?

[ ] **B** I'm Marie Bernard. I'm here for two nights.

[ ] **B** OK.

[ ] **B** It's mbernard87@mymail.org.

[ ] **A** Ah, yes, two nights. What's your cell phone number?

[ ] **B** It's (298) 555-1257.

[ ] **A** Thank you. This is the key. It's for room 7C.

[1] **A** Hi. Welcome to the Tree House Hotel! What's your name?

B PAIR WORK **Choose a hotel in your city. One person is a hotel clerk, and the other person is a visitor. Then change roles.**

Hi. Welcome to the International Hotel. What's your name?

I'm Jae-hoon Park. I'm here for two nights ....

C PAIR WORK **Student A: Go to page 156. Student B: Go to page 158. Follow the instructions.**

# 1.4 MY PROFILE

**LESSON OBJECTIVE**
- write a profile

## 1 VOCABULARY: Jobs

A 1.15 **Listen and repeat.**

## 2 READING

A SCAN **Read the profiles. Circle three job words from exercise 1A.**

B READ FOR DETAILS **Read the profiles again. Complete the chart.**

| First name | Akemi | |
|---|---|---|
| Last name | | Silva |
| City | | |
| Nationality | | |
| Company | | |
| School | | |

C PAIR WORK **One person is Akemi. One person is Frank. How are you different?**

I'm Akemi. I'm a student.

I'm Frank. I'm not a student. I live in Texas ...

**!** Use *but* to connect two different ideas.
*I'm Peruvian,* ***but*** *my home is in the United States.*

**!** People say, *I'm from Paris*. People also say, *I* ***live*** *in Paris*. (= *Paris is my home now.*)

**STUDIO10**
**STORE PROFILES**
*Meet the artists*

**ABOUT AKEMI**

I'm Akemi Tanaka. I live in San Diego, but I'm not American. I'm Japanese. My company is Tanaka Paints. My phone number is (324) 555-6053, and my email is akemit2000@tanakapaints.com. I'm an artist, and I'm a student, too. The name of my school is The Art Institute. It's in California.

**ABOUT FRANK**

My name is Frank Silva. I live in Austin, Texas, in the United States. I'm American and Brazilian. The name of my company is Designs by Frank. It's in my home in Austin. I'm an art teacher, too. The classes are in my home. My phone number is (780) 555-5230, and my email is designsbyfrank@blinknet.com.

## 3 WRITING

A Read the profiles of two people. Where are they from? Who is a student?

**Business Weekly**

Meet the **sales team**

Lima, Peru

Hello. My name is Juan Carlos Fernandez. I am Peruvian. I am from Trujillo, but I live in Lima now. I am a salesperson. The name of my company is Omega Sales. My email is jcfernandez_511@omsmail.com, and my cell phone number is (962) 555-3198.

**Class Connect – find students around the world**

Me, Katya!

Hi! I'm Katya Ivanova. I'm from Russia. My home is in St. Petersburg. It's a great city. I'm an English student. The name of my school is Popov College of English.

@ **email:** kativanova@popovnet.ru
**Twitter:** katya_ivanova98

B PAIR WORK THINK CRITICALLY The two profiles are different. Why? Discuss with a partner.

C WRITING SKILLS Read the rules. Then find two or more examples for the rules in the profiles.

**Use capital letters (A, B, C ...):**

- for *I* (*I'm*)
- for names of people
- for names of places, companies, schools
- for nationalities and languages
- at the beginning of sentences

Use a period ( . ) at the end of statements.

**REGISTER CHECK**

***Hello, Hi,* and *Hey***

Use *hello* in formal writing or speaking, for example at work.

***Hello.** My name is Juan Carlos Fernandez.*

Use *hi* in informal writing or speaking, with friends and family. Use *hey* when you speak to friends and family.

***Hi!** I'm Katya Ivanova.*

### WRITE IT

D Choose a work profile or a personal profile. Then write your profile. Use the profiles in exercise 3A for an example.

E GROUP WORK Work in groups. Read other profiles. Are they work profiles or personal profiles? Say why.

# 1.5 TIME TO SPEAK
## People from history

**LESSON OBJECTIVE**
- meet new people

**A** **Who are the people in the pictures? Tell your partner.**

**B** **Read the conversations (1–3). Then match them to a–c. Which conversation is with three people?**

a an introduction ___ b a greeting ___ c a goodbye ___

1 A Good evening.
B Hello. How are you?
A I'm fine, thanks. And you?
B I'm fine.

2 A Gabi, this is Caio.
B Hi, Gabi. Nice to meet you.
C Nice to meet you, Caio.

3 A See you later.
B Bye.

**C** **PREPARE** **Practice the conversations from exercise B. Then change roles.**

FIND IT

**D** **RESEARCH** **Imagine you're at a party for people from history. Choose a person. You can go online and find the nationality and home city for your person. Create and write down a cell phone number.**

**E** **ROLE PLAY** **Imagine you're the person from exercise D. Meet other people at the party. Write notes.**

**F** **AGREE** **Say the nationality, city or phone number of a person from the party. Other students say the person.**

**G** **DISCUSS** **Who is your favorite person from the party?**

*To check your progress, go to page 152.*

## USEFUL PHRASES

**ROLE PLAY**
Are you (American)?
Yes, I am. / No, I'm not. I'm …
I'm from (city).
How do you spell it?
A What's your cell phone number? B It's …

**AGREE**
The person is from (city). / The phone number is …
It's (name of person).

**DISCUSS**
My favorite person is …
Me, too.

**UNIT OBJECTIVES**

- talk about your family
- describe friends and family
- talk about ages and birthdays
- write a post about friends in a photo
- compare information about friends and family

# GREAT PEOPLE

# 2

## START SPEAKING

**Look at the picture. Say words about the people.**

Server.

American.

Family.

# 2.1 A FAMILY PARTY

**LESSON OBJECTIVE**
- talk about your family

## 1 LANGUAGE IN CONTEXT

A 1.16 **Sara and Liz are at a party. Read and listen to the conversation. How old are David and Emily? Who are Elizabeth One and Elizabeth Two?**

**1.16 Audio script**

**Sara** What a great party, Liz! Are your **children** here?
**Liz** Yes, they are. David … He's my **son**. He's eight. And the girl with him is my daughter Emily. She's ten.
**Sara** And the man … Is he your **husband**?
**Liz** No, he's my **brother** Marcus. My husband isn't here.
**Sara** Oh, OK. Are your **parents** here?
**Liz** No, they're not. Oh, look. Here's my **grandmother**. She's 86. Grandma, this is my friend Sara.
**Grandma** Nice to meet you, Sara. I'm Elizabeth.
**Sara** Nice to meet you. Hey, are you both Elizabeth?
**Liz** Yes, we are! With friends, I'm Liz. But in my family, she's Elizabeth One, and I'm Elizabeth Two!

**REGISTER CHECK**

**Some words for family are formal and informal. Use formal words at work. Use informal words with friends and family.**

| Formal | Informal |
|---|---|
| *grandfather* | *grandpa* |
| *grandmother* | *grandma* |
| *father* | *dad* |
| *mother* | *mom* |

**GLOSSARY**
**both** (*det*) two people/things

## 2 VOCABULARY: Family; numbers

A 1.17 **Listen and repeat the words in the family tree.**

B **Read the sentences below about Liz and her family. Then complete the family tree with the names in bold.**

- Liz = sister of **Marcus**.
- **Kyle** = uncle of Liz.
- **Tim** = cousin of Liz.
- **John** = grandfather of Liz.
- Anna = wife of **Paul**.

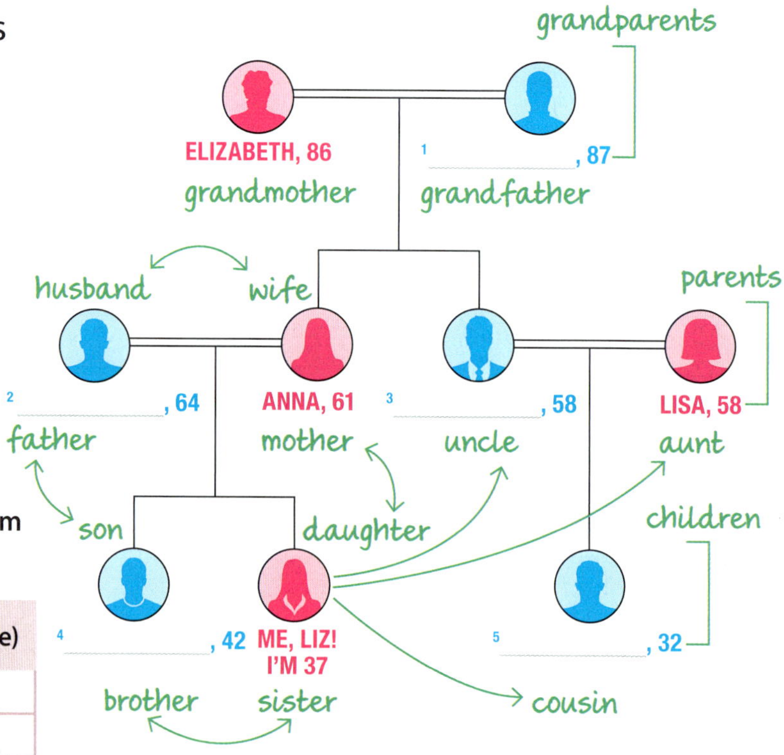


C 1.18 **Complete the table with words from the family tree. Then listen and check.**

| Singular (1 person) | Plural (2+ people) |
|---|---|
| 1 ______ | cousins |
| child | 2 ______ |
| 3 ______ | wives |

D PAIR WORK **Make three more sentences about the people in the family tree. Then compare with a partner.**

E 1.19 **Write the numbers. Then listen and repeat.**

| | | | |
|---|---|---|---|
| 11 eleven | ___ sixteen | 21 twenty-one | ___ sixty |
| 12 twelve | ___ seventeen | 22 twenty-two | ___ seventy |
| 13 thirteen | ___ eighteen | 30 thirty | ___ eighty |
| ___ fourteen | ___ nineteen | ___ forty | ___ ninety |
| ___ fifteen | 20 twenty | ___ fifty | 100 one hundred |

F **Now do the vocabulary exercises for 2.1 on page 141.**

## 3 GRAMMAR: *is / are* in statements and *yes/no* questions

A **Circle the correct answers. Use the sentences in the grammar box to help you.**

1 Use **is** / **are** with *he* and *she*.  2 Use **is** / **are** with *we*, *you*, and *they*.

**_is / are_ in statements and _yes/no_ questions**

| | |
|---|---|
| **Are** your children here? | **Is** he your husband? |
| Yes, they **are**. | No, he**'s** my brother Marcus. |
| He**'s** my son ('s = *is*). He**'s** eight. | **Are** you both Elizabeth? |
| She**'s** my daughter. She**'s** **ten**. | Yes, we **are**. |

B **Complete the sentences.**

1 This ___ my sister. ___ 23.
2 **A** ___ your parents Colombian? **B** Yes, ___ ___.
3 This ___ my grandfather. ___ 88.
4 **A** ___ your mother at home? **B** Yes, ___ ___.
5 We ___ Russian. We live in Moscow.

C **Match the questions with the answers. Then answer the questions so they're true for you.**

1 Are your parents American? *b*
2 Are you 21? ___
3 Is your best friend in class? ___
4 Is your teacher Canadian? ___

**a** Yes. She's from Toronto.
**b** No. They're Colombian.
**c** No, he's at work.
**d** Yes, I am.

D **Now go to page 129. Look at the grammar chart and do the grammar exercise for 2.1.**

## 4 SPEAKING

A PAIR WORK **Draw a simple family tree. Then talk to a partner about people in your family. Ask and answer questions. For ideas, watch Julieth.**

This is Marcos. He's from Mexico City. He's 25.

Is he your brother?

*Who does Julieth talk about? Is your family tree the same or different?*

B GROUP WORK **Tell your group about three people from your family tree. You can show pictures of the people on your phone.**

FIND IT

# 2.2 THEY'RE REALLY FUNNY!

**LESSON OBJECTIVE**
- describe friends and family

## 1 LANGUAGE IN CONTEXT

A **Read the messages. Where is Lara from? Where is she now? Who are the other people in the pictures?**

B **Read the messages again. Find the numbers in the messages. What are they?**

four 12 19 24 85

### Four days with my family

**Hi! I'm Lara. I'm 24. I live with my family in Texas, but we're not in Texas now. We're with Grandma Vera at her home in Miami ☀ Here's a picture of me … and here are pictures of my family 😍**

Look at my mom and dad. My parents are both 50 – not **old**, and not **young**! My mom is **short** and my dad is **tall**. They're not **boring!** They're both really **funny**.

This is Erika. She's my sister – and she's my best friend! ❤ She's 19. She's a student, and she's very **smart**. She's **shy**, but she's **friendly**, too.

This is Justin. He's my brother. He's funny. 😂 He's young (12), but he's not short – he's really tall.

This is my grandmother, Grandma Vera. She's old (85!), and she's very **interesting**. She's a good grandma! ❤

## 2 VOCABULARY: Describing people; *really / very*

A 1.20 **Listen and repeat the adjectives below. Then find them in the messages. Match the adjectives to the people.**

| Age | Appearance | Personality | | |
|---|---|---|---|---|
| old | short | boring | funny | shy |
| young | tall | friendly | interesting | smart |

B **Circle *really* and *very* in the messages. Do they make the adjectives stronger (++) or weaker (--)?**

C Circle the correct word to complete the sentences.

1 A Is he short?
B No, he's not. He's *tall / shy*.

2 A Is she boring?
B No! She's really *short / interesting*.

3 A How old is your grandmother?
B She's 90. She's very *young / old*.

4 A Is Mi-jin a college student?
B Yes. She's really *smart / short*.

5 A Is your cousin interesting?
B Yes, and he's *boring / funny*.

6 A Are your children shy?
B No, they're very *friendly / interesting*.

D **Now do the vocabulary exercises for 2.2 on page 142.**

## 3 GRAMMAR: *is not / are not*

A **Circle the correct answers. Use the sentences in the grammar box and the Notice box to help you.**

1 For negative (-) statements with *he* and *she*, use **'s not / 're not**.

2 For negative statements with *we*, *you*, and *they*, use **'s not / 're not**.

***is not ( = 's not) / are not ( = 're not)***

| | |
|---|---|
| He'**s not** short. | They'**re not** boring! |
| She'**s not** from Miami. | We'**re not** in Texas. |
| Erika **isn't** old. | My parents **aren't** from Miami. |

**!**

**After pronouns (*he, she, we, you, they*), use *'s not* and *'re not*.**

*She'**s not** tall.*

*You'**re not** from South Korea.*

**After nouns (people, places, and things), use *isn't* and *aren't*.**

*Filip **isn't** American.*

*My friends **aren't** boring.*

B **Complete the sentences with a subject (*he, she, you, we, they*) and an affirmative (+) or negative (–) verb.**

1 He's not old. He's young.

2 She's friendly and really funny. ______ shy.

3 ______ from Brazil. We're not from Argentina.

4 ______ Juliana. She's Camila.

5 ______ my cousins. They're not my brothers.

6 ______ American. You're Canadian.

C **Now go to page 130. Look at the grammar charts and do the grammar exercise for 2.2.**

D PAIR WORK **Write two true sentences and two false sentences about a friend or a person in your class. Then exchange sentences with a partner. Correct the false sentences.**

My friend Carina is not tall. She's very funny. She's from Japan. She's smart.

She is very funny, and she's smart. She's tall, and she's not from Japan.

Correct!

## 4 SPEAKING

A **Choose four people, for example, family or friends. Write adjectives to describe them. For ideas, watch Larissa.**

REAL STUDENT

*Are your family or friends the same as Larissa's?*

FIND IT

B GROUP WORK **Talk about your people. You can show pictures on your phone. Ask for more information about people, for example, age, nationality, and city.**

# 2.3 WHEN IS YOUR BIRTHDAY?

**LESSON OBJECTIVE**
- talk about ages and birthdays

## 1 FUNCTIONAL LANGUAGE

A 1.21 **Read and listen. How many parties does Vivian talk about?**

**1.21 Audio script**

**Lucas** This is a really great picture!
**Vivian** Oh, thanks.
**Lucas** Are they your children?
**Vivian** Yes. This is Miranda. **She's eight.**
**Lucas** Miranda. Nice name.
**Vivian** And this is Carlos.
**Lucas** **How old is he?**
**Vivian** **He's three years old.**
**Lucas** **When's his birthday?**
**Vivian** It's March 28. **His party is on March 29.**
**Lucas** Oh, right. He's four this month!
**Vivian** Yeah. And **Miranda's birthday is April 2.**
**Lucas** So two birthday parties in five days.
**Vivian** Yeah, two parties. No, sorry, three parties! One party for Carlos, one party for Miranda, and then one party with the family.
**Lucas** Well, say "**Happy birthday!**" from me!

B **Complete the chart with expressions in bold from the conversation above.**

| Asking about ages and birthdays | Saying ages and birthdays | Giving birthday wishes |
|---|---|---|
| 1 ________ old is he? | She 3 ___ eight. | 6 ________ birthday! |
| When's your birthday? | He's three 4 ________ old. | |
| 2 ________ 's his birthday? | His party is 5 ______ March 29. | |
| When's her birthday? | Miranda's birthday is April 2. | |

## 2 VOCABULARY: Saying dates

A 1.22 **Look at the chart. Listen and repeat the months. What month is your birthday month?**

**Months**

| | | | | | |
|---|---|---|---|---|---|
| January | February | March | April | May | June |
| July | August | September | October | November | December |

**Dates**

| | | | |
|---|---|---|---|
| 1 first | 7 seventh | 13 thirteenth | 19 nineteenth |
| 2 second | 8 eighth | 14 fourteenth | 20 twentieth |
| 3 third | 9 ninth | 15 fifteenth | 21 twenty-first |
| 4 fourth | 10 tenth | 16 sixteenth | 22 twenty-second |
| 5 fifth | 11 eleventh | 17 seventeenth | 30 thirtieth |
| 6 sixth | 12 twelfth | 18 eighteenth | 31 thirty-first |

B 1.23 PAIR WORK **Now listen and repeat the dates. Then say the date of your birthday.**

My birthday is February eighth.

C PAIR WORK **Imagine the dates below are your birthday. Work with a partner. Ask questions and say the birthdays.**

1 May 8
2 November 23
3 August 31
4 April 19
5 January 25
6 June 4

When's your birthday?

It's May eighth.

## 3 REAL-WORLD STRATEGY

A 1.24 **Listen to a conversation. Circle the correct answers.**

1 The conversation is about a *wife / child*.
2 The man says an *age / birthday*.

B 1.24 **Listen again. What number does the man say first? Then what correct number does he say?**

**CORRECTING YOURSELF**

To correct yourself, say *No, sorry* or *Sorry, I mean …* and say the correct word.

*He's twenty. No, sorry, twenty-one.*

*It's March twenty-first. Sorry, I mean May twenty-first.*

C **Read the information in the box above about correcting yourself. What does the man say?**

D PAIR WORK **Student A: Go to page 156. Student B: Go to page 159. Follow the instructions.**

## 4 PRONUNCIATION: Saying numbers

A 1.25 **Listen and repeat the numbers. Then listen again and underline the stress.**

13 thir<u>teen</u> / 30 <u>thir</u>ty
14 fourteen / 40 forty
15 fifteen / 50 fifty
16 sixteen / 60 sixty
17 seventeen / 70 seventy
18 eighteen / 80 eighty
19 nineteen / 90 ninety

B PAIR WORK **Look at the numbers in the chart. Student A says a number. Student B points to the number. Then change roles.**

| 13 | 80 | 40 | 18 | 30 | 60 | 19 |
|---|---|---|---|---|---|---|
| 70 | 15 | 17 | 50 | 90 | 14 | 16 |

## 5 SPEAKING

A PAIR WORK **Match sentences 1–4 to sentences a–d. Then practice with a partner.**

1 How old is your brother? ___
2 When's your birthday? ___
3 My brother is 30 today. ___
4 It's my birthday today. ___

a Happy birthday!
b Say "Happy birthday!" from me.
c It's June 18.
d He's 23.

B PAIR WORK **Say the name of a friend, then say his/her birthday. Make <u>one</u> mistake. Then correct yourself.**

My friend Julia. Her birthday is June fifth. No, sorry, June sixth.

# 2.4 HERE'S MY BAND

**LESSON OBJECTIVE**
- write a post about friends in a photo

## 1 LISTENING

A PAIR WORK **Talk to a partner. Say what you see in the picture on page 19.**

B 1.26 LISTEN FOR GIST **Listen to Isabel talk to a friend, Linda. What do they talk about?**

C 1.26 LISTEN FOR DETAILS **Listen again. Circle the words that Isabel uses to describe the people.**

boring cool friendly funny interesting shy smart

## 2 GRAMMAR: Prepositions of place

A **Look at the picture on page 19 and complete the sentences with the words in the box.**

between in ~~in~~ next to on the left

1. We're not ___in___ Las Vegas! We're ______ Seattle, at college.
2. This is Joshua, on the right. And this is Nuwa, ______ .
3. I'm Isabel. Guy is ______ me.
4. Guy is ______ Nuwa and me.

## 3 PRONUNCIATION: Listening for short forms

A 1.27 **Listen. Write the words you hear. Then write the full forms.**

1. ___Here's___ my band. = ___Here is___
2. ______ in Seattle. = ______
3. ______ really funny. = ______
4. ______ great! = ______

B 1.28 **Complete the conversation with the words in the box. Listen and check.**

I'm It's She's What's When's

1. Nice to meet you, Sara. ______ Elizabeth.
2. **A** ______ your birthday?
   **B** ______ March 14.
3. This is Nuwa. ______ really smart.
4. ______ your name?

## 4 WRITING

**A** **Read the post. How old are the students?**

**SOCIALHUB**

**JING**
September 12 at 2:24pm

We're four college students in Seattle, and we're in a band. The name of the band is *JING*. Joshua is on the right. He's 22, and he's from Chicago. He's really friendly and funny. The first letter in *JING* is for Joshua. I'm Isabel. I'm 20, and I'm the "I" in the band name. I'm next to Joshua. Nuwa is on the left. She's 21. She's Chinese, and she's here for school. She's very interesting and smart. She's the "N." Guy is between Nuwa and me. He's 20, and he's the "G." He's shy, so he's the last letter in the name!

Like Comment Share

35 35

**B** PAIR WORK THINK CRITICALLY **Why is the name of the band "JING"? Is it a good name?**

**C** WRITING SKILLS **Read about two ways to use *and*. Match them (1–2) to the correct example sentence (a–b).**

1 Use *and* to connect words. ___
2 Use *and* to connect two sentences and make one long sentence. ___

a We're four college students in Seattle, and we're in a band.
b She's very interesting and smart.

**D** **Read the post again and underline examples of *and*. Does *and* connect words or sentences?**

### WRITE IT

**E** **Choose a picture of you with three or four people. Write a post about the picture. Say where you are (*in* + city/country). Say where people are in the picture (*next to, on the left/right, between*). Give information about the people. Use *and* to connect words and sentences. Then check your accuracy.**

**ACCURACY CHECK**

After prepositions, use *me*, not *I*.
Guy is next to ~~I~~. ✗
Guy is next to me. ✓
He's between Nuwa and ~~I~~. ✗
He's between Nuwa and me. ✓

# 2.5 TIME TO SPEAK
## True for me

**LESSON OBJECTIVE**
- compare information about friends and family

**A** **Which family members are in the picture? Compare your ideas with a partner.**

**B** **PREPARE Complete the sentences so they're true for you.**

1 My mom is ________________ (nationality).
2 My dad is ________________ (age).
3 My grandmother is ________________ (name).
4 My grandfather is from ________________ (city).
5 My best friend is ________________ (personality).
6 My birthday is in ________________ (month).

**C** **DISCUSS Say your answers from exercise B. Your partner says "*True for me*" or "*Not true for me.*" Then change roles.**

My mom is Brazilian.
Not true for me.

My dad is 50.
True for me.

**D** **Read the instructions. Then talk to people in your class.**

1 Walk around the class. Say hello to someone.
2 Say your answers from exercise B. Your partner says "*True for me*" or "*Not true for me.*"
3 Change roles.
4 Say goodbye.
5 Talk to a new partner.

**E** **PRESENT Who has the same answers? Who has different answers? Tell the class.**

*To check your progress, go to page 152.*

## USEFUL PHRASES

**DISCUSS**

Hello./Hi.
True for me.
Really? (for surprise)
My name is …
Not true for me.
Goodbye.

**PRESENT**

(Name) is the same.
(Name) is different.

**UNIT OBJECTIVES**

- talk about your home
- talk about furniture
- offer and accept a drink and snack
- write an email about a home-share
- choose things for a home

# COME IN

# 3

## START SPEAKING

A **Look at the picture. Where is this house?**

B **Who is in the house?**

C **What is in the house?**

# 3.1 WELCOME TO MY HOME

**LESSON OBJECTIVE**
- talk about your home

## 1 VOCABULARY: Rooms in a home

A 1.29 **Listen and repeat the words in the pictures. Which words are rooms? Which words are things in rooms?**

B PAIR WORK **Talk to a partner. What's your favorite room in the pictures?**

C **Now do the vocabulary exercises for 3.1 on page 142.**

## 2 LANGUAGE IN CONTEXT

A 1.30 **Alina gives a video tour of her family's home. Listen and read. How many rooms does she talk about?**

a six   b seven   c eight

B 1.30 **Listen again. Answer the questions.**

1 What is on the wall?
2 Who is in the kitchen?
3 How many bathrooms are in the apartment?
4 What are the names of the cat and the dog?

C PAIR WORK **What are your favorite rooms? Talk to a partner. For ideas, watch Felipe's video.**

Hi! Welcome to my new home. I mean, my *family's* new home. We live in an apartment, not a house. OK. First, this is the **living room**, with my mom's favorite **picture** on the **wall**. And this is the **dining area**. It's good for family dinners, or pizza with my friends. And this is the **kitchen**, through the **door**! My mom and her friend are in there now. OK, and this is the **bathroom**, the family bathroom. And here, this is my parents' **bedroom**, with a second bathroom. And this is my bedroom, with two **windows**. Oh! This is Milka. She's our cat. And this is Sergei's room. He's my brother. Hey! T-Rex is on Sergei's bed! Bad dog! On the floor! Now! T-Rex is Sergei's dog. OK, now say "hi" to the camera, T-Rex. Welcome to our apartment!

**REAL STUDENT**

*What are Felipe's favorite rooms? Are your favorite rooms the same?*

**ACCURACY CHECK**

Use ***the*** when you talk about a specific thing in your home: ***the*** *floor* in ***the*** *kitchen*, ***the*** *window* (in my room), or ***the*** *picture* on ***the*** *wall*.

## 3 GRAMMAR: Possessive adjectives; possessive *'s* and *s'*

A Circle the correct answers. Use the sentences in the grammar box and the Notice box below to help you.

1 The *'s* in *Sergei's room* = **possession** / ***is***.
2 Possessive adjectives (for example, *my, our, his* ...) go **before** / **after** a noun.
3 Add *'s* to **singular** / **plural** nouns.
4 Add an apostrophe (') after *s* of a **singular** / **plural** noun.

**Possessive adjectives; possessive *'s* and *s'***

| | |
|---|---|
| Welcome to **my** home. | This is **your** bedroom. |
| This is **her** bedroom. | This is **his** bedroom. |
| This is **their** bedroom. | This is my parents**'** bedroom. |
| Milka is **our** cat. | T-Rex is Sergei**'s** dog. |

This is my apartment. **Its** windows are old, but **its** doors are new.

**!** a **noun** = a person or thing, for example, *Katya* or *room*.
Singular nouns are **1 thing**.
Plural nouns are **2+ things**.

B **Complete the sentences. Use the possessive form of the word in parentheses ( ).**

1 Is ___your___ (you) apartment in the city?
2 It's not __________ (my parents) bedroom.
3 What's __________ (John) last name?
4 Maria is __________ (he) wife.
5 __________ (We) home is in Santiago.
6 The __________ (cat) name is Milka.
7 __________ (They) daughter is a college student.
8 What's __________ (she) email address?

C **Now go to page 130. Look at the grammar charts and do the grammar exercise for 3.1.**

D PAIR WORK **Complete the sentences with information about you. Then compare with a partner.**

My dog's name is Friday.

1 __________ name is __________.
2 __________ last name is __________.
3 __________ is my best friend. __________ home is in __________.
4 My __________ home is great. __________ living room is really interesting.
5 __________ is my cousin. The name of __________ company is __________.

## 4 SPEAKING

A **Draw a plan of your home, with all the rooms.**

B GROUP WORK **Talk about the rooms in your homes.**

This is my apartment. This is the door. And this is the living room, with two windows. This is my bedroom.

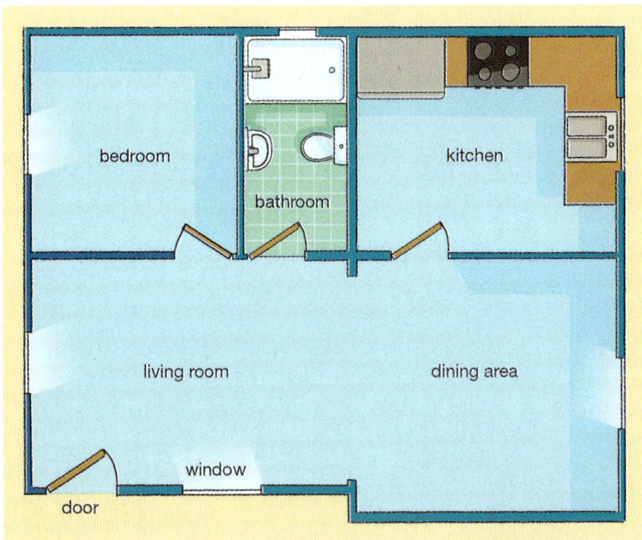

# 3.2 IS IT REALLY A CHAIR?

**LESSON OBJECTIVE**
- talk about furniture

## 1 VOCABULARY: Furniture

A 1.31 **Listen and repeat the words. Then complete the chart below. Some furniture is in more than one room.**

| Bedroom | Living room | Dining area | Kitchen | Bathroom |
|---|---|---|---|---|
| *bed* | | | | |

B PAIR WORK **Work with a partner. Say furniture from exercise 1A. Your partner says where it is in his/her home.**

*A table.*

*In the kitchen. And in the living room.*

C **Now do the vocabulary exercises for 3.2 on page 143.**

## 2 LANGUAGE IN CONTEXT

A PAIR WORK **Choose words to describe the picture in the article.**

| | | | |
|---|---|---|---|
| big | boring | cool | funny |
| great | interesting | new | nice |
| old | small | | |

B **Read the article again. What room/rooms is the furniture for?**

1 A is for a ____________.
2 B is for a ____________.
3 C is for a ____________.

C PAIR WORK **Describe the furniture in one room of your home. Use adjectives from exercise 2A. For ideas, watch June's video.**

*Do you and June talk about the same room and furniture?*

### NO SPACE? NO PROBLEM!

Is your house or apartment small? Is it *really* small? No space for big furniture? No problem! It's time for smart furniture …

**A** This **desk** isn't just a desk. It's a desk and a **bed**. It's great for college students.

**B** Is this one **chair**? Or two chairs? It's both! It's one big chair for you, or it's two small chairs for you and a friend.

**C** Is your living room small? No dining area in your home? This **couch** and **table** are good for a small space. First, it's a nice table for dinner. Then it's a couch!

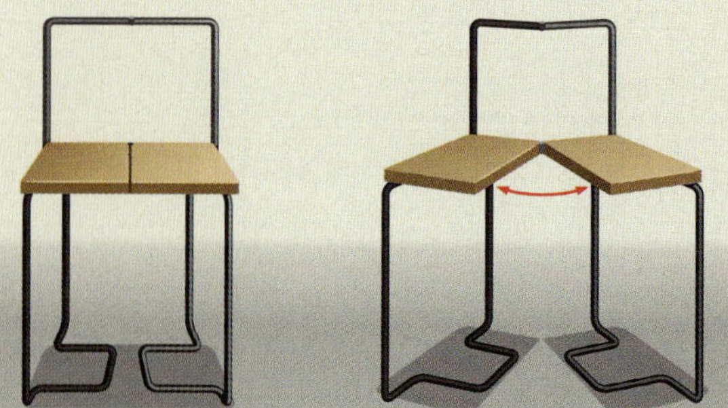

## 3 GRAMMAR: *It is*

A **Circle the correct answers. Use the sentences in the grammar box to help you.**

1 Use *It's* and *It's not* for a **man or woman** / **thing**.
2 To make a question with *It is*, say ***Is it … ?*** / ***It's … ?***

> ***It is* in statements and *yes/no* questions**
>
> **It's** a desk and a bed.
> **It's not** one chair, **it's** two chairs!
>
> **Is it** *really* small?
> Yes, **it is.**
> No, it **isn't**.

B **Complete the sentences. Then match 1–4 with a–d.**

1 **A** Their house isn't old. ______ new. ___
2 **A** Where's Toronto? ______ in the United States? ___
3 **A** We're in your kitchen. ______ really cool. ___
4 **A** Where's your desk? ______ in your living room? ___

a **B** Thanks. ______ small, but it's really nice.
b **B** No, ______ ______. ______ in Canada.
c **B** No, ______ ______. ______ in my bedroom.
d **B** Oh. ______ a big or small house?

C **Now go to page 131. Look at the grammar chart and do the grammar exercise for 3.2.**

D PAIR WORK **Write an affirmative (+) and negative (–) sentence for the rooms and furniture below. Then compare with a partner.**

*My TV is in my bedroom. It's not new, but it's OK.*

1 my TV ______
2 my desk ______
3 my refrigerator ______
4 my bedroom ______
5 my kitchen ______

## 4 SPEAKING

FIND IT

A **Design something for the home. Use the ideas below or your ideas. Draw a picture or find a picture online.**

| an interesting lamp | a big rug | a great shower | a cool desk | a TV for the wall |
|---|---|---|---|---|

B PAIR WORK **Look at your partner's picture. Guess what it is. Is it cool? Is it interesting?**

Is it a lamp?
Yes, it is.

# 3.3 COFFEE OR TEA?

**LESSON OBJECTIVE**

- offer and accept a drink and snack

## 1 VOCABULARY: Drinks and snacks

A 1.32 **Listen and repeat the words. Which things are drinks? Which thing is a snack?**

coffee

a cookie

milk

sugar

tea

## 2 FUNCTIONAL LANGUAGE

A 1.33 **Adam offers a drink and snack to his friend James. Read and listen. Which drink and snack from exercise 1A does James choose?**

**INSIDER ENGLISH**

**Use *sure* in informal speech to say *yes*.**

***Sure****. A cookie, please.*

**Don't say *Sure, please*.**

**1.33 Audio script**

**Adam** **Coffee or tea?**
**James** **Coffee, please.**
**Adam** **With milk?**
**James** **No, thanks.**
**Adam** OK … Here you are.
**James** Thanks. Wow, this is a big cup!
**Adam** It is! **Sugar?**
**James** Yes, please.
**Adam** One? Two?
**James** In that cup? Six! No. Two, please.
**Adam** Just two. And …
**James** Ah! Cookies! Hmm …
**Adam** They *are* small!
**James** Next to the big cup, yeah – they're really small! But sure. **A cookie, please.**
**Adam** Here you are!
**James** Thank you.

B **Complete the chart with expressions in bold from the conversation above.**

| Making offers | Replying to offers |
|---|---|
| Coffee 1 ________ tea? | Coffee, 3 ________ . |
| 2 ________ milk? | 4 ________ , thanks. |
| Sugar? | 5 ________ , please. |

## 3 REAL-WORLD STRATEGY

A 1.34 **Listen to a conversation. What does the man want?**

coffee ☐ tea ☐ milk ☐ sugar ☐ a cookie ☐

B 1.34 **Listen again. Circle the word the man doesn't understand. What does it mean?**

biscuit coffee cookie tea

**ASKING ABOUT WORDS YOU DON'T UNDERSTAND**

To ask about a word, say *Sorry, I don't understand. What's a (word)?*

*Sorry, I don't understand. What's a biscuit?*

C **Read the information on asking about words you don't understand in the box above. Answer the questions.**

1 What does the man say when he doesn't understand?

2 How does he ask about the word?

## 4 PRONUNCIATION: Saying /k/ at the start of a word

A 1.35 **Listen and repeat. Focus on the /k/ sound.**

1 Coffee or tea?
2 This is a big cup!
3 A cookie, please.

B 1.36 **Listen. Which speaker (A or B) says the /k/ sound? Write A or B.**

1 coffee ___
2 cookie ___
3 kitchen ___
4 cup ___
5 couch ___
6 cool ___

C PAIR WORK **Work with a partner. Say the words in exercise 4B. Does your partner say the English /k/ sound?**

## 5 SPEAKING

PAIR WORK **Work with a partner. One person is A. The other person is B. Then change roles.**

A Offer your partner a drink/snack from exercise 1A.

B Ask about a word: "Sorry, I don't understand. What's (a) … ?"

A Point to a picture of the word on page 26: "This is (a) … ."

B Say "Yes, please." or "No, thanks."

# 3.4 HOME-SHARE

**LESSON OBJECTIVE**
- write an email about a home-share

## 1 READING

A **SCAN** **Francisco is a student. He's in Burnaby in Canada for a year. He wants a room in a home-share. Scan the ad. Who is the owner of the house?**

B **READ FOR MAIN IDEAS** **Read the emails. What does Francisco ask questions about?**

**Home-share in Burnaby** « Back to results

One bedroom, with furniture, in a five-bedroom house. Great for a student. Fifteen minutes from Morden College. No pets. From March 1. $650 a month. Contact: John Redmond at jredmond@bestmail.com

Reply Forward

Wednesday, June 7th

Dear Mr. Redmond,

This email is about your home-share in Burnaby. Where is it? Is it big? How many bathrooms are in the house?

Thank you,

Francisco Lopes

Reply Forward

Friday, June 9th

Dear Mr. Lopes,

The house is on Grafton Street in Burnaby. It's very big, with two bathrooms. One bathroom is next to the kitchen and one bathroom is next to the bedroom in my ad. Are you a student?

Sincerely,

John Redmond

Reply Forward

Saturday, June 10th

Dear Mr. Redmond,

Thanks for your email. Yes, I'm a student. How many people live in the house? Who are they? How old are they?

Thank you,

Francisco

Reply Forward

Sunday, June 11th

Dear Mr. Lopes,

Four people live in the house now. Two are students. They are 20 and 22 years old. Two are not students. Mr. Johnson is 36 years old, and Mrs. Smith is 71. She is my wife's mother.

Sincerely,

John

## 2 GRAMMAR: Information questions with *be*

A **PAIR WORK** **Complete the questions with question words from the emails in exercise 1B. Then find John's answers to the questions. Use the questions and answers to have a conversation with a partner.**

1 ________ is it?

2 ________ ________ bathrooms are in the house?

3 ________ ________ people live in the house?

4 ________ are they?

5 ________ ________ are they?

B **Now go to page 131. Look at the grammar chart and do the grammar exercise for 3.4.**

C **PAIR WORK** **THINK CRITICALLY** **Is this a good place for Francisco to live? Why or why not?**

Home-share on **BOND STREET**

Contact owner

## 3 WRITING

**A Francisco writes to the owner of a second home-share. Read the emails. Answer the questions.**

1 Is the owner a woman or a man?

2 How many questions are about the house? the people?

3 Look at the pictures above. Which rooms do you see? Which room is in the email but isn't in the pictures?

4 Is it a good place for Francisco? Why or why not?

Reply Forward

Dear Mrs. Hyland,

This email is about your home-share in Burnaby. Where is it? How many bedrooms and bathrooms are in it? How many people are in the house? Are they students? I'm a student at Morden College, and I'm 22.

Thank you,

Francisco Lopes

Reply Forward

Dear Mr. Lopes,

Thank you for your email. The house is on Bond Street. It's big, with four bedrooms, three bathrooms, and a big kitchen. Three people live in the house now. They are students at Morden College. They are your age – 22.

Sincerely,

Emma Hyland

**B** WRITING SKILLS **Circle the question marks (?) in Francisco's email, above. Then circle the correct answer in the rules, below.**

1 Use **one question mark / two question marks** for each question.

2 The question mark is at **the end / the beginning** of each question.

### REGISTER CHECK

**Formal, polite emails and informal, friendly emails use different words.**

| Formal | Informal |
|---|---|
| *Dear* | *Hello / Hi* |
| *Thank you* | *Thanks* |
| *Sincerely* | *Love* |

## WRITE IT

**C Write an email to the owner of a home-share. Start with:** ***This email is about …*** **Ask questions about the house and the people.**

**D** PAIR WORK **Exchange emails with a partner. Write a reply to your partner. Write about a bad place or a good place.**

**E** PAIR WORK **Read your partner's reply. Is it a good place or a bad place?**

# 3.5 TIME TO SPEAK
## A new home

**LESSON OBJECTIVE**
- choose things for a home

**A** **DISCUSS** Talk about Jason's new home with a partner. Say the rooms you see. Is it a good home for him?

**B** **PREPARE** Talk about the things in the pictures. Which rooms are good places for them?

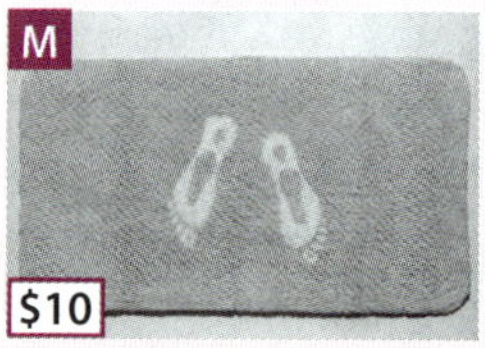

**C** **DECIDE** With a partner, make a list of things to buy for Jason's new home. You have $1,000.

**D** **PRESENT** Compare your lists. Which list is the class' favorite?

*To check your progress, go to page 152.*

## USEFUL PHRASES

**DISCUSS**
This is the (kitchen/…)
It's good for him. / It's not good for him.

**PREPARE**
Where's a good place for a (couch/…)?
In the living room?

**DECIDE**
What's important for Jason?
This is a big/small (TV).
It's $180 ($ = dollars).
It's expensive. ($$$)
It's cheap. ($)
What about this (TV/…)?
This TV is good for Jason.
I agree. / I don't agree.
Good idea!

# REVIEW 1 (UNITS 1–3)

## 1 VOCABULARY

**A Write the words in the correct place in the chart.**

| | | | | |
|---|---|---|---|---|
| artist | chef | French | Mexico | server |
| bookcase | Colombia | Honduran | parents | South Korea |
| ~~Brazil~~ | cousin | hotel clerk | Peruvian | table |
| brother | desk | Japanese | refrigerator | wife |

| Countries | Nationalities | Jobs | Family | Furniture |
|---|---|---|---|---|
| Brazil | | | | |
| | | | | |
| | | | | |
| | | | | |
| | | | | |

**B Write one more word for the categories in exercise 1A.**

## 2 GRAMMAR

**A Complete the sentences with the words in the box.**

're not 's 's Are I'm not Is isn't it is

1 Loretta ______ friendly. She's nice, too.
2 A ______ you shy? B No, ______ .
3 Donna ______ 14. She's only 13.
4 What ______ your last name?
5 They ______ from Chicago. They're from Dallas.
6 A ______ your company in China? B Yes, ______ .

**B Circle the correct answers.**

[1] *My / I* name is Sam, and this is Vic. We're brothers. This is [2] *their / our* apartment. [3] *Vic / Vic's* room is big. [4] *My / His* room is small, but it's OK. It's next to the kitchen! We're in apartment 22B. [5] *We / Our* sister and [6] *her / his* husband are in apartment 23B.

**C Write five things about your home and family. Use possessive adjectives and possessive *'s/s'*.**

## 3 SPEAKING

**A PAIR WORK Think of a person you and your partner know. Think about the person's job, age, nationality, and other information. Describe the person. Your partner guesses the person. Then change roles.**

She's a student. She's 21. She's our friend. She's Peruvian. She's very funny.

Is it Alessa?

**B Write two sentences about your partner's person.**

## 4 FUNCTIONAL LANGUAGE

**A** **Circle the correct answers to complete the conversation.**

**Teacher** Welcome to the college language center. What's your name?
**Sabrina** It's Sabrina Calvo.
**Teacher** How do you [1] *spell / mean* your last name?
**Sabrina** C-A-L-V-O.
**Teacher** Thank you. OK. [2] *How / When* old are you, and [3] *how's / when's* your birthday?
**Sabrina** I'm [4] *21 / 21st.* My birthday [5] *is / are* August 2.
**Teacher** OK. You're [6] *on / in* room 6C. Sorry, I [7] *spell / mean* room 6D. It's next to the library.
**Sabrina** Sorry, I don't [8] *understand / mean.* [9] *Where's / What's* a library?
**Teacher** It's a room with books.
**Sabrina** OK. Thank you.

**B** **Complete the conversation with the words in the box. There is one extra word.**

| milk | please | tea | thanks | yes |
|---|---|---|---|---|

**Server** Coffee or [1] ______________ ?
**Ivan** Tea, [2] ______________ .
**Server** OK. With [3] ______________ ?
**Ivan** No, [4] ______________ .

## 5 SPEAKING

**A** PAIR WORK **Choose one of the situations below. Talk to a partner. Have a conversation.**

1 You are at a hotel. A clerk asks for your personal information. Answer the questions. Look at page 6 for useful language.

*Good evening. Welcome to Hotel 24. What's your name?*

2 You ask a friend about his/her family's ages and birthdays. Your friend answers your questions. Look at page 16 for useful language.

*Is this your daughter? How old is she?*

3 A friend is at your home. Offer him or her a drink and a snack. Look at page 26 for useful language.

*Coffee or tea?*

**B** PAIR WORK **Change roles and repeat the situation.**

**UNIT OBJECTIVES**

- talk about your favorite things
- say how you use technology
- talk about how you communicate
- write product reviews
- talk about your favorite music

# I LOVE IT

# 4

## START SPEAKING

A Look at the people in the picture. Where are they? Why are they here?

B Talk about things you like 🙂 or love ❤. For ideas, watch the video with June and Felipe.

*What do June and Felipe like or love?*

# 4.1 FAVORITE THINGS

**LESSON OBJECTIVE**
- talk about your favorite things

## 1 VOCABULARY: Technology

**!** A **laptop** is a **computer**.

A 1.37 **Look at the pictures above. Listen and repeat the words.**

B PAIR WORK **Look at the pictures again. Which things do you like? Which things <u>don't</u> you like? Tell a partner.**

I like this. I don't like this.

C **Now do the vocabulary exercises for 4.1 on page 143.**

## 2 LANGUAGE IN CONTEXT

A **Read the webpage. What things from exercise 1A do the people talk about? Which thing on the webpage isn't in the pictures above?**

zozo **I love my refrigerator. Am I OK?**

COMMENTS

| | |
|---|---|
| **JJ** | You love a refrigerator! No, you're not OK! We love people – we don't love things. |
| **erico–hello** | I don't agree, JJ! I love my family … and I love my smartwatch. We love people, *and* we love things. |
| **vera** | True. I love my cell phone and the apps on it. I don't have a tablet, but I really want an iPad. Yes, it's OK to love things. But a *refrigerator*? I have a nice refrigerator. I *like* it, but I don't *love* it. |
| **stee33** | I don't love my refrigerator, but I love the things in it! 🙂 |

B **Read the webpage again. Are sentences 1–6 true or false for the people? Circle the correct answer.**

1 I have a refrigerator. For zozo, this is *true / false*.
2 I love things. For erico-hello, this is *true / false*.
3 I have a tablet. For vera, this is *true / false*.
4 I want a tablet. For vera, this is *true / false*.
5 I have a cell phone with apps. For vera, this is *true / false*.
6 I love my refrigerator. For stee33, this is *true / false*.

## 3 GRAMMAR: Simple present statements with *I*, *you*, *we*

A **Circle the correct answers. Use the sentences in the grammar box to help you.**

1 Use the simple present for things that are **generally true** / **finished**.

2 Use ***I*, *you*, or *we*** / ***I'm*, *you're*, or *we're*** with present simple verbs.

3 Use *don't* in **affirmative** / **negative** simple present statements.

4 Simple present verbs have **the same** / **different** spelling after *I*, *you*, and *we*.

**Simple present statements with *I*, *you*, *we***

| | |
|---|---|
| I **love** my watch. | I **don't love** my refrigerator. |
| I **have** a cell phone. | I **don't have** a tablet. |
| You **want** a tablet. | You **don't want** a watch. |
| We **love** our family. | We **don't love** things. |

B **Complete the sentences with the words in the box.**

don't have don't like don't want have love want

1 My new smartwatch is cool. I ____________ it!

2 I ____________ my earphones. They aren't very good.

3 I ____________ 85 apps on my cell phone.

4 We ____________ games on our cell phones. We don't like them.

5 I don't like tablets. I don't have a tablet, and I ____________ a tablet.

6 Your laptop is really old. You ____________ a new laptop.

C **Now go to page 131. Look at the grammar chart and do the grammar exercise for 4.1.**

D PAIR WORK **Complete the sentences. Make them true for you. Then compare with a partner.**

1 I ____________ a smartwatch.

2 I ____________ my cell phone.

3 I ____________ games on my cell phone.

4 I ____________ tablets.

5 I ____________ a new computer.

## 4 SPEAKING

PAIR WORK **What technology do you have? What do you love? What don't you like? Tell your partner. For ideas, watch Anderson's video.**

*I have a good app. It's KickMap. I love it.*

*I like iPhones. I want a …*

REAL STUDENT

*Do you have the same things?*

# 4.2 MY PHONE IS MY WORLD

**LESSON OBJECTIVE**
- say how you use technology

## 1 LANGUAGE IN CONTEXT

A 1.38 **Read and listen. Olivia is at a phone store, TechUBuy. Circle the things she talks about.**

family | friends | her laptop | her phone | school | work

**GLOSSARY**
**phone plan** (*n*) a service you pay for to make calls, send messages, and use the internet on your cell phone

**1.38 Audio script**

**Clerk** Welcome to TechUBuy!
**Olivia** Hi! I want a new phone plan. I love my phone. It's my world! But my plan is expensive.
**Clerk** Do you know which plan you want?
**Olivia** No. I have no idea.
**Clerk** OK. First, I have some questions. What do you do on your phone? Do you **call** your friends?
**Olivia** No. I **chat** with my friends, but I don't *call* them. We **send messages**. And we **leave voice messages**.
**Clerk** Ah, yes. And do you **send emails**?
**Olivia** Yes. I **read emails** on my phone – from friends and for work.
**Clerk** And what else? Do you **listen to music** on your phone?
**Olivia** Yes, I do, and I **watch videos**. I also **use social media** – I **post photos**, **leave comments**, …
**Clerk** OK. Your phone really *is* your world! So, we have three phone plans …

## 2 VOCABULARY: Using technology

A **Read the chart. Which verbs are not in the conversation in exercise 1A?**

**INSIDER ENGLISH**
**Say *What else?* to ask for more information about a topic.**
*And* ***what else?*** *Do you listen to music on your phone?*

| **verbs** + nouns | | |
|---|---|---|
| **buy** apps / games / music / movies<br>**call** friends / family<br>**chat** with friends / family<br>**listen to** music | **play** games<br>**post** photos / comments<br>**read** emails / messages<br>**send** emails / (text) messages | **leave** voice messages / comments<br>**use** apps / social media / technology<br>**watch** movies / videos / TV |
| … on the internet … on my computer / laptop | … on my cell phone / tablet | … on my smartwatch |

I call family on my cell phone.

I listen to music on my phone.

I chat with friends on the internet.

I use apps on my cell phone and tablet.

I play games on my computer.

I read emails on my tablet.

I send text messages on my phone.

I post photos on the internet.

B 1.39 **Look at the pictures. Listen and repeat. Then say three things you do.**

C **Now do the vocabulary exercises for 4.2 on page 144.**

## 3 GRAMMAR: Simple present *yes/no* questions with *I, you, we*

A **Circle the correct answers. Use the sentences in the grammar box to help you.**

1 To make simple present questions, use ***Do* / *Are*** + the subject (for example, *I* or *we*) + a verb.

2 To make negative short answers, use ***do* / *don't***.

**Simple present *yes/no* questions with *I, you, we***

| | |
|---|---|
| **Do** I **post** good photos? | Yes, you **do**. / No, you **don't**. |
| **Do** you **use** social media? | Yes, I **do**. / No, I **don't**. |
| **Do** you **know** which plan you want? | Yes, I **do**. / No, I **don't**. |
| **Do** you and your friends **send** emails? | Yes, we **do**. / No, we **don't**. |

B **Complete the *yes/no* questions. Use the words in parentheses ( ).**

1 ______________________ on your computer? (*you, listen to music*)

2 ______________________ on your phone? (*you, play games*)

3 ______________________ to your teachers? (*you and your friends, send text messages*)

4 ______________________ on social media? (*you, post comments*)

5 ______________________ on your laptop? (*you, watch videos*)

C PAIR WORK **Ask and answer the questions so they are true for you. Say *"Yes, I do."* or *"No, I don't."***

D **Now go to page 132. Look at the grammar chart and do the grammar exercise for 4.2.**

## 4 SPEAKING

A PAIR WORK **What do you do on your phone and the internet? Compare with a partner.**

B PAIR WORK **Look at the cell phone plans. Which plan is good for you? Why? Ask and answer questions with a partner. Use the conversation on page 36 to help you.**

Do you play games on your phone?

No, I don't. I call friends and family, and I send text messages. I don't use social media on my phone. Plan 1 is good for me.

| Plan 1 – $10 / month | Plan 2 – $15 / month | Plan 3 – $20 / month |
|---|---|---|
| 2 GB data | 5 GB data | 10 GB data |
| 100 minutes of talk time | 50 minutes of talk time | 60 minutes of talk time |
| 100 text messages | 200 text messages | 50 text messages |
| Music app | Photo app | 5 games |

# 4.3 WHAT ABOUT YOU?

**LESSON OBJECTIVE**
- talk about how you communicate

## 1 FUNCTIONAL LANGUAGE

A PAIR WORK **How do you communicate with family and friends? Check (✓) the things you use. Then compare with your partner.**

| | | |
|---|---|---|
| ☐ cards | ☐ email | ☐ letter |
| ☐ phone | ☐ social media | ☐ video chat |

B 1.40 **Rocío, a college student in Los Angeles, talks to her new friend Jeff. Read and listen. How do they communicate with family and friends?**

**1.40 Audio script**

**Jeff** So, you're from Chile. Does your family live in Chile, too?

**Rocío** Yes, but LA is my home now! I use technology to chat with my family. I call my parents on my phone, and I send messages to my brothers. It's really nice.

**Jeff** Right. **What about email?**

**Rocío** Yeah. I send emails to my friends in Chile. **How about you?**

**Jeff** I like email, but I use Facebook, too.

**Rocío** OK. I like Instagram.

**Jeff** Oh, yeah? **Do you post photos?**

**Rocío** Yes, photos of LA. My family and friends really like them. **Do you post photos, too?**

**Jeff** No, but I post comments on other people's photos.

**Rocío** Nice comments?

**Jeff** Yes, of course!

C **Complete the chart with expressions in bold from the conversation above.**

| Asking about a new topic | Asking for a response |
|---|---|
| 1 ______ email? | 3 ______ post photos, |
| 2 ______ post photos? | 4 ______ ? |
| Do you send cards? / use social media? | 5 ______ about you? |
| | What about you? |
| | And you? |

D 1.41 PAIR WORK **Put the conversations in the correct order. Listen and check. Then practice with a partner.**

1
___ Yes, I do. Do you use it, too?
___ Yes, it is. I really like it.
_1_ Do you use Instagram?
___ No. Is it interesting?

2
___ No, but I send birthday messages.
___ Yes, to my family and friends. What about you?
___ Hmm … birthday messages are OK, but I like cards.
_1_ Do you send birthday cards to your family?

## 2 REAL-WORLD STRATEGY

**SHOWING YOU ARE LISTENING**

To show you are listening, say *Right*, *Yeah*, or *OK*.

*Jeff* *I use Facebook, too.*

*Rocío* *OK. I like Instagram.*

A **Read about how to show you are listening in the box above. What does Rocío say?**

B 1.42 **Listen to a conversation. How does the man communicate with his family?**

C 1.42 **Listen again. What does the woman say to show she's listening?**

D PAIR WORK **Student A: Go to page 156. Student B: Go to page 159. Follow the instructions.**

## 3 PRONUNCIATION: Saying stressed words

A 1.43 **Listen and repeat the questions. Which words are stressed? Why are they stressed?**

1 What about email? 2 How about you? 3 Do you post photos?

B 1.44 **Listen and underline the stressed words in the questions.**

A Do you use Facebook? (1 word)
B Yeah. How about you? (1 word)
A Me, too. I post photos and comments.
B Do you post videos? (2 words)
A No, but I send videos on WhatsApp.
B Do you use video chat? (2 words)
A Yeah, video chat is great.

C PAIR WORK **Practice the conversation in exercise 3B. Does your partner use stressed words?**

## 4 SPEAKING

A **Think about ways to communicate with people. Which ways do you use? Write a list.**

B PAIR WORK **Talk to a partner about how you communicate. Ask questions to start a new topic. Show you are listening.**

I use Instagram. It's great.

Yeah.

Do you use Instagram, too?

Yes, and I use Snapchat. What about you?

I don't use Snapchat.

# 4.4 GREAT! FIVE STARS

**LESSON OBJECTIVE**
- write product reviews

## 1 LISTENING

A PAIR WORK **Read the definition of "product review." Then answer the questions with a partner.**

1 Do you buy things on the internet?

2 Do you look at or write product reviews?

**GLOSSARY**
**product review** *(n)* people's opinions and comments about things they buy

B 1.45 LISTEN FOR GIST **Listen to product reviews from three vloggers. Match the reviews (1, 2, and 3) to the products below.**

an app ___ a TV ___ a tablet ___

C 1.45 LISTEN FOR MAIN IDEAS **Listen again. How many stars do you think the vloggers give? Circle your answer. Then compare with a partner.**

| Review one: | Review two: | Review three: |
|---|---|---|
| ★☆☆☆☆ / ★★★★☆ | ★★★☆☆ / ★★★★★ | ★☆☆☆☆ / ★★★☆☆ |

D PAIR WORK THINK CRITICALLY **Talk to a partner. Which review is useful to you?**

## 2 GRAMMAR: *a/an*; adjectives before nouns

A **Circle the correct answers. Use the sentences in the grammar box to help you.**

1 Use *a* or *an* with a **singular** / **plural** noun.

2 Use ***a*** / ***an*** before most vowel sounds (*a*, *e*, *i*, *o*, *u*).

3 Use ***a*** / ***an*** before a consonant sound (*b*, *c*, *d*, …).

4 **Use** / **Don't use** *a* or *an* with plural nouns.

***a/an;* adjectives before nouns**

| *a/an* | no *a/an* |
|---|---|
| You take **a photo**. | You take **photos**. (plural nouns) |
| **A tablet** is expensive. | **This tablet** is expensive. (*this* + noun) |
| I have **an uncle**. | I have **two uncles**. (number + noun) |
| We live in **a house**. | **Our house** is small. (possessive adjectives) |
| You have **a new phone**. | His phone **is new**. (*be* + adjective) |

B **Use the words to make sentences. Then check your accuracy.**

1 a / cell phone. / I / new / want ________

2 two / We / in / TVs / our house. / have ________

3 app / really / This / interesting. / is ________

4 you / an / Do / iPad? / have ________

5 like / tablets? / Do / you ________

**ACCURACY CHECK**

**Don't use *a/an* with a plural noun.**

We have computers at work. ✓

We have ~~a computers~~ at work. ✗

C **Now go to page 132. Look at the grammar chart and do the grammar exercise for 4.4.**

## 3 PRONUNCIATION: Listening for the end of a sentence

A 1.46 **Listen. Which sentence do you hear: A or B? Which speaker is finished?**

1 **A** I love games. ↗
  **B** I love games. ↘

2 **A** This tablet is great for games. ↗
  **B** This tablet is great for games. ↘

B 1.47 **Listen. Draw one ↗ and one ↘ for each sentence.**

1 I like it because it's small.

2 It's cheap, but it's nice.

3 It's really fast, and it has a nice design.

4 It's expensive because it's a great product.

## 4 WRITING

A PAIR WORK **Read the product reviews. What are the products? Do you like them? Do you want them?**

### Expensive, but nice

By Linda Valdez ★★★★☆

The earphones are really small. I listen to music on my cell phone with the earphones, and the band is in the room with me! (OK, the band *isn't* in the room with me, but the music *is* really good.) They're great earphones, but they are expensive: $89.99.

### A cheap chair!

By Carl Rogers ★★☆☆☆

This chair is cheap. It's $29.50. I have two chairs – one chair for me, and one chair for my wife. We sit in them and watch TV. I don't like it because it's small, and I'm a big man. I don't sit *in* the chair. I sit *on* it! Is it comfortable? NO!

**GLOSSARY**
**comfortable** (*adj*) good to sit on

B **Read the reviews again. Complete the chart.**

| | Earphones | Chair |
|---|---|---|
| Title | Expensive, but nice | |
| Number of stars | | |
| Price ($) | | |
| Good or bad product? | | |

FIND IT

C **Choose a product you know or find a product on the internet. Find the information in exercise 4B.**

D WRITING SKILLS **Circle the words *but* and *because* in the reviews above. Then circle the correct answer in the rules.**

1 Use *but* to add an idea that is **the same / different**.

2 Use *because* to **give a reason / ask a question**.

**REGISTER CHECK**

**In informal writing, use exclamation points (!) after funny sentences or after words and sentences with a strong feeling, for example, with *love*, *like*, or *don't like*.**

*I don't sit* ***in*** *the chair. I sit* ***on*** *it!*

*Is it comfortable? NO!*

### WRITE IT

E **Write reviews for a good product <u>and</u> a bad product. Use the products below or your own ideas. Write a title, number of stars, and the price.**

an app  a camera  a desk  a game  a lamp  a tablet  a watch

F PAIR WORK **Read a partner's reviews. Do you like their products? Do you want them?**

# 4.5 TIME TO SPEAK
## Playlists

**LESSON OBJECTIVE**
- talk about your favorite music

**A** **Read the text message. What is the message about?**

**B** 1.48 **Use words from the message to complete the definitions (1–5). Then listen and check.**

1 A playlist is a list of your favorite *s*__________ .
2 People in a *b*__________ play music or sing.
3 A *s*__________ is a person in a band. He or she sings the words in a song.
4 *F*__________ music is music that everyone knows.
5 *P*__________ music is music that everyone likes.

**C** **PREPARE** **Talk to a partner. Say the name of one singer, one band, and one song you like.**

**D** **DISCUSS** **Tell your partner about your favorite music. Make a list of singers, bands, and songs you both like.**

**E** **AGREE** **Find singers, bands, and songs that are on your list and on other people's lists. Which music is famous? Which music is popular?**

**F** **DECIDE** **Imagine you're going to the party in the text message. Talk to people in your group. Find songs that everyone likes. Then choose ten songs for the party playlist.**

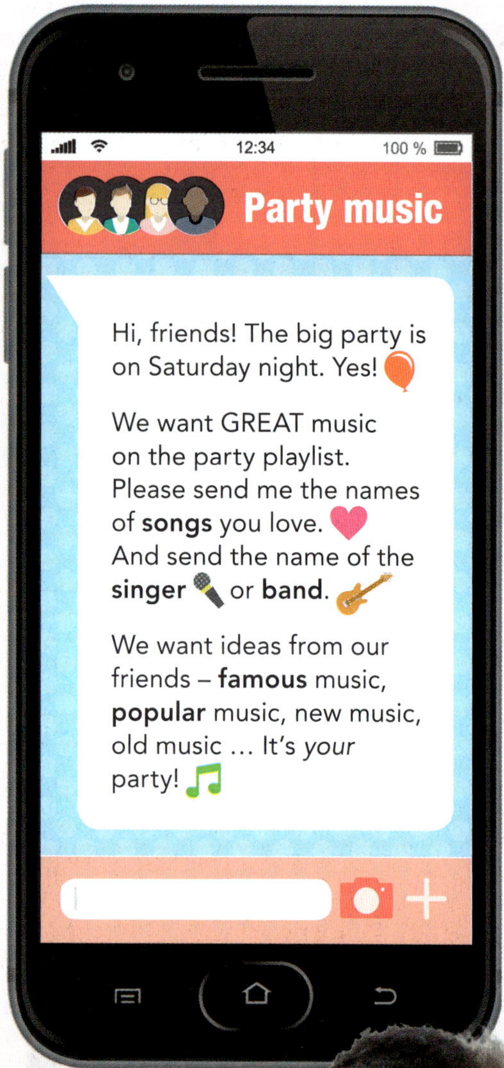

*To check your progress, go to page 153.*

## USEFUL PHRASES

**DISCUSS**
This song is my favorite.
Me, too!
I don't like this song.

**AGREE**
What music do you have on your list?
I have (song/singer/band) on my list.
Let's have this song on the list.
I don't want this song on the list.
What do you think?

**DECIDE**
Do we want (song/singer/band) or (song/singer/band)?
Here are our ten songs for the party playlist.

**UNIT OBJECTIVES**

- talk about weekday and weekend activities
- tell the time and talk about your routines
- show you agree and have things in common
- write a report about your activities
- compare different work weeks

# MONDAYS AND FUN DAYS

# 5

## START SPEAKING

A **Look at the picture and describe the people. Who are they? Where are they?**

B **Are they happy? Is it a fun day?**

C **For you, what is a fun day?**

# 5.1 PLAY OR FAST-FORWARD?

**LESSON OBJECTIVE**
- talk about weekday and weekend activities

## 1 VOCABULARY: Days and times of day; everyday activities

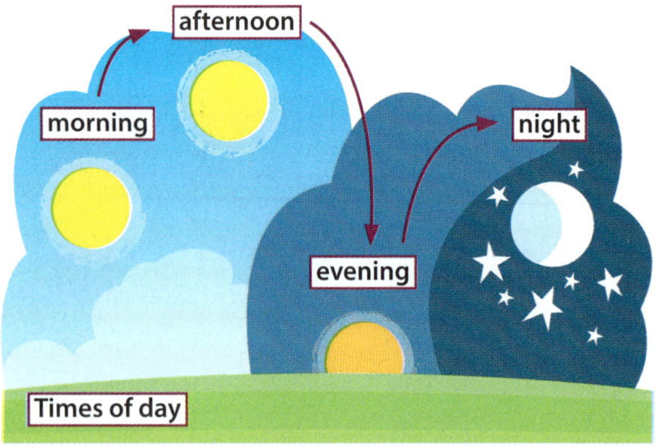


A 1.49 **Listen and repeat. What's your favorite day? What's your favorite time of day?**

| weekdays | | | | | weekend | |
|---|---|---|---|---|---|---|
| Monday | Tuesday | Wednesday | Thursday | Friday | Saturday | Sunday |

B 1.50 **Listen and repeat the sentences.**

1 I go out in the evening.

2 I run on Monday and Friday.

3 I work on the weekend.

4 I study in the morning.

5 I don't play soccer.

C PAIR WORK **Which sentences in exercise 1B are true for you? Tell your partner. Then say two more true sentences about your activities.**

D **Now do the vocabulary exercises for 5.1 on page 144.**

## 2 LANGUAGE IN CONTEXT

A **Read the article. Who are Sam and Justine? What activities does Sam do on weekdays?**

**GLOSSARY**
**after** (*adv*) he works, then he plays soccer
**before** (*adv*) he runs, then he goes to work
**every** (*det*) 100% (of days / evenings)
**way of life** (*phrase*) how you live your life

# PLAY or FAST-FORWARD?

By Matt Newman

**Weekdays** = **work** or **study**. **Weekends** = fun. Right? Not for my brother, Sam! For Sam, *every* day is a fun day! He works from **Monday morning** to **Friday afternoon**, but he usually **runs** in the morning before work. On Monday and **Thursday**, he **plays soccer** after work, and he **goes out** with friends on **Wednesday**. He doesn't go out *every* evening – on **Tuesdays** he stays home and watches TV. His way of life is "play now."

My sister, Justine, is very different. She has fun, but not every day. From Monday to Friday, she works. She doesn't have time for sports, and she hardly ever goes out! It's OK because Justine has free time on the weekend. She chats with family in the afternoon and then goes out with friends at night. Her way of life is work, work, work, and "fast-forward to the weekend."

**Sam and Justine are both happy people, but their ways of life are *very* different. What about you? What's *your* way of life?**

B What's Sam's way of life: "play now", or "fast-forward"? What's Justine's way of life?

C PAIR WORK What's your way of life: "play now" or "fast-forward to the weekend"? Tell your partner. For ideas, watch June's video.

*Are you the same as June?*

## 3 GRAMMAR: Simple present statements with *he, she, they*

A Circle the correct answers. Use the sentences in the grammar box to help you.

1 In affirmative statements with ***he and she*** / ***they***, most simple present verbs end in *-s*.
2 The verb *have* is irregular. In affirmative statements with *he* and *she*, use ***have*** / ***has***.
3 To make negative statements with *he* and *she*, use ***don't*** / ***doesn't*** + verb.

**Simple present statements with *he, she, they***

| | |
|---|---|
| He **works** Monday to Friday. | She **doesn't have** time for sports. |
| She **chats** with family in the afternoon. | They **don't go out** every evening. |
| She **has** fun, but not every day. | My dad **doesn't play** soccer. |
| They **have** fun on the weekend. | |

B Complete the sentences with the words in the box.

doesn't don't has have play plays

1 My friends __________ video games every weekday evening.
2 On weekdays, my sister __________ go out in the evening.
3 Every day, my sister and her husband __________ tea in the morning.
4 Pedro __________ soccer on his college team, but not in every game.
5 My mom __________ a tablet, but she doesn't use it.
6 My grandparents __________ work, so from Monday to Friday they're at home.

C Look at the sentences in exercise 3B and the adverbs of frequency chart. Then circle the correct answers.

1 My friends *often* / *hardly ever* / *never* play video games.
2 On weekdays, my sister is *always* / *sometimes* / *never* at home in the evening.
3 My sister and her husband *always* / *hardly ever* / *never* drink tea in the morning.
4 Pedro *always* / *sometimes* / *never* plays in his college soccer games.
5 My mom *always* / *often* / *never* uses her tablet.
6 My grandparents are *usually* / *hardly ever* / *never* at home on weekdays.

**Adverbs of frequency**

100%
always
usually
often
sometimes
hardly ever
never
0%

D Now go to page 133. Look at the grammar chart and do the grammar exercise for 5.1.

## 4 SPEAKING

A Look at the activities in exercise 1B on page 44. What activities do your family or friends do? When do they do them? Write a list. Use adverbs of frequency.

B PAIR WORK Talk to a partner about your family and friends' activities. Who is "play now"? Who is "fast-forward"?

*My sister is "play now." She often goes out in the evening …*

# 5.2 LISTEN TO YOUR BODY CLOCK

**LESSON OBJECTIVE**
- tell the time and talk about your routines

## 1 VOCABULARY: Telling the time

A 1.51 PAIR WORK **Listen and repeat the times. Then point to a picture and ask *"What time is it?"* Your partner says the time.**

It's eight **o'clock**.

It's five-fifteen.
It's (a) **quarter after** five.

It's three-thirty.

It's ten forty-five.
It's (a) **quarter to** eleven.

It's nine-oh-five.
It's five **after** nine.

It's six-fifty.
It's ten **to** seven.

It's **12:00 p.m.** / It's **noon**.
It's **12.00 a.m.** / It's **midnight**.

! **a.m.** = before 12 noon
**p.m.** = after 12 noon
**to** = before

B **Now do the first vocabulary exercise for 5.2 on page 145.**

**GLOSSARY**
**routine** (*n*) the things you do every day at the same time
**tired** (*adj*) you are sleepy
**late** (*adj*) toward the end of the morning or evening

## 2 LANGUAGE IN CONTEXT

A 1.52 **Read and listen. Alex talks to his doctor. What is Alex's problem? What is your "body clock"?**

**1.52 Audio script**

**Alex** I'm always so tired.
**Doctor** Tell me about your routine, Alex. What time do you **get up**?
**Alex** On weekdays, I usually get up at **7:45**, and I go to class at **8:30**.
**Doctor** Do you **eat breakfast**?
**Alex** No, I don't. But I **drink coffee**.
**Doctor** When do you eat?
**Alex** At noon. Then I **go to class** again in the afternoon. I usually **have dinner** at **9:00**. My parents don't like that.
**Doctor** Well, it is very late. Do they have dinner before you?
**Alex** Yes, they do. Usually at **6:00**.
**Doctor** Does your mom make dinner for you?
**Alex** No, she doesn't. I make it.
**Doctor** OK. What do you do on weekends?
**Alex** On Friday and Saturday, I go out with friends. I usually **go to bed** at **2:00** or **3:00** a.m. And on Sunday, I get up really late and watch TV.
**Doctor** Alex, it's time to listen to your body clock!

B 1.52 PAIR WORK **Listen again. Write notes about Alex's routine. Compare with a partner.**

*He doesn't eat breakfast. He drinks coffee.*

C **Now do the second vocabulary exercise for 5.2 on page 145.**

D PAIR WORK **Is your routine the same as or different from Alex's? Tell your partner. For ideas, watch Josue's video.**

REAL STUDENT

*Is your routine different from Josue's, or the same?*

## 3 GRAMMAR: Questions in the simple present

A **Circle the correct answers. Use the sentences in the grammar box to help you.**

1 With the pronouns *I*, *you*, *we*, and *they*, use **Do / Does**.

2 With the pronouns *he*, *she*, and *it*, use **Do / Does**.

3 In yes/no questions, the word order is ***Do*** **or** ***Does*** **+ person or thing + verb /** ***Do*** **or** ***Does*** **+ verb + person or thing**.

4 In information questions, put the question word(s) (for example, *Where* or *What time*) **before / after** *do* and *does*.

### Questions in the simple present

| *Yes/no* questions | Information questions |
|---|---|
| **Do** I **have** class today? | **How do** I **get** to class? |
| **Do** you **go out** with friends? | **What time do** you **go out** with friends? |
| **Does** he **go** to classes every day? | **When does** he **go** to classes? |
| **Does** it **have** good apps? | **What does** it **have?** |
| **Do** they **have** dinner before you? | **Where do** they **eat** dinner? |

B PAIR WORK **Complete the conversations. Use the audio script on page 46 to help you. Then practice them with a partner.**

1 A ______ ______ do you go to work?
  B I ______ to work at 7:00.
  A Wow! ______ do you go to bed?
  B I usually go to bed after midnight. I'm always tired!

2 A ______ they play soccer?
  B ______, they do. What about you?
  A No, I ______.

3 A ______ Martin have a new job?
  B Yes, he ______.
  A ______ does he work?
  B He ______ in an office.

C **Now go to page 133. Look at the grammar charts and do the grammar exercise for 5.2.**

D **Write three questions about your partner's routine. Use the words in the box to start your questions. Then check your accuracy.**

Do ... ?   What ... ?   What time ... ?
When ... ?   Where ... ?

**ACCURACY CHECK**

**Use *do* or *does* with information questions in the simple present.**

Where Margaret work? ✗
Where does Margaret work? ✓

E PAIR WORK **Ask and answer the questions from exercise 3D with a partner.**

## 4 SPEAKING

A **Think about your routines and your family's routines. What do you do? When do you do it?**

B PAIR WORK **Ask your partner about their routines and their family's routines. Do they listen to their body clock?**

*When do you get up?*

*I usually get up at 7:30, but my sister gets up at 5:00!*

# 5.3 ME, TOO

**LESSON OBJECTIVE**
- show you agree and have things in common

## 1 FUNCTIONAL LANGUAGE

A 1.53 **The men are at work. Read and listen to their conversation. What do both the men do?**

**1.53 Audio script**

A Do you always run at lunchtime?
B Yeah, I usually run for about 30 minutes.
A That's cool. It's good to go out.
B **I agree.** And what about you? Do you run?
A Hardly ever. Well, I play basketball.
B So you run a lot!
A **That's true.** But I don't have the ball a lot! I'm not very good.
B **Me, neither.** But basketball is fun.
A **Yeah, I know.**
B I play with friends.
A **Me, too.** Hey, we have a game on Thursday after work. Play with us!
B Thursday. Um … yeah, OK.
A Great! Now I'm not the only bad player.
B Very funny!

B **Complete the chart with expressions in bold from the conversations above.**

| Showing you agree | Showing you have things in common |
|---|---|
| I [1] ________ .<br>That's [2] ________ . / That's right.<br>[3] ________ , I know. | [4] ________ , neither. (-)<br>Me, [5] ________ . (+) |

C **Choose the correct answers to complete the conversations. Then practice with a partner.**

1 A I play basketball on the weekend.
B *Me, too / Me, neither.* I play on Sunday.

2 A Soccer is great.
B I *agree / right*. Do you play?

3 A This game is boring.
B *Yeah, I know / Me, neither.* The team isn't very good.

4 A I don't get up late on Saturday.
B *Me, too / Me, neither.* I get up at 8.

## 2 REAL-WORLD STRATEGY

**SHORT ANSWERS WITH ADVERBS OF FREQUENCY**

People sometimes answer questions with adverbs of frequency, not complete sentences.

*A Do you always run at lunch?*

*B Usually. And what about you? Do you run?*

*A Hardly ever.*

A **Read about short answers with adverbs of frequency in the box above. Who runs a lot: A or B? Who doesn't run a lot?**

B 1.54 **Listen to a conversation. Who gets up early on the weekend: the man, the woman, or both of them?**

C 1.54 **Listen again. What one-word answer does the man say? What one-word answer does the woman say?**

D PAIR WORK **Student A: Go to page 157. Student B: Go to page 159. Follow the instructions.**

## 3 PRONUNCIATION: Saying syllables in words

A 1.55 **Listen. How many syllables do you hear? Write 1, 2, or 3.**

1 run ___ 2 basketball ___ 3 soccer ___

B 1.56 **Say the words. How many syllables are there? Write 1, 2, or 3. Listen and check.**

1 weekend ___ 3 usually ___ 5 sport ___

2 Wednesday ___ 4 chat ___ 6 morning ___

C **Look at the audio script on page 48. Find more examples of words with one or two syllables.**

## 4 SPEAKING

A **Write a list of things you do often. Write how you feel about the activities.**

chat with friends online – fun

watch TV – interesting

B PAIR WORK **Tell your partner what you do and how you feel about the activities. Your partner says when he/she agrees and when you have things in common. Then change roles and repeat.**

On weekdays, I watch TV in the evening.

Me, too.

It's sometimes interesting.

Yeah, I know.

# 5.4 A HAPPY LIFE

**LESSON OBJECTIVE**
- write a report about your activities

## 1 READING

A **SKIM** Look at the picture and the title. What is the magazine article about?

### WORK, REST, and PLAY = The WRAP test

**Doctors always say, for a happy life, work, rest, and play! OK, but it isn't always easy. What about *your* life? Do you work, rest, and play? Do you work, rest, and play? Or do you work, rest, and play?**

### Look at Cheryl.

She's very busy. She's a salesperson. She works at a store Monday to Friday from 10:00 a.m. to 5:30 p.m. She has a French class in the evening on Tuesdays and Thursdays. After class, she listens to music or watches TV. Then she does her homework. On the weekend, she has free time. She plays soccer with her friends. She often goes out with her sister on Saturday night. On Sunday, she studies French for her class. Then she sometimes plays the guitar.

**What is Cheryl's WRAP?**
**What about you? To find out, take the WRAP test . . .**

B **READ FOR DETAILS** Read the article again. Complete the chart with the correct verbs.

| Work | | Rest | | Play | |
|---|---|---|---|---|---|
| works | at a store | ______ | music | ______ | soccer |
| ______ | a French class | ______ | TV | ______ | with her sister |
| ______ | her homework | | | ______ | the guitar |
| ______ | French | | | | |

C **PAIR WORK** **THINK CRITICALLY** Which WRAP result is true for Cheryl?

1 **work**, rest, and play  2 **work**, rest, and **play**  3 work, **rest**, and **play**

## 2 WRITING

**A** **Read Andre's WRAP report. What does he do on weekdays? What does he do on the weekend?**

### My WRAP report

By Andre Costa

Heading

**Work**

1 I'm a teacher. I work Monday to Friday from 8:00 a.m. to 3:00 p.m.
2 I teach music classes after school on Wednesdays.
3 I study English on Saturday mornings.

**Rest**

1 I watch TV before bed Monday to Thursday.
2 I read books on the weekend.

**Play**

1 I play basketball after work on Thursdays.

**My WRAP result**

I work, rest, and play.

**GLOSSARY**

**from 8:00 a.m. to 3:00 p.m.** = 8:00 a.m. → 3:00 p.m. (7 hours)

**REGISTER CHECK**

**Write *a.m.* and *p.m.* after times.**

*I work Monday to Friday from 8:00 a.m. to 3:00 p.m.*

**Say *in the morning, in the afternoon,* or *at night* after times.**

*Andre says, "I sometimes go to bed at 1:30 in the morning."*

**B** WRITING SKILLS **Look at the heading "Work." Circle the other headings in the report. What do they show?**

a days and times in the report
b different sports in each part of the report
c the different topics in the report

**C** **Look at the numbered lists in the report above. What do the lists show?**

a Andre's test results (= answers)
b Andre's activities
c Andre's classes

**D** **Write notes in the chart below with your information. Use the chart in exercise 1B for an example.**

| Work | Rest | Play |
|---|---|---|
| | | |

### WRITE IT

**E** **Write your WRAP report. Use headings and numbered lists. Include activities, times, and days.**

**F** PAIR WORK **Work with a partner. Read your partner's report. What's his/her WRAP result?**

**G** GROUP WORK **Compare reports in your group. Tell the group about your partner.**

Sora works at a restaurant on the weekend. She ...

# 5.5 TIME TO SPEAK
## Life = 5 + 2

**LESSON OBJECTIVE**
- compare different work weeks

**A** **PREPARE** Read the magazine article about different work weeks. Which week is your favorite: A, B, or C? Tell your partner.

### END OF THE TWO-DAY WEEKEND?

For a lot of people, life = 5 + 2. They work 5 days and have 2 days for the weekend. But is this good? Imagine:

| | |
|---|---|
| Week A | We work 4 long days (10 hours) and have 3 days for the weekend. |
| Week B | We work 6 short days (6½ hours) and have 1 day for the weekend. |
| Week C | We work 7 very short days (5½ hours) and don't have a weekend. |

**B** **DISCUSS** Imagine you have a "week A" life. Talk to a partner. Describe your routine. What do you do, and when do you do it? Then talk about week B and week C.

**C** **DECIDE** Which week is good for your body clock: A, B, C, or "5 + 2"? Why?

**D** **AGREE** Tell the class which week is your favorite. Which week does everyone like? Which week does no one like?

*To check your progress, go to page 153.*

## USEFUL PHRASES

**PREPARE**
Which week is your favorite?
Week … is my favorite.

**DISCUSS**
I have a week A/B/C life.
I get up / have breakfast at …
I work from … to …
Before/After work, I …
I have free time from … to …

**DECIDE**
Week … is good for me because …
I like / don't like week … because …
I want free time on the weekends / in the evenings.
I like long /short work days.

# ZOOM IN, ZOOM OUT

# 6

**UNIT OBJECTIVES**

- talk about places in the city
- talk about nature in your area
- ask for and give directions
- write a fact sheet about a place in nature
- plan a new neighborhood for a city

## START SPEAKING

A **Say things you see in the picture. For ideas, watch Julieth's video.**

B **Do you want to go here? Why or why not?**

C **Do you like cities? Do you like places in nature? Which is your favorite?**

**REAL STUDENT**

*Do you see the same things as Julieth?*

# 6.1 GOOD PLACES

**LESSON OBJECTIVE**
- talk about places in the city

## 1 LANGUAGE IN CONTEXT

A 1.57 **Lucas and Robert are in New York City. Read and listen to their conversation. Where is Lucas from? Where is Robert from? What does Lucas want to do on Saturday?**

B 1.57 **Read and listen again. Are the sentences true or false?**

1 Lucas has a lot of time in New York City.
2 There is no restaurant in the hotel.

**1.57 Audio script**

| | |
|---|---|
| **Lucas** | I'm here, in New York City, for a week. And then I go home to Paris on Sunday. |
| **Robert** | So you don't have a lot of time to see my great city. |
| **Lucas** | No, I don't. There's no free time this week – it's work, work, work! But I have some time on Saturday. |
| **Robert** | OK. There are a lot of places to see and things to do on the weekend. Where is your **hotel**? |
| **Lucas** | It's near Central Park. |
| **Robert** | No way! Central Park is great. There are some interesting museums near the **park**. Oh, and there's a **zoo** in the park! |
| **Lucas** | Cool! What about places to eat? There's no **restaurant** in my hotel. |
| **Robert** | Hmm … for breakfast, there's a nice **café** near here. And there are a lot of great restaurants in this neighborhood, too. |
| **Lucas** | Great. Do you know some good **stores**? I don't have a lot of free time, but … |
| **Robert** | Oh, yeah. There are a lot of great stores in New York. So … no museum, no park, no zoo – just shopping? |
| **Lucas** | Yes! |

**GLOSSARY**
**neighborhood** (*n*) an area of a city

**INSIDER ENGLISH**
Use *No way!* to show surprise.
*No way! Central Park is great.*

## 2 VOCABULARY: Places in cities

A 1.58 **Listen and repeat the words.**

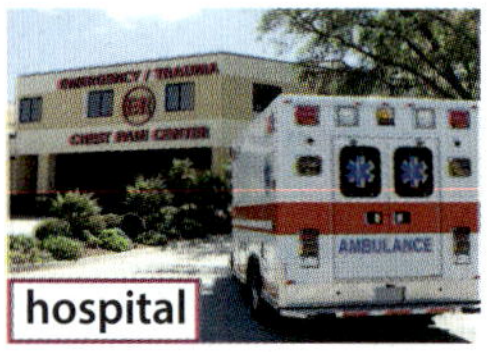

B **Now do the vocabulary exercises for 6.1 on page 145.**

C PAIR WORK **Which three places in cities do you both like? Which three <u>don't</u> you like?**

## 3 GRAMMAR: *There's, There are; a lot of, some, no*

A **Circle the correct answers. Use the sentences in the grammar box to help you.**

1 Use *There's* with **singular / plural** nouns.
2 Use *There are* with **singular / plural** nouns.
3 Use ***an* / *no*** in negative sentences.
4 Use *some* **for exact numbers / when you don't know how many things there are.**

***There's (= There is), There are; a lot of, some, no***

| | | |
|---|---|---|
| **There's** no free time this week. | **There are** some interesting museums near the park. | **no** = zero |
| **There's** a zoo in the park. | **There are** a lot of good places to see on the weekend. | **a/an** = one |
| **There's** a nice café near here. | | **some** = a small number |
| | | **a lot of** = a large number |

B **Circle the correct words to complete the sentences.**

1 *There's / There are* a lot of stores in the mall.
2 *There's / There are* a supermarket near the college.
3 There are *a / some* good cafés on Boston Road.
4 There's *a / a lot of* big hospital in the city.
5 There are *a lot of / no* stores, so it's great for shopping.
6 In my city, there are *a / no* zoos.

C **Now go to page 134. Look at the grammar chart and do the grammar exercise for 6.1.**

D **Write sentences about your city. Use *there is/there are*, *a/an*, *some*, *a lot of*, and *no*. Then check your accuracy.**

There's ______________________________.
There's ______________________________.
There are ______________________________.
There are ______________________________.
There is/are no ______________________________.

**✓ ACCURACY CHECK**

**Use *there are*, not *there is*, before *a lot of* and *some* + plural noun.**

There ~~is~~ some museums in this city. ✗
There are some museums in this city. ✓

E PAIR WORK **Compare your sentences with a partner.**

## 4 SPEAKING

PAIR WORK **Talk about the things in your neighborhood. Then compare with a partner. What's the same? What's different?**

There are some good restaurants near my home.

Same! And there's a movie theater near my home.

# 6.2 CITY LIFE, WILD LIFE

**LESSON OBJECTIVE**
- talk about nature in your area

## 1 VOCABULARY: Nature

A 1.59 **Listen and repeat the words. Which picture is your favorite? Which words describe water?**

B **Cross out the word that does not belong.**

1 lake ~~flower~~ ocean
2 plants trees snow
3 river desert lake
4 grass beach ocean
5 forest ocean trees
6 mountain hill island

C **Now do the vocabulary exercises for 6.2 on page 146.**

## 2 LANGUAGE IN CONTEXT

A **Read the article. Choose a good title.**

1 What's your favorite city? 2 Are you close to nature? 3 Do you like nature?

B PAIR WORK **Take the test. Then compare your answers with a partner.**

**Do I like nature? Sure. We all love flowers and trees. But I live in a big city, so I don't live close to nature ... Or do I? What about you? Take the test. For each sentence, circle all the answers that are true for you.**

| | In your neighborhood | In your city (e.g., in a park) | 1–3 hours from your city | Not near your city |
|---|---|---|---|---|
| There's a lot of **grass**. | A | B | C | D |
| There are a lot of **flowers**. | A | B | C | D |
| There are some **trees**. | A | B | C | D |
| There's a **river**. | A | B | C | D |
| There's a **lake**. | A | B | C | D |
| There's a **forest**. | A | B | C | D |
| There are some **mountains** and **hills**. | A | B | C | D |
| There's a **beach**. | A | B | C | D |
| There's an **ocean**. | A | B | C | D |
| There are a lot of **plants**. | A | B | C | D |

21 25 14

**A** = 3 points, **B** = 2 points, **C** = 1 point, **D** = 0 points

**Are you close to nature?**

**45–60 points**
Nature is everywhere!
**30–44 points**
There's a lot of nature near you.
**15–29 points**
There's some nature near you.
**1–14 points**
There isn't a lot of nature near you.
**0 points**
You only see nature on TV!

C PAIR WORK **Give examples of nature in your city. For ideas, watch Larissa's video.**

REAL STUDENT

*Are your answers the same as Larissa's?*

## 3 GRAMMAR: Count and non-count nouns

A **Circle the correct answers. Use the sentences in the grammar box to help you.**

1 Count nouns have **plural and singular forms** / **no singular or plural form**.
2 Use *a/an* with **singular** / **plural** count nouns.
3 Use ***There's*** / ***There are*** with plural count nouns.
4 Use ***There's*** / ***There are*** with singular count nouns and non-count nouns.

**Count and non-count nouns**

| Singular | Plural | No singular or plural form |
|---|---|---|
| There's a **river** in my city.<br>There's an **ocean** near here. | There are two **rivers**.<br>There are no **oceans** near here.<br>There are some **plants**.<br>There are a lot of **flowers**. | There's no / some / a lot of **grass**.<br>There's no / some / a lot of **water** in the ocean. |

B **Complete the sentences with the correct form of the nouns in parentheses ( ).**

1 There are no ___trees___ (tree) in my neighborhood.
2 There's an ______________ (ocean) three hours from my city.
3 There's a lot of ______________ (nature) in this city.
4 There are some ______________ (restaurant) on my street.
5 There is no ______________ (grass) near my house.
6 There are a lot of ______________ (hotel) in my city.

C **Now go to page 134. Look at the grammar chart and do the grammar exercise for 6.2.**

D PAIR WORK **Change the sentences in exercise 3B so they're true for you and your city. Compare your sentences with a partner.**

There are some trees in my neighborhood.

## 4 SPEAKING

A **Choose a city in your country or in a different country. Think about the nature there.**

B PAIR WORK **Work with a partner. Tell your partner about the place. Does your partner know the place?**

There's a beach in the city.
There are no hills or mountains.
There are a lot of trees ...

I know! It's Tampa, in the U.S.!

# 6.3 IS IT NEAR HERE?

**LESSON OBJECTIVE**
- ask for and give directions

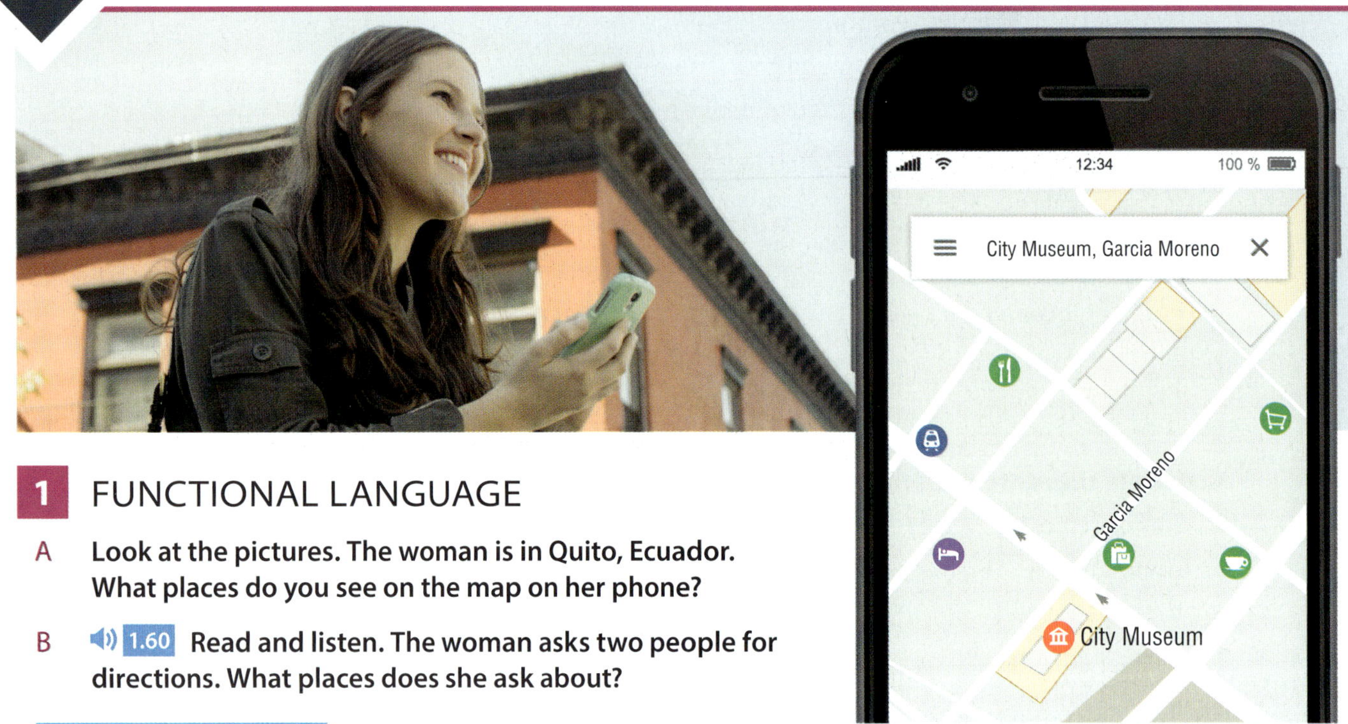


## 1 FUNCTIONAL LANGUAGE

A **Look at the pictures. The woman is in Quito, Ecuador. What places do you see on the map on her phone?**

B 1.60 **Read and listen. The woman asks two people for directions. What places does she ask about?**

**1.60 Audio script**

1 **A** Excuse me. Do you speak English?
**B** Yes, I do.
**A** Oh, good! **Where's** Garcia Moreno Street? **Is it near here**?
**B** Yes, it is. Uh … turn left here. **Go one block**, and then **turn right. That's** Garcia Moreno Street.
**A** OK, great! Thanks.

2 **A** Excuse me. **Is this** Garcia Moreno Street?
**B** Yes, it is.
**A** Where's the City Museum?
**B** **It's that way. Go straight. It's on the left.** Or come with me! It's on my way to the supermarket.

C **Complete the chart with expressions in bold from the conversations above.**

| Asking for directions | Giving directions |
|---|---|
| Where am I? / Where are we? | Turn left. / [4] ______________. |
| I don't understand the map. | [5] ______________ way. |
| [1] ______________ Garcia Moreno Street? | Go one [6] ______________. / Go [7] ______________. |
| Is it [2] ______________? | It's on the right. / [8] ______________. |
| Excuse me. Is [3] ______________ Garcia Moreno Street? | It's over there. / It's here! |
| | [9] ______________ Garcia Moreno Street. |
| | Look on your phone. Zoom in / zoom out. It's here. |

D 1.61 PAIR WORK **Complete the conversations. Then listen and check. Practice with a partner.**

1 **A** Excuse me. *It's / Where's* Central Station? **B** Go one *way / block*. It's on the left.
2 **A** *Is this / Is it* San Gabriel Street? **B** No. *Turn / It's* right. That's San Gabriel Street.
3 **A** Is the language center *go straight / near here*? **B** Yes. It's over *there / go one block*.

## 2 REAL-WORLD STRATEGY

A 1.62 **Listen to a conversation. Where does the man want to go?**

B 1.62 **Listen again. The man wants to check the information. What does he do?**

1 He asks the woman to repeat her words.     2 He repeats the woman's words.

**CHECKING INFORMATION**

To check you understand, say *So, …* and repeat the information.

*It's that way. Turn left here. Go one block, and then turn right.*

*So, turn left here. Go one block, and then turn right.*

C 1.63 **Read about checking information in the box above. Then listen to the directions. Check the information.**

1 Turn right here. Then turn right again.   *So, turn right here. Then turn right again.*

D PAIR WORK **Student A: Go to page 157. Student B: Go to page 159. Follow the instructions.**

## 3 PRONUNCIATION: Saying /ɪr/ and /er/ sounds

A 1.64 **Listen and repeat. Focus on the sound of the letters in bold.**

/ɪr/ Is it n**ear** h**ere**?     /er/ Wh**ere** is th**eir** house?

B 1.65 **Listen. Write A for words with /ɪr/. Write B for words with /er/.**

| | | | |
|---|---|---|---|
| 1 clear ____ | 3 chair ____ | 5 there ____ | 7 year ____ |
| 2 they're ____ | 4 earphones ____ | 6 parent ____ | 8 square ____ |

C 1.66 PAIR WORK **Listen to the conversations. Then practice with a partner.**

1 **A** Where's Bl**air** Street?

**B** It's n**ear** h**ere**. Go to the town squ**are** and then turn right.

2 **A** Where are your p**are**nts?

**B** **They're** over th**ere**, on the ch**air**s.

## 4 SPEAKING

A PAIR WORK **Put the conversation in order. Then practice it with a partner.**

____ So, go straight. Then turn left. It's on the left.

____ Yes.

____ Excuse me. Where's the Park Hotel?

____ It's that way. Go straight. Then turn left. It's on the left.

B **Work alone. Choose one of the situations below.**

1 Imagine you are at the City Museum in Quito, Ecuador. Look at the map on the cell phone on page 58. Choose a place to go.

2 Imagine you are in another city. You can go online and find a map of the city. Choose where you are and a place to go.

FIND IT

C PAIR WORK **Ask a partner for directions. You can use your phone to help you. Then change roles.**

# 6.4 A FOREST IN THE CITY

**LESSON OBJECTIVE**
- write a fact sheet about a place in nature

## 1 LISTENING

A **Look at the pictures. Where is the woman? What do you see?**

B 1.67 LISTEN FOR DETAILS **Listen to the podcast *Walk with Yasmin*. Where is the forest?**

C 1.67 LISTEN FOR EXAMPLES **Listen again. Check (✓) the words Yasmin says.**

| | | | | |
|---|---|---|---|---|
| **Forest** | ☐ animals | ☐ grass | ☐ an ocean | ☐ a river |
| | ☐ flowers | ☐ a mountain | ☐ plants | ☐ trees |
| **City** | ☐ hospitals | ☐ museums | ☐ restaurants | ☐ stores |
| | ☐ hotels | ☐ people | ☐ schools | ☐ zoos |

## 2 PRONUNCIATION: Listening for important words

A 1.68 **Read the sentences below. Focus on the underlined words. Then listen. Which sentence do you hear, A or B?**

**A** There are some tall trees and a lot of big plants here.

**B** There are some tall trees and a lot of big plants here.

B 1.69 **Underline the important words in each sentence. Listen and check.**

1 There's a river near me. (1 word)

2 There are a lot of interesting animals here. (3 words)

3 I'm on a mountain in a forest. (2 words)

4 There's an ocean and some beautiful beaches. (3 words)

## 3 WRITING

A **Read the fact sheet. What is in Tijuca Forest?**

### FACT SHEET: Tijuca Forest

Tijuca Forest is in Rio de Janeiro, Brazil.

It is a nice, big forest. It is 39 square kilometers.

There are a lot of plants and trees in the forest.

It has nice rivers and waterfalls.

It has a lot of interesting animals and birds.

There are some mountains in the forest. One famous mountain is Corcovado Mountain.

There is a tall statue on Corcovado Mountain. It is the Christ statue.

Brazilians love the forest, and people from many countries visit it.

Tijuca Forest is very important to Rio de Janeiro.

Capuchin monkey

Taunay Waterfall

Tropical flowers

Christ the Redeemer

B PAIR WORK THINK CRITICALLY **There are no contractions in the fact sheet (for example, *It's, There's*). Why not?**

C **Read the sentences from the fact sheet. Underline two opinion adjectives and one size adjective.**

It has a lot of interesting animals and birds.

It is a nice, big forest.

D WRITING SKILLS **Read the rules below. Circle *before* or *after*. Use the sentences in exercise 3C to help you.**

1 *Some, a lot of,* and *no* go **before** / **after** opinion adjectives (for example, *good, nice, interesting*).

2 Opinion adjectives usually go **before** / **after** size adjectives (for example, *big, small, tall*).

**REGISTER CHECK**

***Really*** **and** ***very*** **make adjectives stronger. Use** ***very*** **in writing.** ***Really*** **is common in speaking.**

*Tijuca Forest is* ***very*** *important to Rio de Janeiro.*

FIND IT

E **Choose a natural area to write about. You can go online to find facts about where it is, how big it is, what nature is there, and who goes to it. Use *very*. Do not use contractions. Remember to write adjectives in the correct order.**

### WRITE IT

F **Write a fact sheet about a place in nature. Write five or six sentences. Use the fact sheet in exercise 3A for an example.**

6.5

# TIME TO SPEAK
## A good place to live

**LESSON OBJECTIVE**

- plan a new neighborhood for a city

**A** **PREPARE** **Talk to a partner. What do you see in the pictures?**

**B** **DISCUSS** **Which places in the pictures are important to have near your home? Write numbers 1–8 next to the pictures.**

1 = very important ➔ 8 = not very important

**C** **DISCUSS** **Imagine that city planners want ideas for a new neighborhood in your city. Work with a partner. Choose <u>one</u> person from the list below. What does your person want in the new neighborhood? Write notes.**

- You have young children.
- You are over 60 and you don't work.
- You are a young person in your first apartment.
- You are a college student in a home-share.

**D** **PRESENT** **Present your ideas for the new neighborhood to the class. Which things does everyone think are important in a city?**

*To check your progress, go to page 153.*

## USEFUL PHRASES

**DISCUSS**

I have children. A school is really important.
What about … ? Me, too. I agree. / I disagree.
I think … is good for the neighborhood.
I want … for the neighborhood.
I like / don't like …
I think … are very important / not very important.

**PRESENT**

We want …
Everyone in the class likes …

# REVIEW 2 (UNITS 4–6)

## 1 VOCABULARY

A **Look at the groups of words in 1–6. In each group, circle the word that does not belong. Then match the groups with the categories (a–f).**

| | | | | | | | | |
|---|---|---|---|---|---|---|---|---|
| 1 | grass | mountain | river | song | tree | ___ | a | technology |
| 2 | call friends | get up | hill | play soccer | work | ___ | b | music |
| 3 | album | band | camera | playlist | singer | ___ | c | places in cities |
| 4 | afternoon | hotel | Monday | morning | night | ___ | d | nature |
| 5 | app | laptop | morning | phone | tablet | ___ | e | things we do |
| 6 | café | hospital | restaurant | run | store | ___ | f | days and times of day |

B **Match each word you circled in 1–6 to a different category (a–f). Then add <u>one</u> extra word to the categories.**

## 2 GRAMMAR

A **Make questions and answers. Use the words in parentheses ( ) and *do/does/don't/doesn't*.**

1 A ________________ you ________________ video games?
 B Yes, I sometimes ________________ games on my cell phone. (play)

2 A Where ________________ you ________________ at lunchtime?
 B I usually ________________ at home. (eat)

3 A ________________ your grandfather ________________ ?
 B Yes, he ________________ at the hospital. (work)

4 A ________________ you and your family ________________ soccer?
 B No, we ________________ it. (like)

5 A What ________________ your parents ________________ on TV?
 B Not a lot! They ________________ usually ________________ TV. (watch)

6 A ________________ your children ________________ phones?
 B My daughter has a cell phone, but my son ________________ one. (have)

B PAIR WORK **Ask and answer <u>five</u> questions about things you and your family do.**

C **Circle the correct answers.**

I [1] *work / works* in a hotel. It's an expensive hotel with [2] *a / some* really nice rooms. It's next to a big park. [3] *There's / There are* a lot of trees, and [4] *there's / there are* a lake, too. It's really nice in the park, so I [5] *often / never* go at lunchtime, and I [6] *have / has* lunch near the lake.

D **Write a description of a nice place. Write how often you go there.**

## 3 SPEAKING

A PAIR WORK **Talk about a place. Describe it or say what you do there. Your partner guesses the place. Then change roles.**

> There's a couch, and there are some chairs. I often watch TV in the evening.

> It's your living room.

B **Write three sentences to describe a place from exercise 3A. Then compare with a partner.**

## 4 FUNCTIONAL LANGUAGE

A **Circle the correct answers.**

**Felix** Your photos are great.

**Maya** Thanks. My phone has a good camera.

**Felix** [1] *See / So*, all the pictures are from the camera on your cell phone.

**Maya** Yes, that's [2] *fine / right*. I always use my cell phone camera.

**Felix** [3] *Hey. / Yeah.*

**Maya** [4] *What / Where* about you?

**Felix** I always use my phone, too. I don't have a different camera.

**Maya** [5] *Me, / My* neither. I don't want a different camera. They're really big …

**Felix** Yeah, I [6] *know / do*. And they're expensive.

**Maya** [7] *That's / There's* true.

B **Complete the conversation with the words in the box. There are two extra words.**

| turn | way | to | me | you | near |
|---|---|---|---|---|---|

**A** Excuse [1] ______________. Where's the zoo?

**B** The zoo?

**A** Yes. Is it [2] ______________ here?

**B** Yes. It's that [3] ______________. Go one block, and then [4] ______________ left.

## 5 SPEAKING

A PAIR WORK **Choose one of the conversations below. Ask and answer the questions with a partner.**

**1** What technology do you have? How often do you use it?

I have a laptop, a phone, and a TV. I use my laptop every day. I send emails, and I …

**2** What do you on weekdays? When do you do fun things?

On weekdays, I go to work. I get up at 7:00 a.m., and then I …

**3** What's a good place to go to in or near your city? Where is it?

There's a new Chinese restaurant near here. It's really good.

Yeah. Where is it?

B PAIR WORK **Change roles and repeat the conversation.**

UNIT OBJECTIVES

- talk about activities around the house
- ask and answer questions about travel
- share news on the phone
- write a blog about things happening now
- ask what people are doing these days

# NOW IS GOOD

# 7

## START SPEAKING

A Say what you see in the picture. Who are the people? Are they at work or do they have free time? Where are they?

B Are they busy now? Do they have a busy life?

C Talk about things:

- they do *and* you do.
- you do, but they don't.
- they do, but you don't.

# 7.1 A GOOD TIME TO CALL

**LESSON OBJECTIVE**
- talk about activities around the house

## 1 LANGUAGE IN CONTEXT

A 2.02 **David calls his sister Ariana on the phone. Read and listen. Circle the correct answers.**

1 Ariana is *the mother / the daughter.*
2 Jason is *Ariana's son / Ariana's husband.*
3 Stevie is *Ariana's son / Ariana's daughter.*
4 Julia is *Ariana's sister / Stevie's sister.*

**2.02 Audio script**

**David** Hi, Ariana. It's David. Are you busy? Is this a good time to call?
**Ariana** Um, well, I'm **cooking** breakfast right now, and Jason's **helping** the children— Jason, Stevie isn't drinking his milk.
**David** Oh, yeah. It's a school day today.
**Ariana** That's right, so …
**David** What time do they leave for school?
**Ariana** Usually at 8:00, but we're running late today — Jason, give this to the kids, OK? Thanks. — OK, David, they're eating breakfast now.
**David** Do they like their classes?
**Ariana** Yes, and they're learning a lot — Julia, you're not eating. Please eat your breakfast now! — Sorry, David. This isn't a good time to talk.

B 2.02 **Read and listen again. Is David busy now? Why does Ariana say *"This isn't a good time to talk."*?**

**GLOSSARY**
**kids** (*n*) children (informal)
**running late** (*phrase*) you are late

## 2 VOCABULARY: Activities around the house

A 2.03 **Look at the pictures. Listen and repeat.**

1

I'm cleaning the kitchen.

2

I'm cooking dinner.

3
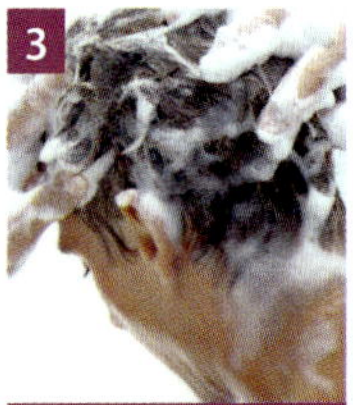
I'm washing my hair.

4

I'm brushing my teeth.

5

I'm doing the dishes.

6

I'm helping my daughters. They're taking a bath.

B **Add the words in the box to the verbs.**

| breakfast | the dog | my hair | my homework | ~~my room~~ | a shower |
|---|---|---|---|---|---|

1 **clean** the kitchen / *my room*
2 **cook** dinner / ______
3 **wash** my hair / ______
4 **brush** my teeth / ______
5 **take** a bath / ______
6 **do** the dishes / ______

C **Now do the vocabulary exercises for 7.1 on page 146.**

D PAIR WORK **Do you do your homework and talk on the phone? What other activities do you do at the same time? For ideas, watch June's video.**

REAL STUDENT

*Do you do the things June does?*

## 3 GRAMMAR: Present continuous statements

A **Circle the correct answer. Use the sentences in the grammar box to help you.**

1 Use the present continuous to talk about **things happening right now or around now / finished things**.
2 Sentences 1, 2, and 3 in the grammar box are about **right now / around now**.
3 Sentence 4 is about **right now / around now**.
4 To make the present continuous, use *am/is/are* and a **verb + *-ing* / verb + *-s***.

**Present continuous statements**

| | |
|---|---|
| 1 I'**m cooking** breakfast right now. | 3 Julia, you'**re not eating** your breakfast. |
| 2 Jason, Stevie **isn't drinking** his milk. | 4 They'**re learning** a lot at school this year. |

B **Complete the sentences in the present continuous. Use an affirmative or negative form of the verbs in parentheses ( ).**

1 He ______________________ (take) a bath. He's in the shower.
2 I ______________________ (do) my homework now. It's really difficult.
3 Carola isn't studying right now. She ______________________ (watch) TV.
4 My parents ______________________ (wash) the car. They're having lunch now.
5 I ______________________ (brush) my hair. I'm brushing my teeth.
6 You ______________________ (help) your friends with their English. You're really nice!
7 My cat loves milk. It ______________________ (drink) milk right now.

C **Now go to page 135. Look at the grammar chart and do the grammar exercise for 7.1.**

D **Think about four of your friends. What are they doing or not doing now? Write sentences about each person. Then check your accuracy.**

*Teresa isn't studying. She's playing games on her phone.*

**✓ ACCURACY CHECK**

**Use the present continuous for things you're doing now. Use the simple present for things you do regularly.**

Just a minute. ~~I talk~~ on the phone. ✗
Just a minute. I'm talking on the phone. ✓
I talk on the phone every day. ✓
I'm talking on the phone every day. ✗

## 4 SPEAKING

A **Think of what you're usually doing at the times of day below. Is it a good or bad time to call you?**

- Monday, 7:30 a.m.
- Tuesday, 10:00 a.m.
- Wednesday, 1:30 p.m
- Thursday, 3:30 p.m.
- Friday, 9:30 p.m
- Saturday, 11:00 a.m.
- Sunday, 6:00 p.m.

B PAIR WORK **Take turns choosing times in exercise 4A. For each time, "call" your partner and ask, *"Is this a good time to call?"* Listen to the answers. Is your partner a busy person?**

*Hi, is this a good time to call?*

*No, sorry. I'm having dinner with my family.*

# 7.2 TEXTING ON THE RUN

**LESSON OBJECTIVE**
- ask and answer questions about travel

## 1 VOCABULARY: Transportation

**A** 2.04 **Look at the pictures. Listen and repeat.**

take the bus/ train/subway

go to a store / your parents' house

walk

be at the bus stop / train station

carry a bag

wait

ride your/my bike

be on the bus/train/subway

drive

**B** **Circle the correct words to complete the sentences.**

1 I *ride my bike / am at the bus stop* to class every day.
2 I'm *waiting / walking* for a friend right now.
3 We *are on the train / take the subway* to work on Fridays.
4 Are you *carrying / walking* right now?
5 I'm *at the train station / to the mall* right now.

**C** **Now do the vocabulary exercises for 7.2 on page 147.**

**D** GROUP WORK **How do you usually get to the places in the box? For ideas, watch Julieth's video.**

English class | the supermarket | work/college | your best friend's house

REAL STUDENT

*Do you use the same transportation as Julieth?*

## 2 LANGUAGE IN CONTEXT

**A** **Read the text messages. Where is Inna going? Why?**

**B** **Read the text messages again. Correct the sentences.**

1 Inna is sending text messages to ~~her father~~. Rob
2 Inna is taking the bus to the mall. ______
3 Inna's dad is waiting at his house. ______
4 Inna is carrying a big bag. ______
5 Today is Inna's dad's birthday. ______

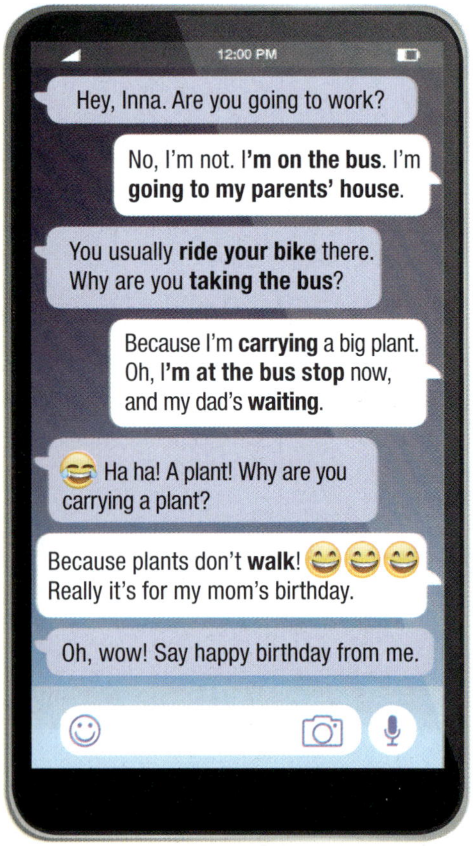


**INSIDER ENGLISH**

People often write *ha ha* (the sound of a laugh) in informal writing. It means they think something is funny.

## 3 GRAMMAR: present continuous questions

A **Circle the correct answer. Use the questions in the grammar box to help you.**

1 Use *are* and *is* **at the beginning / in the middle** of *yes/no* questions.

2 Use *are* and *is* **before / after** question words (for example, *What* or *When*) in information questions.

**Present continuous questions**

| *Yes/no* questions | Information questions |
|---|---|
| **Are** you **going** to work? | **Why is** he **carrying** a plant? |
| **Is** she **carrying** a plant? | **Who are** they **waiting** for? |
| **Are** they **waiting** at the bus stop? | **What are** you **doing**? |

B **Complete the questions with the present continuous form of the verbs in the box. Then match the questions and the answers below.**

carry do go listen ride

1 ________ Josh ________ his bike in the park right now?

2 What ________ Kim and Todd ________ ?

3 ________ the children ________ to music right now?

4 Why ________ Jamal ________ a big bag?

5 Where ________ Lydia ________ now?

___ a Because he's taking a lot of books to class.

___ b Yes, they are.

___ c She's walking to her friend's house.

___ d No, he isn't. He's running by the lake.

___ e They're driving to the beach.

C **Now go to page 135. Look at the grammar charts and do the grammar exercise for 7.2.**

D PAIR WORK **Imagine what people in your family are doing right now. Ask and answer questions.**

*What's your sister doing right now?*

## 4 SPEAKING

FIND IT

A **Imagine you're going somewhere and carrying something interesting or funny. Use the ideas below or your own ideas. Then decide where you are going and your transportation.**

a big bag a small chair an expensive picture

B PAIR WORK **What is your partner doing? Ask and answer questions.**

*Hi, Anna. What are you doing?*

*I'm carrying 100 cookies. I'm at the subway station.*

# 7.3 A NEW LIFE

**LESSON OBJECTIVE**

- share news on the phone

## 1 FUNCTIONAL LANGUAGE

A Look at the people. Are they having a long or a short conversation? How long are your phone calls?

B 2.05 Luana is calling her friend Jennifer. Read and listen. What's new in Luana's life?

**2.05 Audio script**

**Jennifer** **Hello.**

**Luana** **Hi**, Jennifer. **It's** Luana.

**Jennifer** **Hey**, Luana!

**Luana** **How's it going?**

**Jennifer** **Not bad, thanks. How are you doing?**

**Luana** **Good, thanks.** Well, I'm busy.

**Jennifer** Really? What are you doing these days?

**Luana** I have a new job, in Monterrey.

**Jennifer** Oh, wow! *Monterrey*? So you're not living in Mexico City now.

**Luana** That's right. I'm living in Monterrey. I live in a new building. It's expensive, but it's very nice. And I have a new boyfriend.

**Jennifer** Really? Great! You have a new *life*! I want to hear all about it!

C Complete the chart with expressions in **bold** from the conversation above.

| Answering the phone and greeting people | Asking people how they are | Responding |
|---|---|---|
| 1 Hello . | How's it 5 ________ ? | |
| 2 ________ , Jennifer. | *(How's = How is)* | Not 8 ________ , thanks. |
| 3 ________ Luana. | How 6 ________ you | 9 ________ , thanks. |
| 4 ________ , Luana! | 7 ________ ? | I'm fine. |
| | How are you? | |

D 2.06 PAIR WORK Put the phone conversation in the correct order. Listen and check. Then practice with a partner.

___ Good, thanks. How's it going?
3 Hey, Andrew! How are you doing?
1 Hello.
___ Not bad.
___ Hi, Francisco. It's Andrew.

## 2 REAL-WORLD STRATEGY

**REACTING TO NEWS**

People often say *oh* after they hear good news, ordinary news, and bad news.

| **Good news** | **Ordinary news** | **Bad news** |
|---|---|---|
| *Oh, wow!* | *Oh.* | *Oh, no!* |

**Luana** *I have a new job.* **Jennifer** *Oh, wow!*

**Luana** *I'm busy.* **Jennifer** *Oh.*

**Luana** *My apartment is very expensive.* **Jennifer** *Oh, no!*

A **Read the information in the box about reacting to news. Then look at the examples. What does Jennifer think is: good news, ordinary news, and bad news?**

B 2.07 **Listen to a conversation. What news does the man give?**

Ordinary news: He's in his car. Good news: ____________

Bad news: ____________

C 2.07 **Listen again. How does the woman react to the different types of news?**

D PAIR WORK **Student A: Go to page 157. Student B: Go to page 160. Follow the instructions.**

## 3 PRONUNCIATION: Saying *-ing* at the end of the word

A 2.08 **Listen. Complete the words.**

1 How are you do______? 2 I'm liv______ in Dallas. 3 Where are you go______?

B 2.09 **Listen. Focus on the *-in* and *-ing* sounds. Circle the phrase you hear.**

1 a learn in Spanish b learning Spanish

2 a call in the restaurant b calling the restaurant

3 a help in my school b helping my school

4 a study in nature b studying nature

5 a carry in a bag b carrying a bag

6 a shop in malls b shopping malls

C 2.10 PAIR WORK **Listen to the conversations. Then practice with a partner. Listen for the *-ing* sound.**

1 A How are you do**ing**?
  B Not bad. I'm work**ing** in Monterrey now.

2 A Are you liv**ing** in Mexico City now?
  B No, I'm liv**ing** in Monterrey.

3 A Where are you go**ing**?
  B We're go**ing** to the Italian restaurant over there.

## 4 SPEAKING

PAIR WORK **Imagine you're calling your partner. Start the call, and then talk about some news. Use some of the questions below. React to the things your partner says. Then change roles.**

How are you doing?
What are you doing right now?
Are you busy?
What about you?

Hey, Ali. It's Clara.

Hey, Clara! How are you doing?

# 7.4 CHAOS!

**LESSON OBJECTIVE**
- write a blog about things happening now

## 1 READING

A **SKIM** **Skim the text. Where is the man? What is on his laptop?**

# JAMIE'S BLOG

HOME ABOUT BLOG

**Bloggers sometimes write from difficult places: mountains, deserts, rainforests …**
**So today, my blog is from a difficult place, too. I'm writing from my living room.**

Why is it difficult to write in here? Well, my brother's playing soccer (yes, in the living room.) The ball is going *BOOM-BOOM-BOOM* on the wall near my table and chair. My sister's doing her homework. Every two minutes, she asks me a question: "What's 15% of 500? What's 50% of 320?" So, really, *I'm* doing her homework.

The TV is on, but I don't know why. My mom's talking about work on the phone, so she isn't watching TV. And my dad isn't watching it. He's in the kitchen: *PSSSSSS, CRASH, BANG!* He's cooking – I think. And the cat doesn't like TV. But she likes laptops. She's walking on my laptop … and now she's going to sleep! How do I work in this place? It's chaos!

B **READ FOR DETAILS** **Read the blog again. Find words to complete the chart.**

| | | | |
|---|---|---|---|
| 5 people in the family | me | | |
| | | | |
| 3 technology words | | | |
| 2 pieces of furniture | | | |
| 2 rooms | | | |
| 1 animal | | | |

C **PAIR WORK** **THINK CRITICALLY** **Which people from exercise 1B are busy? having fun?**

## 2 WRITING

A **Jodi is a college student. She's helping at a school for a week. Read her blog. What <u>six</u> things are the children doing? What <u>three</u> things is Jodi doing? What <u>one</u> thing are the children <u>and</u> Jodi doing?**

# Jodi's Blog

Home About Blog

## Busy!

April 11

I'm helping a teacher at a school this week. Today, I'm writing my blog on a school bus. We're going to the beach. There are 25 kids on the bus, and they're nine and ten years old. Wow, they're making a lot of noise! They're busy, too. Some kids are talking. Some kids are playing music on their phones. Some are singing. Three boys are playing games on a tablet. Also, the children are eating cookies.
What about me? Well, I'm cleaning their hands and washing their faces.
And I'm answering millions of questions from the kids. They're happy.
The teacher is happy, too.
But this is difficult for me.
Am I getting old?

**GLOSSARY**

**noise** (*n*) a sound or sounds, usually loud
**millions** (*quantifier*) a lot (informal)

B **WRITING SKILLS** **People use *also* and *too* to add information. <u>Underline</u> the words *also* and *too* in the blog. Then circle the correct words in the rules, below.**

Use *too* at the **beginning / end** of a sentence.

Use a comma (,) **before / after** you write *too*.

Use *also* at the **beginning / end** *of a sentence.*

Use a *comma* (,) **before / after** you write *also*.

### REGISTER CHECK

**People sometimes use *And*, *Also*, or *But* at the beginning of sentences in speaking and informal writing. In formal writing, people usually don't begin sentences with these words.**

***And** I'm answering millions of questions from the kids.*

***Also**, the children are eating cookies.*

***But** this is difficult for me.*

## WRITE IT

C **Imagine you're in a very busy place: at home, at college, at work, on a bus, or at a party. Write a blog about the activities happening around you. Use the title "Busy!"**

D **PAIR WORK** **Compare your blog with a partner. How many activities does your partner describe?**

# 7.5 TIME TO SPEAK

## Your life these days

**LESSON OBJECTIVE**

- ask what people are doing these days

**A** **PREPARE** Read the note and questions below. Which topic is interesting for you? Which topic is boring?

**You are with a group of people. They are your friends, but you hardly ever see them. What do you say? Here are some ideas!**

| Topics | Main question | Follow-up questions |
|---|---|---|
| Work and school | Are you going to college? | Are your classes easy or difficult? Are you doing a lot of homework these days? |
| | What classes are you taking? | Do you like your classes? Why or why not? |
| | Where are you working these days? | Are you working every day? Is your job interesting? Is it difficult? |
| Free time | What are you reading these days? | Is it good? Who's the writer? |
| | What are you watching on TV? | Is it interesting? Is it funny? Who's in it? |
| | What music are you listening to? | Who's your favorite singer? What's your favorite band? |
| | Do you play video games? | Which games are you playing right now? |
| | Are you going out a lot these days? | Where do you go? What's your favorite place? |
| | Are you playing sports? | What sports do you play? Where? |
| Home life | How is your family? | Are you living with them now? |
| | Are you living in a new place? | Is it an apartment or house? Do you like it? Is it close to work/school? |
| | Are you cooking a lot these days? | Do you cook for other people? |

**B** **ROLE PLAY** Imagine you are at a party. Talk to different people about different topics. Ask and answer some of the questions from the chart.

**C** **AGREE** Talk about popular things from your conversations. What are a lot of people doing these days?

*To check your progress, go to page 154.*

## USEFUL PHRASES

**PREPARE**

I like / don't like …

I think … is interesting/boring. And you?

**ROLE PLAY**

Hi, [name]. How's it going?

Hey, [name]! What are you doing these days?

**AGREE**

(Work and school / free time / home life) is a popular topic.

A lot of people are doing …

**UNIT OBJECTIVES**

- talk about your skills and abilities
- say what you can and can't do at work or school
- say why you're the right person for a job
- write an online comment with your opinion
- talk about what people in your country are good at

# YOU'RE GOOD!

# 8

## START SPEAKING

A **Look at the picture. Where is this person? What is he doing?**

B **Do you think this is a difficult activity? Do you think it's fun?**

C **Talk to a partner about fun or difficult activities you do. For ideas, watch Anderson's video.**

**REAL STUDENT**

*What does Anderson do? Do you think it's fun, difficult, or both?*

# 8.1 SHE LIKES MUSIC, BUT SHE CAN'T DANCE!

**LESSON OBJECTIVE**
- talk about your skills and abilities

## 1 VOCABULARY: Verbs to describe skills

A 2.11 **Listen and repeat the skills in the pictures. Which are fun skills? Which are difficult skills?**

dance

draw

fix things

read music

paint

play the guitar

sing

skateboard

snowboard

speak two languages

surf

swim

B **Now do the vocabulary exercises for 8.1 on page 147.**

## 2 LANGUAGE IN CONTEXT

A 2.12 **Read and listen. Who are Mia and her dad talking about? What do they choose to buy? Do you think it's a good idea?**

**2.12 Audio script**

**Dad** So, Mia. You know it's your mom's birthday next month, right?
**Mia** Oh wow! Let's buy her something really cool. Do you have any ideas?
**Dad** Hmm. How about some art classes? She can **draw**.
**Mia** Or what about singing lessons? She likes music and can **play the guitar**.
**Dad** I don't think that's a good idea. She thinks she can't **sing**, and she's very shy about it.
**Mia** Hmm. What about dance lessons? Can she **dance** well?
**Dad** No, she can't. She's terrible at it. It's really funny – she can **read music**, but she can't dance!
**Mia** *You* can't dance, Dad. I know! Let's buy you both some dance lessons!
**Dad** Great idea! Wait a minute – what?

**INSIDER ENGLISH**

**You can use *So* to start talking about a topic.**

***So**, Mia. You know it's your mom's birthday next month, right?*

**GLOSSARY**

**terrible** (*adj*) very bad

B 2.12 **Read and listen again. What can Mia's mom do? What can't she do? Complete the sentences.**

1 Mia's mom can ______________, ______________, and ______________.

2 She can't ______________ and ______________.

C PAIR WORK **Talk to a partner. Which things in exercise 1A do you often do? Which things do you never do? For ideas, watch Larissa's video.**

REAL STUDENT

*Do you often do the same things as Larissa?*

## 3 GRAMMAR: *can* and *can't* for ability; *well*

A **Circle the correct answers. Use the sentences in the grammar box and the information in the Notice box to help you.**

1 Use ***can* / *can't*** to talk about things you don't do well or don't know how to do.

2 Use ***can* / *can't*** to talk about things you do well or know how to do.

3 With *he*, *she*, and *it*, **do / do not** add *-s* to the verb after *can* or *can't*.

**can and can't (= can not) for ability**

| | | |
|---|---|---|
| I **can** swim. | I **can't** play the guitar. | **Can** you fix things? |
| She **can** draw. | He **can't** sing well. | **Can** he surf? |
| We **can** surf well. | They **can't** read music. | **Can** they speak two languages? |

**!** ***Well* is the adverb of *good*.**
*She can sing* ***well****.* (= *she's good.*)
*I can't dance* ***well****.* (= *I'm not good.*)

B **Circle the correct answers to complete the sentences.**

1 I swim every day. I *can* / *can't* swim well.

2 Sorry. My dad *can* / *can't* fix your car. He's not a mechanic.

3 You can draw really well, Tomas. What other things *can* / *can't* you do?

4 She *can* / *can't* drive, and she doesn't have a car.

5 You *can* / *can't* skateboard really well! Can you teach me?

6 **A** Can you play the guitar, Robbie?
**B** No, I *can* / *can't*.

C **Now go to page 136. Look at the grammar chart and do the grammar exercise for 8.1.**

D **Write five questions to ask people in your class about their skills. Use vocabulary from exercise 1A. Then check your accuracy.**

1 Can you ______________________________?

2 Can you ______________________________?

3 Can you ______________________________?

4 Can you ______________________________?

5 Can you ______________________________?

**ACCURACY CHECK**

**Do not use *to* between *can/can't* and a verb.**

Can you ~~to~~ fix bikes? ✗
Can you fix bikes? ✓

## 4 SPEAKING

A GROUP WORK **Ask and answer your questions from exercise 3D. Say how well you do the skills.**

Can you play the guitar?

No, I can't. What about you?

Yes, I can. I can play it really well.

B GROUP WORK **What skill can everyone in your group do? Who can do it really well?**

# 8.2 HAPPY WORKERS = GREAT WORKERS?

**LESSON OBJECTIVE**
- say what you can and can't do at work or school

## 1 LANGUAGE IN CONTEXT

A **Look at the offices in the pictures on pages 78 and 79. How are they different from other offices? Do you like them? Are they good places to work?**

B **Read the article. What activities can you do in a happy office?**

### *Not just an office … an* OFFICE

Who can you find in all great **companies**? Great **workers**. And what's true for all great workers? They're happy because happy people do a great job.

How can companies make their workers happy? They can pay them a lot of money, of course, but money can't make people happy – not always. A great company can also give its workers a happy **office**. Happy offices aren't just ordinary offices with desks, phones, and computers – and they're not *just* for work.

What can you do in a happy office? The short answer is, you can **work hard** *and* have fun. You can run or play basketball with **your coworkers** and **have a meeting** at the same time. This is a great way to **think** of new ideas. You can work in a cool room with big chairs and no table or **take a break** in a room with a lot of plants (like a forest!) In some offices, you can come to work with your dog!

**GLOSSARY**
**all** (*det*) 100% of something
**pay** (*v*) give someone money for their work
**ordinary** (*adj*) usual, normal

## 2 VOCABULARY: Work

A 2.13 **Find the words below in the article. Then listen and repeat.**

company workers office work hard have a meeting think take a break your coworkers

B **Match the words from exercise 2A with the definitions.**

1 a workplace, with desks and chairs ______
2 the people you work with ______
3 a business – for example, Microsoft or Toyota ______
4 the people in a company ______
5 do a lot of work ______
6 stop work for a short time – for example, to have coffee ______
7 have ideas, or find answers to problems ______
8 get together with people at work and talk about business ______

C **Now do the vocabulary exercises for 8.2 on page 148.**

FIND IT

D GROUP WORK **What other activities can you do in a happy office? Which companies have happy workers? You can go online to find examples.**

## 3 GRAMMAR: *can* and *can't* for possibility

A **Circle the correct answers. Use the sentences in the grammar box to help you.**

1 Use *can* to talk about things that are **possible** / **not possible**.

2 Question words (*Who*, *What*, *Where*, *Why*, and *How*) go **before** / **after** *can* or *can't* to ask about possibility.

**_can_ and _can't_ for possibility**

| | |
|---|---|
| You **can** work hard and have fun. | What **can't** they do in the office? |
| She **can** take a break any time. | How **can** companies make their workers happy? |
| Your dog **can't** come to work with you. | Where **can** you have a meeting? |

B **Put the words in the correct order to make questions. Then match them to the answers (a–e) below.**

1 we / have / lunch? / can / Where ______

2 the / restaurant? / How / get / to / can / I ______

3 can / What / eat? / we ______

4 have / the / meeting? / we / can / When ______

5 I / this / message? / send / can / How ______

___ **a** We can have some cookies.

___ **b** You can email it from your phone.

___ **c** Tuesday is good for me.

___ **d** In the company restaurant.

___ **e** Go straight, and then turn left.

C **Now go to page 136. Look at the grammar chart and do the grammar exercise for 8.2.**

D **Write questions about a company or school to ask if it's a good place to work or study.**

1 What can ______?

2 Where can ______?

3 How can ______?

## 4 SPEAKING

PAIR WORK **Talk to a partner about things you can and can't do at your company or school. Ask your questions from exercise 3D.**

What can you do at lunchtime?

You can go to …

# 8.3 ARE YOU THE RIGHT PERSON?

**LESSON OBJECTIVE**

- say why you're the right person for a job

## 1 FUNCTIONAL LANGUAGE

A **Look at the picture. Where are the people? What are they doing?**

B 2.14 **Read and listen. What three things can the man do well?**

2.14 Audio script

A Can we speak in English for five minutes?
B Yes, we can.
A Great. So, are you the right person for this job?
B Yes. **I think so.**
A Why? In a very short answer, please.
B Because I can work well with people on a team. **I think that** teamwork is very important.
A I see. **Why do you think** it's important?
B Because a company is a big team. I mean, it's a group of people, and you work with them every day.
A And why are *you* good on a team?
B Because I like people, and I can communicate well.
A That's great. **I think that** good communication is important. But **I don't think** it's the only important thing. What other things can you do well?
B I can speak two languages. I mean, I speak Spanish and English.

C **Complete the chart with expressions in bold from the conversation above.**

| Asking for opinions | Giving opinions |
|---|---|
| What do you think ? | I think [2] ______ . |
| [1] ______ do you think (that) … ? | I don't think so. |
| | I [3] ______ (that) … |
| | I [4] ______ think (that) … |

D 2.15 PAIR WORK **Complete the conversations with words from exercise 1C. Listen and check. Then ask and answer the questions with a partner. Answer with your ideas.**

1 A I think video games are great. What do you think?
 B I ______ they're very cool. They're boring.
2 A ______ do you ______ cell phones are important?
 B They're useful. We communicate with our phones.
3 A Do you think soccer is a good sport?
 B No. I ______ . I like basketball.
4 A Are you good at music?
 B I ______ . I sing and play the guitar really well.

## 2 REAL-WORLD STRATEGY

### EXPLAINING AND SAYING MORE ABOUT AN IDEA

Use *I mean* to explain or say more about an idea.

*A company is a big team. I mean, it's a group of people, and you work with them every day.*

*I can speak two languages. I mean, I speak Spanish and English.*

A Read about explaining and saying more about an idea in the box above. Look at what the man says. What idea does he explain? What idea does he give more information about?

B 2.16 Listen to a conversation. What does Lori want to do? When does she have free time?

C 2.16 Listen to the conversation again. Complete the chart with the sentences you hear.

| Idea | Explanation/more information |
|---|---|
| I work really hard. | I mean, I [1] ________ about [2] ________ ________ a day. |
| I'm not busy. | I mean, I [3] ________ in a restaurant [4] ________ ________, but I have free time in the [5] ________. |

D PAIR WORK **Student A: Go to page 157. Student B: Go to page 160. Follow the instructions.**

## 3 PRONUNCIATION: Saying groups of words

A 2.17 Listen for the space (= short pause) between the words ( / ). Which sentences do you hear, A or B?

1 A Can we speak in English / for five minutes?
  B Can we speak in / English for five minutes?
2 A What other things can / you do well?
  B What other things / can you do well?

B 2.18 Listen to the sentences. Write a pause mark (/) in each sentence.

1 I'm good on a team because I can communicate well.
2 I can speak two languages and I can play the guitar.
3 I work in a restaurant at night but I'm free in the mornings.
4 I think that good communication is important but I don't think it's the only important thing.

C PAIR WORK Practice the sentences in exercise 3B with a partner. Take turns. Can your partner hear the spaces between the words?

## 4 SPEAKING

A Choose a job from the box or your own idea. Think about why you are the right person for the job.

| | | |
|---|---|---|
| an art teacher | a chef at a restaurant | a hotel clerk |
| a singer in a band | a soccer player | |

B PAIR WORK Tell a partner your job from exercise 4A. Your partner interviews you for the job. Then change roles.

Are you the right person for this job?

I think so. I …

# 8.4 COMPUTERS AND OUR JOBS

**LESSON OBJECTIVE**
- write an online comment with your opinion

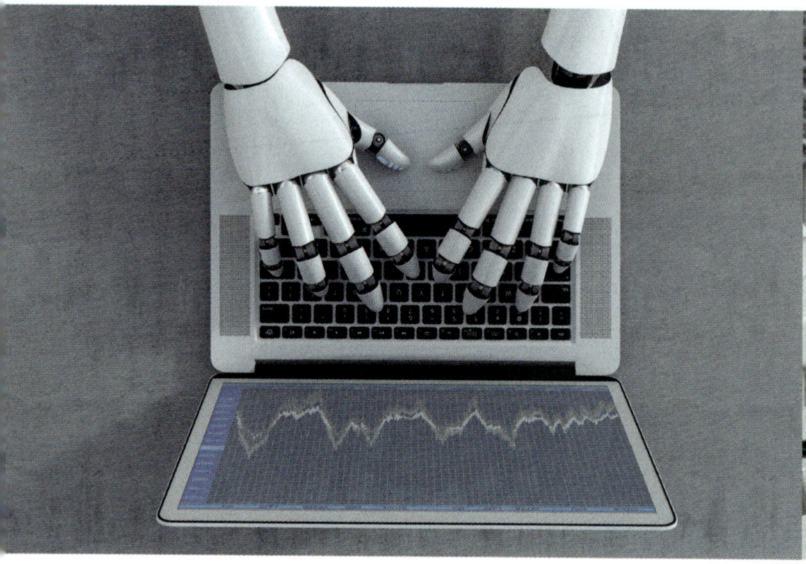

## 1 LISTENING

A **Chris is the host of the podcast *Technology Talks*. Look at the pictures above. What is today's podcast about?**

B 2.19 LISTEN FOR DETAILS **Listen to the podcast. Who is Joanna Ramos? What does she say computers <u>can't</u> do?**

C 2.19 LISTEN FOR SUPPORTING DETAILS **Listen again. Check (✓) the supporting details Joanna gives.**

| Jobs for computers | New jobs for people |
|---|---|
| ☐ make cars | ☐ make computers |
| ☐ drive cars | ☐ start computer companies |
| ☐ call people on the phone | ☐ make cars |
| ☐ talk | ☐ be a computer's voice |
| ☐ think | ☐ make phones |

D PAIR WORK THINK CRITICALLY **Who thinks computers are a good thing: Joanna or Chris?**

## 2 PRONUNCIATION: Listening for *can* and *can't*

A 2.20 **Listen. Write the missing words.**

1 What ________ computers do?
2 They ________ make cars.
3 A computer ________ make 100% of a car.

B 2.21 **Listen. Do you hear *can* or *can't*? Circle the correct words.**

1 can / can't
2 can / can't
3 can / can't
4 can / can't

## 3 WRITING

A **Read three people's online comments about the podcast. Which person thinks Joanna is correct? Which person doesn't think Joanna is correct? What's your favorite comment?**

TECHNOLOGY TALKS:
### Interview with Joanna Ramos

JUNE 1, 11:30 A.M.

**Kaito, Tokyo**

I don't think Joanna Ramos is right. Computers *are* a problem. Robots are taking all our jobs! They can say hello to people in stores and hotels, they can cook, they can play music, they can clean buildings, they can make cars … What jobs CAN'T they do? Joanna says, "People make computers." Well, I think robots can make computers now. They're *very* smart.

**Ruby, Miami**

Computers and robots can do a lot of things, but they don't have feelings: they're not happy, and they're not sad. Feelings are important for many jobs. For example, teachers, doctors, and nurses work with people, so feelings are important. I don't like the idea of robot doctors!

**Arturo, Mexico City**

Computers are cheap. I mean, companies pay people for their work, but they don't pay their robots or computers. And computers work hard. But I think Ruby is right. Computers don't have feelings. Joanna is right, too. She says, "They are taking *some* of our jobs." Not *all* of them. She also says, "There are a lot of new jobs, too." That's true. It's not a problem.

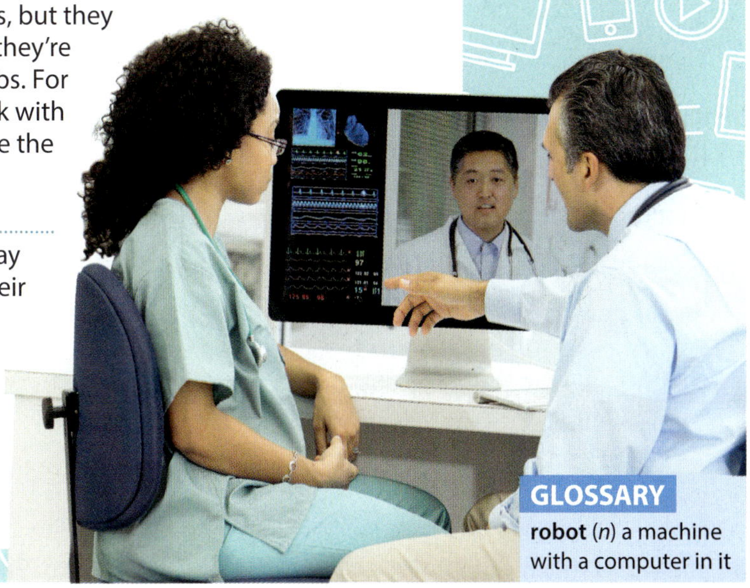

**GLOSSARY**

**robot** (*n*) a machine with a computer in it

B WRITING SKILLS **Sometimes we want to write another person's words. Their words are quotations. Read the rules below. Then circle all the capital letters and punctuation marks in sentences 1–3.**

- Use quotation marks (" ") around other people's words.
- Put a comma (,) after *says*.
- Start the quotation with a capital letter (A, B, C, …).

1 Joanna says, "People make computers."
2 She says, "They are taking *some* of our jobs."
3 She also says, "There are a lot of new jobs, too."

**REGISTER CHECK**

**In informal writing and speaking, people often use *says* to quote (= give) another person's words.**

**In an online comment:** *Joanna says, "People make computers."*

**In formal writing, people often use *said*.**

**In a newspaper article:** *Joanna Ramos said, "A computer can't make 100% of a car."*

### WRITE IT

C **Read the ideas from Joanna's interview in exercise 1C. Then write an online comment. Give your opinion about computers and jobs. Quote some of Joanna's words.**

D GROUP WORK **Read your group's comments. Do you have the same or different ideas?**

# 8.5 TIME TO SPEAK
## National skills

**LESSON OBJECTIVE**
- talk about what people in your country are good at

**A** **PREPARE** Match the skills in the box to the pictures. Which three skills are <u>not</u> in the pictures?

| cook | dance | make movies | paint | play soccer | sing | snowboard | surf |
|---|---|---|---|---|---|---|---|

1

3

5

2

4

**B** **DISCUSS** Where can people do the things from exercise A really well? For each skill, say the name of a city, region/area, or country. Then compare your ideas with your group.

**C** **DECIDE** Read the information in the box on the right. Talk to a partner about the question in the box. Together, think of <u>three</u> skills for the video.

**D** **AGREE** Compare everyone's ideas. Choose your class' <u>three</u> favorite ideas for the video.

**CAN YOU HELP US?**
We want to make a YouTube™ video about our country and why it's great. The title is "We're good!" The video is about the skills people have here. What can we do *really* well in this country? Please send us your ideas!

*To check your progress, go to page 154.*

## USEFUL PHRASES

**DISCUSS**
Where can people cook really well?
Chinese food is always great.
I think people can cook really well in Rome and Naples.
What do you think?

**DECIDE**
What can we do really well in this country?
We can do … well.
I agree. / I disagree.
Our three skills for the video are …

**AGREE**
What are your ideas?
Good idea!
Our three favorite skills are …

**UNIT OBJECTIVES**

- talk about travel and vacations
- make travel plans
- ask for information in a store
- write a description of a place
- plan a vacation for someone

# PLACES TO GO

# 9

## START SPEAKING

A Look at the picture. Where is the woman? Is it difficult to get to this place?

B What do you do in your free time? Do you go to new places?

C Think of a place you like. Talk about it. Say why it's good. For ideas, watch Julieth's video.

*What's Julieth's place? Do you agree it's a good place to go?*

# 9.1 I LOVE IT HERE!

**LESSON OBJECTIVE**
- talk about travel and vacations

## 1 LANGUAGE IN CONTEXT

A **Kaitlin and her friends are on vacation. Read Kaitlin's posts. Where do they go?**

B **Read again. Check (✓) the sentences that are true. Correct the false ones.**

- [ ] 1 Kaitlin takes a bus to San Diego.
- [ ] 2 They go to their hotel on Thursday.
- [ ] 3 They are in San Diego on Friday.
- [ ] 4 They go to a zoo on Saturday.
- [ ] 5 Kaitlin and her friends have a bad vacation.

### FROM MY SMALL **TOWN** TO A BIG **CITY**

PROFILE
LOG OUT

THURSDAY MORNING

Goodbye to my small **town**. San Diego, here I come! I have my **ticket** and my seat on the **plane**. I'm next to the window!

THURSDAY AFTERNOON

Now I'm in San Diego, and this is our hotel. These are my friends in front of the hotel.

FRIDAY

Today we're in the **country**, not in the **city**! We're at this cool **ranch** near San Diego. It's a really big **farm**.

SATURDAY

We're at the San Diego Zoo. These birds are funny. They're talking. They say, "Hello. How are you? Hello. How are you?"

SUNDAY

Now I'm on a **tour** of San Diego Bay. I'm on a **boat** with my friends. They're not listening to the tour guide because they're talking.

A fun **vacation**? I think so. I love it here! 😄

**GLOSSARY**
**tour guide** (*n*) this person takes you to a place and tells you about it

## 2 VOCABULARY: Travel

A 🔊 2.22 **Listen and repeat the words. Which words are places?**

| boat | country | farm | plane | ranch | ticket | tour | town | vacation |
|---|---|---|---|---|---|---|---|---|

B **Now do the vocabulary exercises for 9.1 on page 148.**

C PAIR WORK **Which places do you like from Kaitlin's vacation? Which places <u>don't</u> you like? Why?**

## 3 GRAMMAR: *This* and *These*

A **Circle the correct answer. Use the sentences in the grammar box to help you.**

1 Use *This bird* and *These birds* to talk about **birds around you / birds you can't see.**

2 *This* and *these* go **before / after** a noun.

3 ***This / these*** goes before a singular noun. ***This / these*** goes before a plural noun.

4 You **can / can't** use *this* and *these* at the beginning of a sentence.

| ***This* and *These*** | |
|---|---|
| **This** ticket is expensive. | **These** birds are funny. |
| We're at **this** cool ranch. | I don't like **these** pictures. |

B **Kaitlin writes a postcard about a museum. Write *this* or *these* to complete Kaitlin's postcard.**

Dear Grandma,

I'm in San Diego! It's great. [1] ______________ postcard shows Balboa Park in the city. The park is very big, and it has 15 museums! [2] ______________ museums are for art, technology, transportation, and history. We're at the Mingei International Museum right now. You can see it in [3] ______________ photo on the right. [4] ______________ museum is interesting because it has local art – the artists are from [5] ______________ city. I'm looking at some cool pictures now. [6] ______________ pictures show places in San Diego. [7] ______________ artists are *really* good. [8] ______________ is my favorite room in the museum.

Love, Kaitlin

C **Now go to page 136. Look at the grammar chart and do the grammar exercise for 9.1.**

## 4 SPEAKING

FIND IT

A **Choose five pictures on your phone or draw some simple pictures of places you know. Think about the people and places in the pictures.**

B PAIR WORK **Tell your partner about your pictures.**

*This is a picture of my mom and my aunt. They're walking in the country. This hill is very big. What else? This is my favorite aunt. She's…*

# 9.2 SAN FRANCISCO, HERE WE COME

**LESSON OBJECTIVE**
- make travel plans

## 1 LANGUAGE IN CONTEXT

A 2.23 **Kaitlin is making a vacation video. Read and listen. Where is she now? Where is she going? How is she going there?**

B 2.23 **Read and listen again. Check (✓) the sentences that are true. Correct the false ones.**

- ☐ **1** The plane is expensive, and the bus is cheap.
- ☐ **2** You can take a bus to San Francisco at night.
- ☐ **3** It's Friday night. Kaitlin is sleeping in a hotel.

Hello again from San Diego! Today is Tuesday, and we want to **leave** on Friday. Our **destination** is San Francisco. But how do we **travel**? Do we **fly** or take the bus?

Well, the **flight** is two hours. But you have to **arrive** at the **airport** a long time before the flight. You need to **check in** two hours before. So in total, by plane, the **trip** is about five hours. That's not bad. And I like to fly. *But* … the ticket is expensive.

The bus *isn't* expensive. It *is* a long trip – it's 12 hours. But we can take a night bus. And it arrives in San Francisco the next morning. That's good because we don't need to **stay** in a hotel on Friday night.

So, we're taking the bus. We just need to buy our tickets **online**. And then, San Francisco, here we come … on the bus.

## 2 VOCABULARY: Travel arrangements

A 2.24 **Listen and repeat the sentences. Then match the sentences (a–h) to the pictures (1–8.)**

- **a** Stay in a hotel. ___
- **b** Arrive at the airport. ___
- **c** Check in at the airport. ___
- **d** Fly to another airport. You can sleep on the flight. ___
- **e** Leave your house. Ready to travel? ___
- **f** Have a great trip! ___
- **g** Arrive at your destination. ___
- **h** Buy tickets online. ___

B **Now do the vocabulary exercises for 9.2 on page 149.**

C PAIR WORK **Imagine you're going from San Diego to San Francisco. What's a good way to go? Why?**

## 3 GRAMMAR: *like to, want to, need to, have to*

A Circle the correct answer. Use the sentences in the grammar box to help you.

1 Use *want to* + verb and *like to* + verb to talk about **necessary things / things you choose to do**.
2 Use *need to* + verb and *have to* + verb to talk about **necessary things / things you choose to do**.
3 After *like to, want to, need to,* and *have to,* use **verb + *-ing* / verb**.

***like to, want to, need to, have to***

| | |
|---|---|
| I **like to** fly. | She **wants to** take a bus. |
| You **need to** check in before the flight. | He **has to** buy tickets. |
| We **want to** leave on Friday. | My mom **likes to** sleep on a flight. |

B Circle the correct answer to complete the sentences.

1 I always sit by the window because I *need to / like to* look outside. It's interesting!
2 My cell phone isn't old, but I *need to / want to* buy a new one.
3 My wife isn't happy because she *has to / wants to* work this weekend.
4 On Fridays, we *like to / need to* watch TV after dinner.
5 He starts work at 6:30, so he *needs to / wants to* get up really early.

C Now go to page 137. Look at the grammar chart and do the grammar exercise for 9.2.

D PAIR WORK Write four sentences that are true for you. Use *like to, want to, need to,* and *have to*. Then compare your sentences with a partner and check your accuracy.

**ACCURACY CHECK**

Use *to* with *want, like, need* and *have* when they are before another verb.

I like fly. ✗
I like to fly. ✓

## 4 SPEAKING

A Work alone. Imagine you have to take a trip for one of these reasons: vacation, work, or to visit family. Where do you want to go? How do you want to travel: on a bus, a train, or a plane? For ideas, watch Larissa's video.

REAL STUDENT

*Do you want to travel the same way as Larissa?*

B PAIR WORK Tell your partner about your trip. Talk about the things you need to do for your trip.

I have to take a trip for work.

Where do you have to go?

Buenos Aires, and I want to go by plane. I like to fly.

You can buy your ticket online ...

# 9.3 THEY'RE TWO FOR $15

**LESSON OBJECTIVE**
- ask for information in a store

## 1 FUNCTIONAL LANGUAGE

A 2.25 **Andy arrives at the airport in Mexico City. Read and listen. What does he want to buy? What does he want to drink? What place does he ask about?**

**2.25 Audio script**

**Andy** Hello. I need a travel guide for Mexico City. **Where are the travel guides?**
**Clerk** Sorry, can you say that again?
**Andy** Travel guides – where are the travel guides?
**Clerk** Oh, OK. They're here, with the books and magazines.
**Andy** OK. **How much is that?**
**Clerk** **It's $9.99.**
**Andy** Great. I need to buy a travel guide for Guadalajara, too. **Is it the same price, $9.99?**
**Clerk** Yes, it is. But good news! **They're two for $15.**
**Andy** Great! I want both, please. Hey, **what time does the café open?** I really need some coffee.
**Clerk** **It opens in about 10 minutes.**
**Andy** OK. **And where is the men's restroom?**
**Clerk** It's over there, next to the café. But first you need to buy your books!

**INSIDER ENGLISH**

People often say *restroom* in public places and *bathroom* in people's homes. *Restroom* is more polite.

**At an airport:**
*Where is the men's restroom?*

**At a friend's house:**
*Sorry, where's your bathroom?*

**GLOSSARY**

**travel guide** (*n*) a book with information about where to go and what to see in a city or country

B Complete the chart with expressions in **bold** from the conversation above.

| Asking for information | Giving information |
|---|---|
| 1 ________ the travel guides? | 6 ________ $9.99. |
| 2 ________ that? | 7 ________ $15. |
| 3 ________, $9.99? | 8 ________ about 10 minutes. |
| 4 ________ the café open? | |
| 5 ________ the men's restroom? | |

C 2.26 **Complete the conversations with words from the chart above. Listen and check.**

1 A Excuse me. ________ is this smartwatch?
B ________ $125.49.
A What about this big smartwatch? Is it the ________?
B No, it isn't. ________ $149.00.

2 A ________ flight 248 arrive?
B It arrives ________ 30 minutes.
A OK, thanks. Oh, and ________ the women's ________?
B It's over there.

## 2 REAL-WORLD STRATEGY

**ASKING SOMEONE TO REPEAT SOMETHING**

To hear information again, ask, *Sorry, can you say that again?* or *Can you repeat that, please?*

*Andy* *Where are the travel guides?*

*Clerk* *Sorry, can you say that again?*

A **Read the information in the box. What question does the clerk ask? Why?**

B 2.27 **Listen to a conversation. Does the woman understand the man the first time? What question does she ask? How much is the cell phone?**

## 3 PRONUNCIATION: Saying prices

A 2.28 **Listen and repeat the prices. Where does the speaker put stress in each price?**

**1** $6.19 / $6.90
**2** $15 / $50
**3** $17.30 / $70.13
**4** $19 / $90
**5** $2.16 / $2.60
**6** $14 / $40

B 2.29 **Listen and write the prices. Then practice the conversation with a partner.**

**A** I love that picture! How much is it?
**B** It's $__________ .
**A** $__________ ! That's cheap!
**B** No, it's $__________ .
**A** Oh …

C PAIR WORK **Work with a partner. Ask to buy your friend's cell phone, bag, or Student's Book. Make a mistake with the price. Use the conversation in exercise 3B for an example. Then change roles.**

## 4 SPEAKING

FIND IT

PAIR WORK **Imagine you want to buy something. Look at the items below, or go online and find an item. Take turns being the customer. Ask for information, and ask the store clerk to repeat something. Then change roles.**

$29.99, or two for $50

$6, or two for $10.50

$13, or two for $20

$45, or two for $79

Excuse me. How much is this mug?

It's $6, or two for $10.50.

Sorry, can you repeat that, please?

# 9.4 A GREAT DESTINATION

**LESSON OBJECTIVE**
- write a description of a place

## 1 READING

A **RECOGNIZE TEXT TYPE** **Read the text. What is it from?**

☐ a travel guide ☐ an email ☐ a review ☐ a student's homework

## TravelSmart PLACES TO GO **NEAR PUNO**

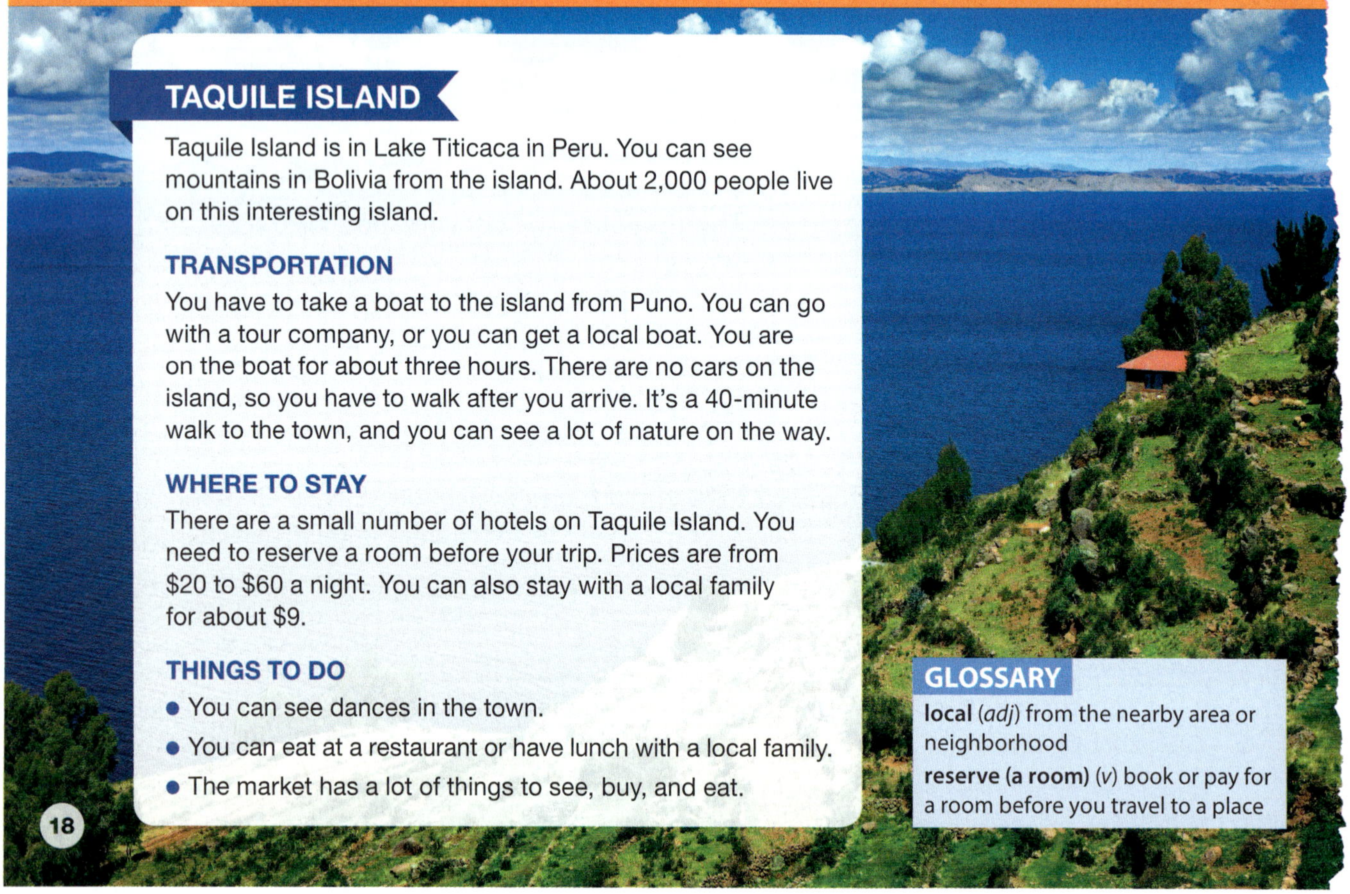

### TAQUILE ISLAND

Taquile Island is in Lake Titicaca in Peru. You can see mountains in Bolivia from the island. About 2,000 people live on this interesting island.

**TRANSPORTATION**

You have to take a boat to the island from Puno. You can go with a tour company, or you can get a local boat. You are on the boat for about three hours. There are no cars on the island, so you have to walk after you arrive. It's a 40-minute walk to the town, and you can see a lot of nature on the way.

**WHERE TO STAY**

There are a small number of hotels on Taquile Island. You need to reserve a room before your trip. Prices are from $20 to $60 a night. You can also stay with a local family for about $9.

**THINGS TO DO**

- You can see dances in the town.
- You can eat at a restaurant or have lunch with a local family.
- The market has a lot of things to see, buy, and eat.

18

**GLOSSARY**

**local** (*adj*) from the nearby area or neighborhood

**reserve (a room)** (*v*) book or pay for a room before you travel to a place

B **SCAN** **Find the numbers in the text. What do these numbers mean?**

2,000 three 40 $20 to $60 $9

C **READ FOR DETAILS** **Read the text again. Circle the correct answers.**

1. Taquile Island *is* / *isn't* in Bolivia.
2. You *can* / *can't* get a boat to the island.
3. You *can* / *can't* drive on the island.
4. There are *no* / *some* hotels on the island.
5. There *are* / *aren't* restaurants on the island.
6. You *can* / *can't* meet local people.

D **PAIR WORK** **THINK CRITICALLY** **Why do people like to go to Taquile Island? Do you want to go there? Why or why not? Give examples from the text to explain your answer.**

## 2 WRITING

A Read Cameron's review of Taquile Island. What does he say not to do?

**DestinationsNow** About | Hotels | Restaurants | Search

### Taquile Island

Lake Titicaca, Puno, Peru

**Reviews (365)** Write a review

| | |
|---|---|
| Very good | 673 |
| Good | 575 |
| OK | 6 |
| Bad | 0 |
| Very bad | 0 |

Search review topics

Cameron T.

3 weeks ago

**You have to see Taquile Island!**

This island is really nice. It's not very big. There is only one town on the island. There are a lot of small homes on the hills, and there's a lot of nature. I like to walk, and you have to walk a lot on Taquile. Walk to the top of the island and see the ocean. You can see Peru on one side and Bolivia on the other side. You can even see snow on the mountains in Bolivia. Don't take a tour with a travel company. Take a local boat and stay with a family. The people are very friendly. You don't need to eat at the restaurants in town. The food is OK, but the family gives you a great breakfast, lunch, and dinner. Talk with the family. You can learn a lot about Taquile this way. Don't forget your camera. You can take a lot of pictures of this wonderful place!

**GLOSSARY**

**wonderful** (*adj*) really good

B WRITING SKILLS **Read the information about imperative verbs below. Then underline all the sentences beginning with an imperative verb in Cameron's review in exercise 2A.**

You can use imperative verbs to give someone advice. An imperative verb is a verb with no subject (e.g. *he, she*).

\+ **Walk** to the top of the island and see the ocean.

– **Don't take** a tour with a travel company.

**REGISTER CHECK**

People often use imperative verbs in informal writing to give advice.

In a website review: *Walk to the top of the island.*

People usually use verb forms with subjects in formal writing.

In a travel guide: *You can walk to the top of the island.*

### WRITE IT

C **Choose a place for people to visit in your area. Write a review of the place. Say what people can do and see. Use imperative verbs to give advice. Use Cameron's review in exercise 2A for an example.**

D PAIR WORK **Read your partner's review. Do you want to visit your partner's place? Why or why not?**

9.5

# TIME TO SPEAK
## Vacation plans

**LESSON OBJECTIVE**

- plan a vacation for someone

**A** **DISCUSS** Look at the pictures. What do you think these people like to do on vacation? For each person, say three things. Compare your ideas with a partner. Find a new idea for each person.

Jim

Minako

Carter

**B** **DECIDE** Work in pairs. Choose Jim, Minako, or Carter. Imagine they are coming to your country on vacation for two weeks. What do you think they want to do? Make a list of things to do and places to go.

**C** **PREPARE** Imagine you are helping this person plan a vacation. Look at your list from exercise B. What do you need to do? Make a plan.

**D** **AGREE** Work in groups: Group Jim, Group Minako, or Group Carter. Present your plan. Which plan is your group's favorite?

*To check your progress, go to page 154.*

## USEFUL PHRASES

**DISCUSS**

I think Jim/Minako/Carter likes to … on vacation.

What do you think Jim/Minako/Carter likes to do?

My three ideas for Jim are …

I agree. / I disagree.

Let's think of one new idea for Minako.

**DECIDE**

A good thing to do / place to go is …

On the first day, he/she can …

**AGREE**

We're planning a vacation for …

This is our plan.

Our favorite plan is … because it's interesting/fun/nice.

# REVIEW 3 (UNITS 7–9)

## 1 VOCABULARY

**A Write the words in the chart. There are five words or phrases for each group.**

| | | | | |
|---|---|---|---|---|
| airport | clean my room | do homework | paint | take a break |
| be on the subway | company | draw | play the guitar | take the bus |
| brush my hair | dance | have a meeting | sing | do the dishes |
| check in | destination | office | take a bath | workers |

| Activities around the house | Transportation/Travel | Skills | Work |
|---|---|---|---|
| | | | |
| | | | |
| | | | |
| | | | |
| | | | |
| | | | |

**B Add one more word or phrase to each group in exercise 1A.**

## 2 GRAMMAR

**A Put the words in the correct order to make sentences.**

1 my / right / cleaning / I'm / room / now. ______

2 aren't / homework. / The / doing / children / their ______

3 bus? / Is / waiting / she / a / for ______

4 days. / hard / is / these / father / My / working ______

5 watching / TV / not / right now. / They're ______

6 you / these / reading / What / days? / books / are ______

**B** PAIR WORK **Tell a partner two or three things you are doing these days. For example, what you're reading or watching on TV, what classes you're taking, or what games/sports you're playing.**

**C Complete the sentences with *can* or *can't*.**

1 My brother usually goes out for dinner because he ______ cook.

2 I ______ swim really well. I usually swim in the evening after work.

3 Juan ______ speak four languages: Spanish, Portuguese, French, and Italian.

4 My sister ______ skateboard, and she doesn't want to learn.

5 I ______ drive a car. It's easy.

6 My grandfather ______ use a computer. He doesn't have one, and he doesn't want one.

**D** PAIR WORK **Talk to a partner. Say two things you can do and two things you can't do.**

## 3 SPEAKING

A PAIR WORK **You're going to play a guessing game with your partner. Follow the instructions.**

1 Work alone. Choose one of these places, but <u>don't</u> tell your partner: in a room at home, in an office, in a classroom, on a train or a bus, in a car. Now, imagine you're in the place.

2 Talk to your partner. Say what you can and can't do in the place. Say what you're doing there now.

3 Your partner guesses the place. You can say *"Yes."* or *"No."*

I can sleep here, and I can use my phone. I can't cook here, but I can go places. Right now, I'm studying here.

Is it a classroom?

No!

B **Write about your partner's place in exercise 3A. Describe what he/she can and can't do there.**

## 4 FUNCTIONAL LANGUAGE

A **Circle the correct answers.**

**Robert** Hi, Marina! [1] *I'm / It's* Robert.

**Marina** Hey, Robert! How are you [2] *do / doing*?

**Robert** Not [3] *bad / fine*, thanks. And you?

**Marina** [4] *I'm / It's* fine. What are you doing these days?

**Robert** Well, I'm planning a trip to Rio for five days.

**Marina** [5] *Oh, wow! / Oh no!* That's great!

**Robert** Yeah, and the hotel's a good price.

**Marina** Really? [6] *How much / When* is it?

**Robert** $189.99 a night.

**Marina** [7] *I don't think / I think* that's a good price. That's really, really expensive!

**Robert** [8] *I think / I think so* it's good. [9] *I mean / I say*, it's a five-star hotel.

**Marina** [10] *Oh. / Oh no!* [11] *Where / What* is it?

**Robert** In Copacabana.

## 5 SPEAKING

A PAIR WORK **Choose <u>one</u> of the situations below. Talk to a partner. Have a conversation.**

1 Start a telephone conversation. Ask how your partner is and what he/she is doing these days. Look at page 70 for useful language.

Hi, Ji-un. How are you?

2 Talk about things people do in unusual offices. Give your opinion about these things. Look at page 80 for useful language.

In some offices, you can play computer games. I don't think that's a good idea. I mean, people need to work!

3 You're at an airport and need information about prices, locations, and times. Look at page 90 for useful language.

Excuse me. How much are these travel guides?

B PAIR WORK **Change roles and repeat the situation.**

**UNIT OBJECTIVES**

- make outdoor plans for the weekend
- discuss what clothes to wear for different trips
- suggest plans for evening activities
- write an online invitation
- plan and present a fun weekend in your city

# GET READY

# 10

## START SPEAKING

A Look at the picture. Imagine you're doing this. Say things you can do to get ready before you do it.

B Do you have big plans for the future? What are they? For ideas, watch Larissa's video.

**REAL STUDENT**

*Are your plans the same as Larissa's?*

# 10.1 WHITE NIGHTS

**LESSON OBJECTIVE**
- make outdoor plans for the weekend

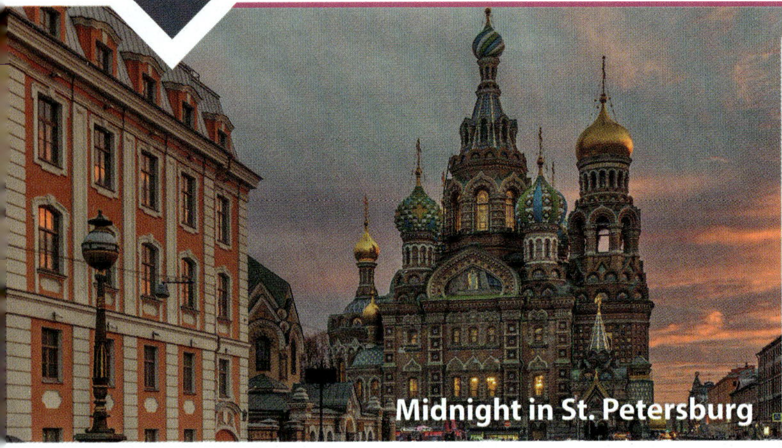

Midnight in St. Petersburg

Reply  Forward

**To:** sofiaperez@mymail.com
**From:** averin.yana@grabmail.org
**Subject:** Your trip

Hi Sofia,

You're going to be here next weekend! I'm very happy because you're going to see St. Petersburg during the White Nights. It's light for about 24 hours in June. We live *outside* – all day and *all night*.

So, here's the plan. On Friday evening, I'm going to **meet** you at the airport and then **take** you out to dinner. We're going to **eat** outside at Marketplace. It's my favorite restaurant.

On Saturday, we're going to **look at** art at the Street Art Museum. And, of course, we can **go** shopping on Nevsky Prospect. And then in the evening, we're going to **get together** with some of my friends in Kirov Park. We can **take** a walk in the park, and then we're going to **have** a picnic – at midnight!

What else do you want to do? I'm not going to be home tonight, but we can talk tomorrow.

See you soon!

Yana

**GLOSSARY**
**light** (*adj*) the sun is in the sky

## 1 LANGUAGE IN CONTEXT

A PAIR WORK **Look at the picture. Where is it? What time is it? What's unusual about it?**

B **Read the email and answer the questions.**

1 Why is Yana happy?
2 What are the "White Nights"?
3 When does Yana want to talk to Sofia?

## 2 VOCABULARY: Going out

A 2.30 **Find these verbs in the email. Then complete the phrases with the verbs. Listen and check.**

eat   get together   go   have   look at   meet   take (2x)

1 ________ art

2 ________ a walk

3 ________ someone out to dinner and ________ outside

4 ________ someone at the airport

5 ________ shopping

6 ________ with friends and ________ a picnic

B **Now do the vocabulary exercises for 10.1 on page 149.**

C GROUP WORK **How often do you do the activities in exercise 2A? Tell your group.**

## 3 GRAMMAR: Statements with *be going to*

A **Circle the correct answer. Use the sentences in the grammar box to help you.**

1 Use *be going to* to talk about **things you're doing right now** / **future plans**.

2 Make future statements with *be going to* + **a verb** / **a noun**.

**Statements with *be going to***

| | |
|---|---|
| I'**m going to be** home tomorrow. | I'**m not going to be** home tonight. |
| It'**s going to be** light all night. | It **isn't going to be** light all night. |
| You'**re going to meet** me at the airport. | My friends **aren't going to go** shopping. |
| We'**re going to get together** with some of my friends. | They'**re not going to eat** outside this weekend. |

B **Complete the sentences with *be going to* and the affirmative or negative form of the verb in parentheses ( ).**

1 I ____________________ (be) home tomorrow. I have to work at the office.

2 My parents ____________________ (take) me to lunch on Saturday. They're busy.

3 My friends and I ____________________ (go) on a trip to Rio next year. We have our tickets!

4 I ____________________ (study) a lot next week. I have an important test.

5 My friend ____________________ (meet) me tonight. She's sick.

C PAIR WORK **Change the sentences in exercise 3B so they're true for you. Then compare with a partner.**

*I'm not going to be home tomorrow. I have to go to college.*

D **Now go to page 137. Look at the grammar chart and do the grammar exercise for 10.1.**

## 4 SPEAKING

A PAIR WORK **What can you do outside in your city? Make a list.**

*We can eat outside at a lot of restaurants.*

*True. And we can watch movies outside.*

B PAIR WORK **Make outdoor plans with your partner for next weekend. Then share your plans with the class.**

*Next Saturday, we're going have a picnic in ...*

# 10.2 BUT IT'S SUMMER THERE!

**LESSON OBJECTIVE**
- discuss what clothes to wear for different trips

## 1 VOCABULARY: Clothes; seasons

A 2.31 **Listen and repeat the clothes. Then look at the people in your class. How many of the clothes can you see?**

B 2.32 PAIR WORK **Look at the seasons below. Listen and repeat. What seasons do you have where you live? When are they?**

C **Now do the vocabulary exercises for 10.2 on page 149.**

## 2 LANGUAGE IN CONTEXT

A 2.33 **Read and listen. Sofia and her friend discuss Sofia's trip to St. Petersburg. What clothes do they talk about?**

**2.33 Audio script**

**Rena** So, are you ready for your trip? What clothes are you going to take?
**Sofia** Yeah, I am! I'm going to take a big **coat**, and I need to buy a **hat**.
**Rena** Really? But it's **summer** there!
**Sofia** Yes, but it's Russia, not Florida! It's not hot in the summer.
**Rena** True, but it's not *cold*. So, are you going to take **pants** and some **sweaters**?
**Sofia** Yes, I am. No. I don't know. I usually wear **shorts** in the summer here, but … Oh, I know! I can take my **fall** or **spring** pants.
**Rena** Good idea. And what are you going to wear on your feet?
**Sofia** I need some new **shoes**. We're going to walk outside a lot. Or maybe **boots**.
**Rena** When are you going to leave? I mean, are you *really* ready for this trip?

**INSIDER ENGLISH**

You can say, *Oh, I know!* when you think of a good idea or an answer to a problem.

***Oh, I know!*** *I can take my fall or winter pants.*

**GLOSSARY**

**wear** (*v*) have clothes on your body

B PAIR WORK What season is it now? What clothes do you usually wear? For ideas, watch Anderson's video.

*Are your answers the same as Anderson's?*

## 3 GRAMMAR: Questions with *be going to*

A **Circle the correct answers. Use the sentences in the grammar box to help you.**

1 A *yes/no* question with *be going to* begins with ***Am*, *Is*, or *Are* / *What*, *Where*, or *When*.**

2 For information questions with *be going to*, put the question word **before / after** *is*, *are*, or *am*.

### Questions with *be going to*

| *Yes/no* questions | | Information questions |
|---|---|---|
| **Are** you **going to take** some sweaters? | Yes, I **am**. / No, I**'m not**. | **What are** you **going to take**? |
| **Is** Sofia **going to see** a friend? | Yes, she **is**. / No, she**'s not**. | **When are** you **going to leave**? |
| | | **Where is** Sofia **going to go**? |
| | | **Who are** you **going to meet**? |

B **Put the words in the correct order to make questions.**

1 are / going to / this weekend? / What / you / do ______

2 study / Are / tonight? / going to / you ______

3 have / you / What / for dinner? / are / going to ______

4 on TV? / going to / are / watch / you / What ______

5 tomorrow? / go / you / are / Where / going to ______

6 going to / your / next week? / see / Are / friends / you ______

C **Now go to page 138. Look at the grammar chart and do the grammar exercise for 10.2.**

D PAIR WORK **Read the Accuracy check box. Then ask and answer the questions in exercise 3B with a partner.**

**ACCURACY CHECK**

**Do not use *be going to* in short answers.**

*Are you going to wear a dress to the party?*

*No, I'm not ~~going to~~.* ✗

*Yes, I am.* ✓

## 4 SPEAKING

A **Look at the trips. Choose two, and plan what clothes you're going to take with you.**

- A two-week trip to Miami, Florida, in the summer. (29°C / 84°F)
- A one-week trip to Vienna, Austria, in the winter. (2°C / 36°F)
- A five-day trip to Vancouver, Canada, in the spring. (20°C / 68°F)
- A two-week trip to Manaus, Brazil, in the rainy season. (30°C / 86°F)

B PAIR WORK **Ask questions about your partners' trips.**

Where are you going to go?

First, I'm going to go to Miami this summer.

Oh, great! What clothes are you going to take?

# 10.3 LET'S MEET AT THE HOTEL

**LESSON OBJECTIVE**
- suggest plans for evening activities

## 1 FUNCTIONAL LANGUAGE

A **Jonathan is in Mexico City for a meeting with his coworker, Antonio. They're making plans to go out in the evening. What do you think they are saying?**

B 2.34 **Read and listen. Where are Antonio and Jonathan going to have dinner? Where are they going to meet? What time are they going to meet?**

**2.34 Audio script**

| | |
|---|---|
| **Antonio** | So, Jonathan, **why don't we go out tonight?** |
| **Jonathan** | **OK, sounds good.** |
| **Antonio** | Do you like Mexican food? |
| **Jonathan** | I love it! Are there any good Mexican restaurants in town? |
| **Antonio** | Um, in Mexico City? Yeah, I know one or two places! |
| **Jonathan** | I'm sure you do! |
| **Antonio** | There's a very good restaurant near your hotel. Why don't we go there? |
| **Jonathan** | **Good idea.** |
| **Antonio** | So **let's meet at the hotel.** |
| **Jonathan** | OK. What time? Eight o'clock? |
| **Antonio** | Um … **I'm sorry, but I can't.** How about eight-thirty? |
| **Jonathan** | **Yes, sure.** |

C **Complete the chart with expressions in bold from the conversation above.**

| Making suggestions | Accepting suggestions | Refusing suggestions |
|---|---|---|
| 1 ____________ go out tonight? | OK, 3 ____________ good. | I'm sorry, 6 ____________ . |
| 2 ____________ meet at the hotel. | Good 4 ____________ . | Sorry, I'm busy. |
| | Yes, 5 ____________ . | |

D 2.35 **Complete the conversations with words from exercise 1C. Listen and check. Then practice with a partner.**

1 **A** ____________ take a break.
  **B** OK, sounds ____________ .
2 **A** ____________ have lunch?
  **B** ____________ , but I can't.
3 **A** Coffee?
  **B** ____________ idea.

## 2 REAL-WORLD STRATEGY

**SAYING WHY YOU CAN'T DO SOMETHING**

After you say, *I'm sorry, but I can't*, you can give a reason with *I have to.*

*Jonathan* *What time? Eight o'clock?*

*Antonio* *I'm sorry, but I can't. I have to go home first. How about eight-thirty?*

A **Read the information in the box above. Why can't Antonio meet at eight o'clock?**

B 2.36 **Listen to a conversation. What are the man and woman going to do, and when?**

C 2.36 **Listen again. Why can't the woman have a meeting on Monday?**

D PAIR WORK **Student A: Go to page 158. Student B: Go to page 160. Follow the instructions.**

## 3 PRONUNCIATION: Saying the letter *s*

A 2.37 **Listen and repeat. How is the letter *s* different in the words?**

/s/ sorry /z/ busy

B 2.38 **Read and say the words below. Which sound does the letter *s* have? Write /s/ or /z/. Some words have two sounds. Then listen and check.**

1 restaurants ____ ____
3 tickets ____
5 station ____
7 jeans ____

2 movies ____
4 shoes ____
6 season ____ ____
8 shorts ____

C 2.39 PAIR WORK **Listen and repeat the sentences. Focus on the /s/ and /z/ sounds. Then practice the sentences with a partner.**

1 Are there any restaurants in town?
2 I'm sorry, but I can't. I'm busy tonight.
3 Are there any movies on TV tonight?
4 Why don't we get tickets at the station?

## 4 SPEAKING

PAIR WORK **Imagine your partner is in your town or city on a business or study trip. He/She is staying at a hotel in the city. Suggest something to do in the evening. Also suggest a place to go and a time to meet. Then change roles.**

# 10.4 A 24-HOUR CITY

**LESSON OBJECTIVE**
- write an online invitation

## 1 LISTENING

A PAIR WORK **Look at the city in the pictures on pages 104 and 105. What do you think you can you do there?**

B 2.40 LISTEN FOR DETAILS **Listen to the start of a TV travel show about Montevideo. Which two cities does the woman talk about? Which two neighborhoods in Montevideo does she talk about?**

C 2.40 LISTEN FOR EXAMPLES **Listen again. Check (✓) the places the woman says.**

- ☐ restaurants
- ☐ places to go dancing
- ☐ hotels
- ☐ the ocean
- ☐ the beach
- ☐ museums

D PAIR WORK THINK CRITICALLY **The woman says, "This really is a day-and-night city." Look at the places in exercise 1C. Where do people usually go: in the day? at night? at night *and* in the day?**

## 2 PRONUNCIATION: Listening for *going to*

A 2.41 **Listen to the sentences. Do you hear *going to* or *gonna*? Circle the correct words.**

1 I'm not *going to* / *gonna* go dancing now.

2 We're *going to* / *gonna* walk by the ocean in Old City.

B 2.42 **Listen. What do you hear? Circle *going to* or *gonna*.**

1 *going to* / *gonna*

2 *going to* / *gonna*

3 *going to* / *gonna*

4 *going to* / *gonna*

C **People often use *gonna* in informal conversations. Circle the correct answer.**

People usually say *gonna* when they are ***at work* / *talking to friends*.**

## 3 WRITING

A **Read the online invitation. What does Ramon say his friends can wear? Which night is a surprise?**

Reply Forward

**From:** Ramon
**Subject:** Montevideo Nights

### MESSAGE FROM RAMON

| | |
|---|---|
| **EVENT** | Montevideo Nights |
| **HOST** | Ramon |
| **WHEN** | Friday and Saturday, December 19–20 |
| **WHERE** | Montevideo, Uruguay |
| **MEET** | Hotel Central, Friday, December 19 at 9:30 p.m. |

This is a city that never sleeps. *You're* not going to sleep, either! Meet me at the front door of the hotel. Don't be late! And don't eat dinner first because we're going to eat at a nice restaurant in the Pocitos neighborhood. Then we're going to go dancing – all night! Early in the morning, about 5:00 a.m., we're going to watch the sunrise at the beach and then go for a morning walk by the ocean. It's a great place for a picnic – a breakfast picnic. And then why don't we play soccer on the beach? A lot of people play soccer on the beach in the summer. You can wear shorts and a T-shirt, but a sweater is good for the early morning. On Saturday night, we're going to … well, it's a surprise! See you Friday night!

**GLOSSARY**

**sunrise** (*n*) early in the morning, when the sun is first in the sky

**surprise** (*n*) something you don't know about

B **WRITING SKILLS** **Look at the contractions in two of Ramon's sentences below. Then <u>underline</u> all 10 contractions in his message. Work with a partner and say the full forms.**

<u>You're</u> not going to sleep, either! (*You're = You are*)

<u>Don't</u> be late! (*Don't = Do not*)

**REGISTER CHECK**

Many speakers of English use contractions in informal writing. In formal writing, people often use the full forms.

### WRITE IT

FIND IT

C **Plan an exciting day or night out for your friends. You can look online for ideas. Then write an online invitation. Use Ramon's invitation for an example. Describe where you are going to go and what you are going to do. Use contractions.**

D GROUP WORK **Read the other invitations in your group. Which events do you want to go to? Why?**

# 10.5 TIME TO SPEAK
## 48 hours in your city

**LESSON OBJECTIVE**
- plan and present a fun weekend in your city

**A** **PREPARE** Look at the pictures. Can you do these things in your country? When can you do them? Think about seasons, days, and times of day.

**B** **RESEARCH** Work with a partner. Choose a season or a month. Think of fun things to do in your city in that season/month during the day, at night, and outside. Write a list.

**C** **AGREE** Plan a fun weekend (48 hours) in your city. Choose activities from exercise B. Make a plan for Saturday and Sunday.

**D** **DISCUSS** Work with another pair and compare your plans. Ask and answer questions about their plan.

**E** **PRESENT** With your partner, present your 48-hour plan to the class. Which plan do you want to do?

*To check your progress, go to page 155.*

## USEFUL PHRASES

**RESEARCH**

Let's talk about the summer / February / the rainy season.

What fun things can we do during the day? at night? outside?

**DISCUSS**

We're going to have breakfast in the park.

Are you going to have a picnic?

**PRESENT**

We're planning a fun weekend in (season/month).

First, we're going to …

On Saturday/Sunday, …

## UNIT OBJECTIVES

- describe people, places, and things in the past
- talk about colors and memories
- talk about movies and actors
- write an email about things you keep from your past
- talk about TV shows from your childhood

# COLORFUL MEMORIES

# 11

## START SPEAKING

A Look at the picture. Where is the boy? How old is the boy now?

B Is the boy happy? Why or why not?

C Talk about a happy time in your life. For ideas, watch Felipe's video.

REAL STUDENT

*What time does Felipe talk about? Do you remember the same time?*

# 11.1 FLASHBACK FRIDAY

**LESSON OBJECTIVE**
- describe people, places, and things in the past

## 1 LANGUAGE IN CONTEXT

A **Mason writes about two old pictures from his past. Read his posts and the comments. Circle the topics he writes about.**

| | |
|---|---|
| his school | his first job |
| the season | a toy |
| his family | his favorite food |

B **Read again. Check (✓) the sentences that are true. Correct the false ones.**

- ☐ 1 Flashback Friday is for pictures from the past.
- ☐ 2 The yard is at Mason's parents' house.
- ☐ 3 Bethany is Mason's friend now.
- ☐ 4 Mason drives a car these days.

**Mason Clark** It's Flashback Friday! Here are two of my favorite memories from 2009. I was eight. This was in the summer. I was with my sister, and we were on vacation at my grandparents' house. My parents weren't there. It was **exciting**! #flashbackfriday #2009 #summervacation

**Fay L. Wright** You were really **cute**!

**Bert Chow** Your grandparents' yard was **beautiful**!

**Mason Clark** Yeah, it was **wonderful**. It was usually **quiet**, but not in the summer. We were **noisy** kids!

**Mason Clark** And this was my old go-kart. My grandpa made it for me. Well, it wasn't old in 2009 – it was **new** then! It was **slow**, but to me, at eight, it was really **fast** and exciting. #go-kart #2009 #bestgrandparents

**Sam Lopez** My go-kart was **awful**, but yours is great.

**Bethany Clark** Hey, Mason is still driving it today! 😂

**Mason Clark** Don't listen to my sister! I have a real, *fast* car now. 🙂

👍 13 ❤ 2

**GLOSSARY**
**memories** (*n*) things you think about from your past
**yard** (*n*) the outdoor area in front of or behind a house

## 2 VOCABULARY: Describing people, places, and things

A 🔊 2.43 **Listen and repeat the adjectives in bold. Which adjectives in Mason's posts describe people, places, and things?**

**new** shoes

**cute** dog

**wonderful** vacation

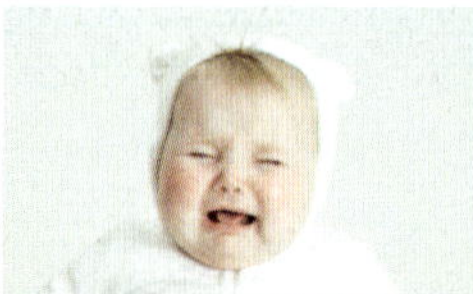
**noisy** baby

**fast** car

**exciting** book

**beautiful** day

**awful** day

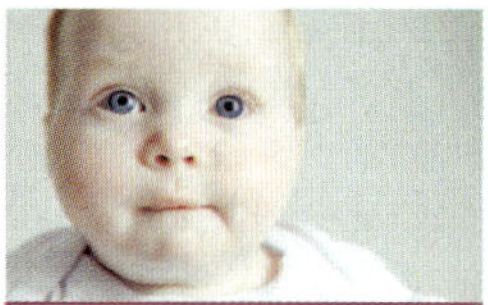
**quiet** baby

**slow** car

B **Now do the vocabulary exercises for 11.1 on page 150.**

C GROUP WORK **Think about a person, place, or thing from your past. Describe it to your group. Use the adjectives in exercise 2A. For ideas, watch Anderson's video.**

REAL STUDENT

*Is Anderson's memory happy? Is your memory happy, too?*

## 3 GRAMMAR: Statements with *was* and *were*

A **Circle the correct answer. Use the sentences in the grammar box to help you.**

1 Use *was* and *were* to talk about people, places, or things in the **past / future**.

2 *Was* and *were* are the simple past forms of ***go* / *be***.

3 *Was* and *were* are **affirmative / negative**.

4 *Wasn't* and *weren't* are **affirmative / negative**.

**Statements with *was* and *were***

| | |
|---|---|
| I **was** in the yard. | My parents **weren't** there. |
| We **were** on vacation. | It **wasn't** old. |

B **Read another Flashback Friday post. Complete the post with *was*, *wasn't*, *were*, or *weren't*.**

**Ethan Collins**
March 14 at 3:37 p.m.

I remember a visit to my uncle's farm in August 1998. It [1] ______ a big farm – just a nice, small one. There [2] ______ a lot of animals, only ten or fifteen. They [3] ______ farm animals, not pets, so they [4] ______ friendly, but my uncle's dog [5] ______ really nice. He [6] ______ only two or three, so he [7] ______ very old, but he [8] ______ smart. His real name [9] ______ Jake, but my name for him [10] ______ "Fluffy Duffy." It's an awful name, but I [11] ______ seven at the time, and to me, Fluffy Duffy [12] ______ a beautiful name! We [13] ______ great friends. #flashbackfriday #1998 #bestfriend

Fluffy Duffy

Like Comment Share

35 8

**GLOSSARY**
**remember** (*v*) think about something from the past

C **Now go to page 138. Look at the grammar chart and do the grammar exercise for 11.1.**

D PAIR WORK **Write sentences with *was* or *were*. Use the words in parentheses ( ). Then check your accuracy. Which sentences are true for you?**

*When I was a child ...*

1 (My friends / wonderful) ______.

2 (My hometown / beautiful) ______.

3 (My brother's car / awful) ______.

4 (My cat / really cute) ______.

**✓ ACCURACY CHECK**

Do not forget to use *was*, *wasn't*, *were*, or *weren't* before adjectives when describing the past.

He cute. ✗

He was cute. ✓

## 4 SPEAKING

A **Choose one or two of your memories. Think about the ideas below or your own ideas. Write notes.**

ages animals the people the place the season the year things

B PAIR WORK **Talk about your memories. You can begin, *"I remember ..."***

*I remember my sister's birthday party. It was July 2006. She was thirteen. The party was very noisy, and ...*

# 11.2 OUR OLD PHONE WAS WHITE

**LESSON OBJECTIVE**

- talk about colors and memories

## 1 LANGUAGE IN CONTEXT

A PAIR WORK **Look at the picture of the child. Describe it with one word.**

B 2.44 **Emilio talks to his wife, Paula. Read and listen. Where was Emilio in the picture? Which rooms does Paula remember?**

**2.44 Audio script**

**Emilio** Here's another picture of me.

**Paula** Cute! How old were you?

**Emilio** I don't know. Two?

**Paula** And where were you? Were you at home?

**Emilio** No, I wasn't, because our phone was **black**. Hmm … so where was the **green** phone? Oh, yeah! It was at my grandparents' house, in the kitchen.

**Paula** Hey, I remember our old phone, too. It was **white**.

**Emilio** Wow, you remember the color, too! Was it big? Our old phone was *really* big.

**Paula** Yeah, it was. I remember a lot! The phone was in the living room, next to the couch. The couch was **brown**. And the living room walls were **orange**. Oh, yeah, and my bedroom walls were **pink** and green. Yuck! It's really easy to remember the colors of things – even ugly colors!

**GLOSSARY**

**ugly** (*adj*) not nice to look at

C 2.44 **Read and listen again. Then answer the questions.**

1 How many phones does Emilio talk about?

2 Paula remembers the color of her phone, living room walls, bedroom walls – and which other thing?

**INSIDER ENGLISH**

**You can say, *Oh, yeah,* when you remember something.**

*Where was the green phone?* ***Oh, yeah!*** *It was at my grandmother's house.*

***Oh, yeah,*** *and my bedroom walls were pink and green.*

## 2 VOCABULARY: Colors

A 2.45 PAIR WORK **Listen and repeat the colors. Which colors are in the conversation above? What's your favorite color?**

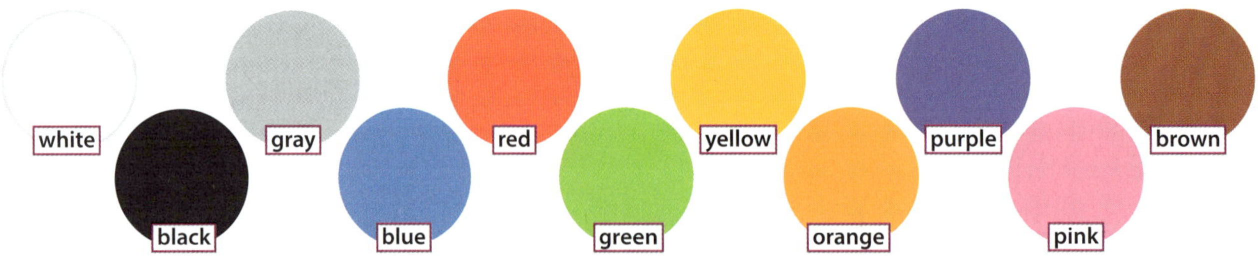


B **Now do the vocabulary exercises for 11.2 on page 150.**

C PAIR WORK **Tell your partner the colors of <u>two</u> things from your home.**

## 3 GRAMMAR: Questions with *was* and *were*

A **Circle the correct answers. Use the questions in the grammar box to help you.**

1 In *yes/no* questions, *was* and *were* go at the **beginning** / **end** of the question.

2 In information questions, *was* and *were* go **before** / **after** the question word(s) (for example, *How old* and *When*).

**Questions with *was* and *were***

| *Yes/no* questions | Information questions |
|---|---|
| **Were** you at home? | How old **were** you? |
| No, I **wasn't**. | I **was** two. |
| **Was** the phone in the kitchen? | What color **were** the walls? |
| Yes, it **was**. | They **were** orange. |

B PAIR WORK **Put the words in the correct order to make questions. Then ask and answer the questions with a partner.**

1 color / your old phone? / was / What ______

2 was / the phone? / Where ______

3 in the kitchen? / the refrigerator / Was ______

4 the walls / color / in the kitchen? / were / What ______

5 big? / Were / the bedrooms ______

6 your home / nice? / Was ______

C **Now go to page 139. Look at the grammar chart and do the grammar exercise for 11.2.**

## 4 SPEAKING

A **Draw a picture or plan of a room in your house from your past. Include furniture and your favorite things.**

B PAIR WORK **Work with a partner. Ask and answer questions about your rooms.**

This is the bedroom. There was a bed, a desk, and two windows.

What color was the bed?

My bed was white.

# 11.3 I HAVE NO IDEA

**LESSON OBJECTIVE**
- talk about movies and actors

## 1 FUNCTIONAL LANGUAGE

A **Look at the picture of the woman. Do you know her name? What else do you know about her?**

B 2.46 **Read and listen. What does the man want to remember? Does he remember it?**

**2.46 Audio script**

**A** I'm going to watch *Titanic* tonight.
**B** The movie?
**A** Yeah. With Leonardo DiCaprio, and … who was the other actor? The woman?
**B** Um, **I have no idea.**
**A** She's from England.
**B** Sorry, **I'm not sure.**
**A** Her first name is Kate, **I think.**
**B** Let me think. **Maybe** it's Kate Hudson? No, she's American. Why don't we look online?
**A** Good idea. Let's see … *Titanic* actor, woman … Kate Winslet!
**B** Oh, yeah.
**A** What was the name of that other movie she was in? With Johnny Depp.
**B** Oh no … Not again!

**GLOSSARY**
**actor** (*n*) a man or woman in a movie, TV show, or play

C **Complete the chart with expressions in bold from the conversation above.**

| Expressing uncertainty | |
|---|---|
| **Very unsure** | **A little unsure** |
| I have [1] ________ . | Her first name is Kate, I [3] ________ . |
| I'm [2] ________ . | I think her first name is Kate. |
| I don't know. | [4] ________ it's Kate Hudson? |

D 2.47 PAIR WORK **Complete the conversations with the correct words from the box. Listen and check. Then practice with a partner.**

don't Maybe no not think

1 **A** When was the movie *Titanic* in theaters?
**B** I ________ know. ________ it was in 1997?
2 **A** How many movies was Kate Winslet in?
**B** I have ________ idea.
3 **A** Where was Melinda yesterday?
**B** I ________ she was at home.
4 **A** Where are the restrooms?
**B** Sorry, I'm ________ sure.

## 2 REAL-WORLD STRATEGY

**TAKING TIME TO THINK**

When you need time to think about an answer, say, *Let me think*, *Uh*, or *Um*.

*Um, I have no idea.*

*Let me think. Maybe it's Kate Hudson?*

A **Read the information in the box about taking time to think. Which <u>two</u> expressions does the woman use?**

B 2.48 **Listen to a conversation. What is the man sure about? What <u>isn't</u> he sure about?**

C 2.48 **Listen again. Which <u>two</u> expressions does the man use when he needs time to think?**

D PAIR WORK **Student A: Go to page 158. Student B: Go to page 160. Follow the instructions.**

## 3 PRONUNCIATION: Saying /oʊ/ and /ɑː/ vowel sounds

A 2.49 **Listen and repeat the words. How are the vowel sounds different?**

/oʊ/ know /ɑː/ not

B 2.50 **Listen. Write A for words with /oʊ/, for example *know*. Write B for words with /ɑː/, for example *not*.**

1 don't ___ 3 no ___ 5 home ___

2 on ___ 4 go ___ 6 concert ___

C 2.51 PAIR WORK **Look at the letters in bold below. Listen and repeat. Then practice the conversations with a partner.**

1 A Was M**o**na at the c**o**ncert yesterday?
B N**o**, she wasn't. She was at h**o**me.

2 A Where is Leonard**o** DiCapri**o** fr**o**m?
B I have n**o** idea.

3 A D**o**n't g**o**!
B Sorry, I have to g**o** h**o**me.

4 A Are we **o**n the right bus? It's very sl**o**w.
B I d**o**n't kn**o**w.

## 4 SPEAKING

GROUP WORK **Think of a movie. Ask other people in your group about the actors in it. Then change roles.**

Who was in the first *Avatar*?

I have no idea.

Um, was Zoe Saldana in it?

Yes, she was.

# 11.4 THINGS WE KEEP

**LESSON OBJECTIVE**

- write an email about things you keep from your past

## 1 READING

**A** Look at the pictures. What things can you see? Are the things old or new? Do you have some of these things?

**B** READ FOR MAIN IDEAS Read the article. What is it about?

### PICTURING MEMORIES

**Terry Lawrence is a travel writer for Pak Airlines in-flight magazine. Today she takes a break from travel writing and tells Pak Airlines readers about what she does in her free time.**

**I love to travel, I love to write – and I love to take pictures! I often take pictures of people and their favorite things. I have hundreds of pictures of people and the things they keep. People around the world keep things from childhood, for example toy cars, books, and games. These were their first favorite things. And me? I like to keep photographs, of course! Here are some of my favorite pictures.**

Meet Tom Bradley and his toy cars. They were birthday gifts. They're old, but he plays with them today – with a little help!

Many parents keep their children's things, like baby shoes or a child's first clothes. Rosa Ortiz keeps her daughter's shoe and her son's shoe in her car. They were one and two years old at the time. Now they're 12 and 13!

Many people keep books and comic books. This is Doug and one of his comic books, but it's not his favorite. Doug leaves his favorite comic book at home – it's very expensive!

**GLOSSARY**

**childhood** (*n*) the time when you were a child

**keep** (*v*) have something for a long time

**C** READ FOR DETAIL Read again. Then read these sentences from the article. What do the underlined words mean? Circle the answers.

1 These were their first favorite things.
*These* = **a** children **b** birthday gifts **c** things from their childhood

2 They're old, but he plays with them today.
*They* and *them* = **a** toy cars **b** shoes **c** games

3 They were one and two years old at the time.
*They* = **a** Rosa's cars **b** Rosa's parents **c** Rosa's children

4 It's not his favorite.
*It* = **a** Doug **b** Doug's comic book **c** Doug's house

**D** PAIR WORK What things do you keep? Why? Do you keep the same things from the article, too? Tell a partner.

## 2 WRITING

A Read Angie's email to her brother. What things from the past does she find in a box?

Reply Forward

Hi Eddie,

Do you remember this postcard? It was in a box under my bed. It was from Grandpa Bowman in 1969. He was in Saudi Arabia. His postcards were always exciting, and this one was my favorite. The desert is really beautiful. Do *you* have any of his old postcards?

There was also a lot of homework from my school days in the box. Hey, I was smart! Well, usually. My math homework was awful! 😱 I don't think I want to keep it.

Your old soccer ball was in the box, too. ⚽ Why do I have it? I don't know. There's some writing on it. Maybe it's the autograph of a famous soccer player. Do you want it?

Love,

Angie

**GLOSSARY**

**autograph** (*n*) name in handwriting, usually of a famous person

**REGISTER CHECK**

Use emojis (small pictures) in texts, social media posts, and informal emails. Do not use them in formal emails, for example, emails for college or work.

*My math homework was awful!* 😱

B PAIR WORK THINK CRITICALLY **Why does Angie's email have three paragraphs?**

C WRITING SKILLS **Read the topic sentence from the email below. The topic sentence tells you what the paragraph is about. Read the email again and underline the three topic sentences.**

Do you remember this postcard? (= this paragraph is about a postcard.)

### WRITE IT

D **Imagine you have a box of old things from your childhood. Write an email to a friend about two or three things in the box. Use a new paragraph for each thing. Write a topic sentence for each paragraph. You can use emojis.**

E PAIR WORK **Read your partner's email. What interesting things do they write about in their email?**

# 11.5 TIME TO SPEAK
## TV memories

**LESSON OBJECTIVE**

- talk about TV shows from your childhood

**A** **PREPARE** Work with a partner. Talk about old TV shows you remember from your childhood. Write notes.

**B** **AGREE** Compare your ideas with other students. Which shows do a lot of people remember?

**C** **DISCUSS** Choose a TV show from your conversations in exercise A or B. What do you remember about it? Talk about the names, places, and things in the show.

FIND IT

**D** **PREPARE** Prepare a presentation about your TV show from exercise C. Include the ideas below and your own ideas. You can go online and find information you don't remember.

TV show
- When was it on TV?
- Who were the characters (names, ages, personalities)?
- What were the places in the show?
- Why was the show popular?

**E** **PRESENT** Present your memories of the TV show to the class with your partner. Which shows does everyone remember?

*To check your progress, go to page 155.*

## USEFUL PHRASES

**DISCUSS**

I remember … from my childhood.

What about you?

Let's talk about the characters in …

What were their names?

I liked that show because …

**AGREE**

What do you remember?

A lot of people / I remember …

**PRESENT**

We're talking about …

Our show was really popular.

It was on TV in (year).

**UNIT OBJECTIVES**

- talk about snacks and small meals
- talk about meals in restaurants
- offer and accept food and drink
- write a restaurant review
- create a menu for a restaurant

# STOP, EAT, GO

# 12

## START SPEAKING

A **Which meal do you think these men are eating: breakfast, lunch, or dinner? Is it a big meal or a small meal? Are they enjoying their food?**

B **For a good meal, you need good food – and what else? Do you see these things in the picture?**

C **Talk about a good meal you remember. You can talk about where and when it was, who you were with, and why it was good.**

# 12.1 BACKPACKING AND SNACKING

**LESSON OBJECTIVE**
- talk about snacks and small meals

## 1 VOCABULARY: Snacks and small meals

A 2.52 PAIR WORK **Listen and repeat. Then choose something you want to eat now.**

apple

beef

butter

chicken

crackers

orange

potato

soup

banana

bread

cheese

coconut

lamb

pineapple

sandwich

tomato

> **!** To make these words plural, add *-s* or *-es*:
> *banana* → *bananas*  *tomato* → *tomatoes*  *sandwich* → *sandwiches*
> Some nouns are non-count, for example *cheese* and *soup*.

B **Now do the vocabulary exercises for 12.1 on page 151.**

C PAIR WORK **Look at the pictures in exercise 1A and find:**

- seven words for fruit and vegetables
- three words for meat
- two words for dairy products
- two words for grain products
- two words for small meals

## 2 LANGUAGE IN CONTEXT

A **Read the blog. Where was Tyler yesterday? Where was he last week?**

B **Read again. Check (✓) the sentences that are true. Correct the false ones.**

☐ 1 Tyler's breakfast and lunch were big.

☐ 2 There was meat in Tyler's sandwich.

☐ 3 There were dairy products in Tyler's breakfast, lunch, and dinner.

☐ 4 There are dairy products and fruit in *locro*.

**TRAVEL WITH TYLER**

Hello from Salvador, Brazil! I'm happy to be here after a really long trip. Yesterday, I took the bus from Aracaju. I didn't eat a lot for breakfast before the trip – just some **bread** and **butter**. Then I was on the bus for seven hours. We stopped in a lot of places, but I stayed on the bus, so I didn't have a big lunch. I ate some **crackers** and a **banana**, and I drank a bottle of warm water (yuck!)

I arrived in Salvador in the afternoon, and I was *really* hungry, so I didn't wait. I had dinner at the bus station! I went to a food stand, and I bought a *bauru* **sandwich**. It's bread with **beef**, **cheese**, and **tomatoes**. I needed it! And I liked it – I'm going to eat it again tomorrow.

South American food is great. Last week, in Quito, Ecuador, I tried *locro*. It's a **soup** with **potatoes** and cheese. I love the fruit in South America, too, but because I'm "backpacking and snacking," it's not always easy to eat. You can't eat **pineapples** and **coconuts** on a bus!

**GLOSSARY**
**food stand** (*n*) a place to buy food on the street
**hungry** (*adj*) you need to eat

## 3 GRAMMAR: Simple past statements

A **Circle the correct answers. Use the sentences in the grammar box to help you.**

1 Use the simple past to talk about **finished events** / **events that are happening now**.
2 After *I*, *you*, *he*, *she*, *we*, *they* and *it*, simple past verbs have **the same** / **different** spelling.
3 Simple past verbs can be regular or irregular. To make most regular past simple verbs, add **-*d* or -*ed*** / **-*s***.
4 To make negative statements in the simple past, use ***don't*** / ***didn't*** + verb (for example, *eat*, *drink*, or *have*).

**Simple past statements**

| | |
|---|---|
| Yesterday, I **took** the bus from Aracaju. | I **didn't eat** a lot for breakfast. |
| I **had** some soup. He **had** a big dinner. | She **didn't like** the sandwich. |
| She **wanted** an orange. We **wanted** some apples. | They **didn't drink** the coffee. |

**!** **Irregular past simple verbs do not end in -*ed*. For example, *I took the bus*, not *I ~~taked~~ the bus*.**

***eat*** → ***ate*** ***drink*** → ***drank*** ***have*** → ***had*** ***go*** → ***went*** ***take*** → ***took*** ***buy*** → ***bought***

**For more irregular verbs, go to page 161.**

B **Read the information about irregular verbs in the Notice box. Then circle the correct words.**

1 It was a really big sandwich, but I *ate* / *eat* it all.
2 We *have* / *had* fish for dinner last night.
3 She didn't *buy* / *bought* food at the supermarket.
4 I was hungry and really *needed* / *need* some food.
5 We *arrive* / *arrived* at the restaurant at 5:30, but it wasn't open.
6 Was the cheese good? I didn't *tried* / *try* it.

C **Now go to page 139. Look at the grammar charts and do the grammar exercise for 12.1.**

D PAIR WORK **Complete the sentences so they're true for you. Then compare with a partner.**

1 For breakfast, I ate ______________________, and I drank ______________________.
2 Last week, I bought ______________________ at the supermarket.
3 The last movie I watched was ______________________.
4 Last weekend, I went to ______________________ with ______________________.

## 4 SPEAKING

A PAIR WORK **Talk about the food in exercise 1A. Say which things you like and which you don't like. For ideas, watch June's video.**

*Do you like/not like the same things as June?*

B PAIR WORK **Give examples of snacks and small meals you ate last week. Ask your partner questions about what they ate.**

Yesterday, I ate a sandwich for lunch.

Was it good?

# 12.2 WHAT DID YOU EAT?

**LESSON OBJECTIVE**
- talk about meals in restaurants

## 1 VOCABULARY: Food, drinks, and desserts

A 2.53 **Look at the pictures. Listen and repeat.**

B PAIR WORK **Which things in exercise 1A are drinks? Which are desserts? Which ones do you like? Which don't you like?**

C **Now do the vocabulary exercises for 12.2 on page 151.**

D GROUP WORK **What do you usually eat and drink for breakfast, lunch, and dinner? Tell your group. For ideas, watch Anderson's video.**

REAL STUDENT

*What's Anderson's food routine? Is your routine the same or different?*

## 2 LANGUAGE IN CONTEXT

A 2.54 **Jackie and Yoo-ri are writing comments on a restaurant review card. Read and listen. Did they like their meal?**

B 2.54 **Read and listen again. What did Jackie and Yoo-ri eat? What did they drink?**

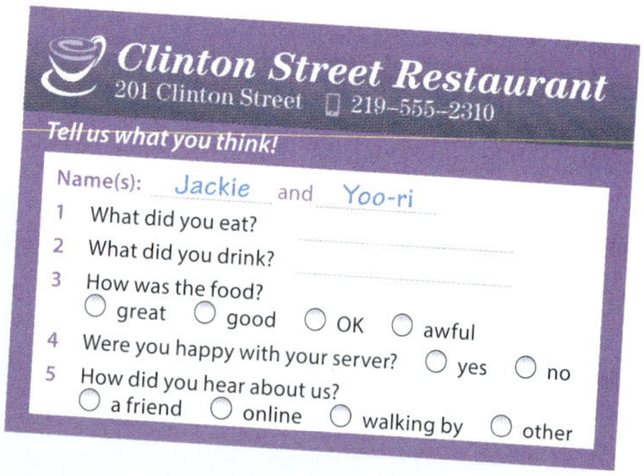

Clinton Street Restaurant
201 Clinton Street 219-555-2310
Tell us what you think!
Name(s): Jackie and Yoo-ri
1 What did you eat?
2 What did you drink?
3 How was the food?
○ great ○ good ○ OK ○ awful
4 Were you happy with your server? ○ yes ○ no
5 How did you hear about us?
○ a friend ○ online ○ walking by ○ other

**2.54 Audio script**

**Jackie** Look, a comment card. Let's do it.
**Yoo-ri** OK. We have time before dessert.
**Jackie** Number one. "What did you eat?" You had **fish** and **rice**. Did you have any vegetables?
**Yoo-ri** Yeah. I had beans, **black beans**.
**Jackie** That's right. And I had the **steak** with potatoes and **green beans**. OK. Number 2. "What did you drink?" I just had **water**. Did you have apple **juice**?
**Yoo-ri** No, I didn't have any juice. I had a **soda**.
**Jackie** Oh, yeah. OK, number 3. "How was the food?" My steak was great, but I didn't like the potatoes. The green beans were OK. Did you like the fish?
**Yoo-ri** Yes, I did. It was wonderful, and the rice and beans were good, too. But my soda was warm.
**Jackie** Hmm … I'm going to check "good." Ah, the server is coming with dessert. Oh, wow! Look at our **chocolate cake** and **ice cream**.
**Yoo-ri** Yum! Change "good" to "great!"

**INSIDER ENGLISH**

**Some people use *waiter* for a man and *waitress* for a woman. But these days, many people use the word *server* for a man or a woman.**

## 3 GRAMMAR: Simple past questions; *any*

A **Circle the correct answers. Use the information in the grammar box and the Notice box to help you.**

1 In simple past *yes/no* questions, use ***Did*** / ***Do*** + verb.

2 In simple past information questions, the question word and *did* go **before** / **after** the person or thing.

3 You can use *any* with ***yes/no*** / **information** questions in the simple past.

**Simple past questions**

| *Yes/no* questions | Information questions |
|---|---|
| **Did** you **have** apple juice? | **How did** you **hear** about us? |
| **Did** she **like** the fish? | **What** did they **eat**? |
| **Did** they **eat** any ice cream? | |

**!** **Use *some* in affirmative statements. Use *any* in *yes/no* questions and negative statements.**

*I had **some** soup for lunch.*
*Did you have **any** dessert?*
*They didn't have **any** juice.*

B PAIR WORK **Complete the conversations with the simple past form of the verbs in parentheses ( ). Then practice with a partner and make the answers true for you.**

1 A ______ you ______ (eat) breakfast?
 B Yes, I ______ .

2 A What ______ you ______ (have) for lunch?
 B I ______ an egg sandwich.

3 A ______ your friends ______ (go out) for dinner last night?
 B No, they ______ .

4 A What ______ your sisters ______ (buy) at the mall?
 B They ______ some shoes. They ______ any lunch.

5 A ______ your teacher ______ (give) you any homework?
 B No, she ______ .

C **Now go to page 140. Look at the grammar charts and do the grammar exercise for 12.2.**

D PAIR WORK **Write questions with these words. Use your ideas for the words in parentheses ( ). Then ask and answer the questions with a partner.**

what / do / (time or day) have (food item) / for (meal) / yesterday where / go / (time or day)

## 4 SPEAKING

A PAIR WORK **You're going to ask your partner about a meal they had in a restaurant. Ask the questions from the comment card and the box below. Then think of <u>two</u> more questions.**

| | |
|---|---|
| Where did you eat? | Was the food expensive? |
| Did you have any dessert? | Was the restaurant busy? |
| Did you wait for a table? | Who did you eat with? |

**Clinton Street Restaurant**
201 Clinton Street 219-555-2310

*Tell us what you think!*

Name(s): ______ and ______
1 What did you eat? ______
2 What did you drink? ______
3 How was the food?
 ◯ great ◯ good ◯ OK ◯ awful
4 Were you happy with your server? ◯ yes ◯ no
5 How did you hear about us?
 ◯ a friend ◯ online ◯ walking by ◯ other

B PAIR WORK **Ask and answer the questions from exercise 4A about a meal you ate last week or a favorite meal you had in the past.**

Where did you eat?

I had dinner at The Fish Dish.

# 12.3 PLEASE PASS THE BUTTER

**LESSON OBJECTIVE**
- offer and accept food and drink

## 1 FUNCTIONAL LANGUAGE

A 2.55 **Elisa has dinner in two different places on different nights. Read and listen to two conversations. What food and drink does Elisa want? What doesn't she want?**

**2.55 Audio script**

1 **Elisa** I really like this fish, Dan. It's so good!
**Dan** Thanks. **Do you want** some more?
**Elisa** Yes, please. Thanks. **Can I have** some bread, please?
**Dan** **Of course.** Here. **Would you like** some potatoes?
**Elisa** No, thanks, but **please pass** the butter.
**Dan** OK. **Here you are.**

2 **Server** **What would you like to eat?**
**Elisa** **I'd like** the chicken and rice, please.
**Server** **All right.** And what would you like to drink?
**Elisa** **Do you have** iced tea?
**Server** Yes. **We have** small and large iced teas.
**Elisa** I'd like a large iced tea, please. It's so hot today!

**GLOSSARY**
**more** (*det*) another piece (of fish, for example)
**iced tea** (*n*) cold tea

B **Complete the chart with expressions in bold from the conversations above. Then read the information in the Accuracy check box. What food does Elisa request with *some*?**

| Offering food and drink | Requesting food and drink |
|---|---|
| 1 ______ some more? | 4 ______ some bread, please? |
| 2 ______ some potatoes? | 5 ______ the butter. |
| 3 ______ ______ to eat? / to drink? | 6 ______ the chicken and rice, please. |
| What would you like for dessert? | 7 ______ iced tea? |

**Responding to requests**
Of 8 ______ .
Here. / Here 9 ______ .
All 10 ______ . / OK.
11 ______ small and large iced teas.

**ACCURACY CHECK**

Use *any* in questions.
*Did you have any vegetables?*
You can use *some* when a question is a request.
Can I have ~~any~~ bread? ✗
Can I have some bread? ✓

C 2.56 PAIR WORK **Put the two conversations in the correct order. Listen and check. Then practice with a partner.**

1
___ Yes, please. It's good!
___ OK. Here you are.
___ Would you like some more chicken?
___ And please pass the potatoes.

2
___ No, sorry.
___ What would you like for dessert?
___ I see. OK, I'd like ice cream and coffee, please.
___ Let me think. Do you have any chocolate cake?

## 2 REAL-WORLD STRATEGY

### USING *SO* AND *REALLY* TO MAKE WORDS STRONGER

Use *so* before adjectives to make them stronger. Use *really* before some verbs to make them stronger, for example: *like, love, don't like, need (to), want (to), have to.*

*Elisa* *I really like this fish, Dan. It's so good!*

*Elisa* *I'd like a large iced tea. It's so hot today!*

A **Read the information in the box above about making words stronger. What adjectives does Elisa use with *so*? What verb does she use with *really*?**

B 2.57 **Listen to a conversation. What does the man ask for?**

C 2.57 **Listen again. What words does he use after *so* and *really*?**

## 3 PRONUNCIATION: Saying /h/ and /r/ sounds

A 2.58 **Listen and repeat the words. Focus on the /h/ and /r/ sounds. How are they different?**

/h/ have /r/ really

B 2.59 **Listen. What sound do you hear? Write /h/ or /r/.**

1 ___ ear 3 ___ ight 5 ___ appy 7 ___ ad
2 ___ ave 4 ___ ead 6 ___ ice 8 ___ ed

C 2.60 PAIR WORK **Listen. Then practice the conversations with a partner. Does your partner say /h/ and /r/ clearly?**

1 **A** How is your food?
**B** It's good. I really like this rice.

2 **A** Where did you go last night?
**B** We had dinner at The Happy Home restaurant.

3 **A** How did you hear about us?
**B** I had an email from a friend. He really likes the food here.

## 4 SPEAKING

A PAIR WORK **Have a conversation. Use exercise 1C for an example. Choose one of these situations:**

- You're at a friend's home. One person offers food. The other person asks for things.
- You're at a restaurant. One person is a server. The other person orders a meal.
- You're at a café. One person is a server. The other person orders a drink and a snack.

Would you like some chicken, Matias?

Yes, please.

B GROUP WORK **Have your conversation again, in front of another pair. Listen. What situation in exercise 4A is it? What food and drink do they talk about?**

# 12.4 WHAT DID THE REVIEWERS SAY?

**LESSON OBJECTIVE**

- write a restaurant review

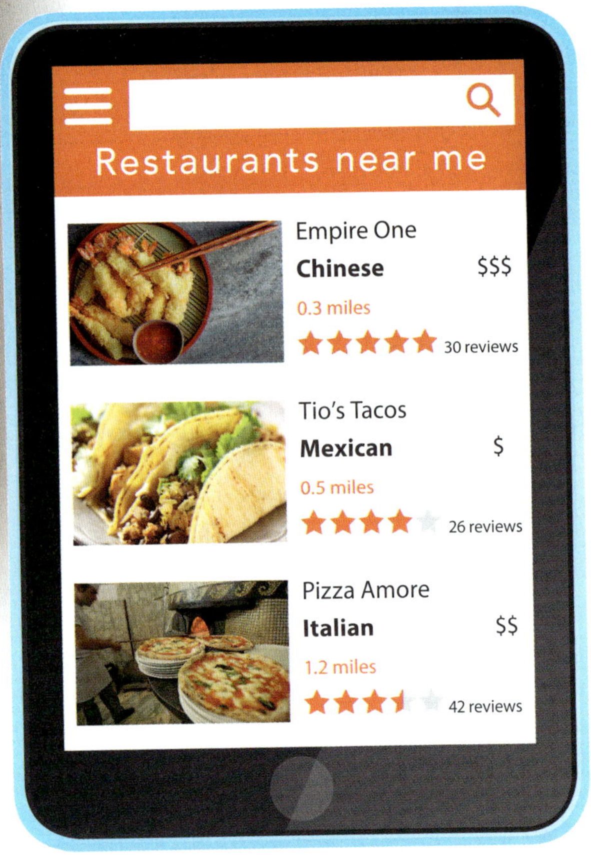


## 1 LISTENING

A **Look at the pictures. What are the people doing? Do you use similar apps?**

B 2.61 LISTEN FOR DETAILS **Listen to the conversation. What food does Mara want to eat?**

C 2.61 LISTEN FOR SUPPORTING DETAILS **Circle the reasons for each statement. Sometimes, there is more than one answer.**

1 Eric wants to eat at a restaurant near where they are.
   a He likes to eat in the car. b His favorite restaurants are in the area. c He's hungry.
2 Mara and Eric don't go to Fish Around.
   a Mara doesn't like fish. b Mara ate there in the past. c Eric had a bad meal there.
3 They don't go to Kayla B's Kitchen.
   a The food was bad. b It took a long time to get food. c The restaurant isn't new.
4 They go to Tio's Tacos.
   a It has good reviews. b Mara had a good meal there before. c It's Eric's favorite restaurant.

## 2 PRONUNCIATION: Listening for *Do you want to … ?*

A 2.62 **Listen and repeat. Focus on the underlined words. How is the pronunciation different than the written words?**

1 Where do you want to eat? 2 Do you want Chinese, Mexican, or Italian food?

B 2.63 **Listen to three speakers. How do they say *want to*? Match the speaker (1–3) with the pronunciation (a–c).**

a wanna ___ b /dʒu/ want ___ c /dʒu/ wanna ___

## 3 WRITING

A **Read two reviews of the restaurant Fish Around. What did Frank and Julieta eat? What was their favorite thing?**

# Fish Around

Los Angeles, United States

$$ Fish ★★★★★ 98 reviews

**Frank B.** ★★★★

**Los Angeles, USA** This is a nice restaurant. It's big, and it has a lot of windows, so it's very light. There are some tall plants in the dining area, but it isn't a "forest." I had vegetable soup, fish, and rice. The soup was good. I love fish, and the fish was great! My brother had fish and vegetables, and he liked his meal, too. We both had dessert. He had cake and I had ice cream. The servers were so friendly. We were really happy with our meal, and it wasn't expensive.

---

**Julieta F.** ★★★

**Buenos Aires, Argentina** I think this is a good restaurant, but I didn't choose it. My friends like fish, so they wanted to eat here. I like meat, but there wasn't any meat on the menu. Was the food good? Well, my friends liked it. They had fish, vegetables, rice, and dessert. I had fish and potatoes. The potatoes were OK. The fish was … well, it was fish! For dessert, I had pineapple cake and coconut ice cream. Wow! It was so good! I'm giving this restaurant three stars because the dessert was so great. The servers were nice. The price was OK – not cheap, but not expensive.

B PAIR WORK THINK CRITICALLY **Did Frank and Julieta like their meals? Why or why not?**

C **Read the sentences from the reviews. Underline the things the people ate.**

My brother had fish and vegetables.

I had vegetable soup, fish, and rice.

**REGISTER CHECK**

**In informal writing, you can sometimes ask and answer your own questions.**

*Was the food good? Well, my friends liked it.*

D WRITING SKILLS **Read the rules about writing lists, below. Circle the correct answers. Use the sentences in exercise 3C to help you. Then underline all the lists of food in the reviews.**

1 To list two things, you can join them with *and*. **Do / don't** use a comma (,) between two things.

2 To list three or more things, you can use a comma (,) between the things. Use *and* **before / after** the last thing.

## WRITE IT

E **Write a review of a restaurant you like. You can write about:**

- the restaurant's appearance
- the food you ate
- your opinion about the food
- your opinion about the servers
- the price of the food

F GROUP WORK **Read other people's reviews. Would you like to eat at any of the restaurants?**

# 12.5 TIME TO SPEAK

## Recipe for a great restaurant

**LESSON OBJECTIVE**

- create a menu for a restaurant

**A** **DISCUSS** Talk about a great restaurant you went to, and say why you liked it. Then talk about a bad restaurant, and say why you didn't like it.

**B** **PREPARE** Talk about what makes a great restaurant. Think about the things you discussed in exercise A and the things below. Then compare your ideas with other people.

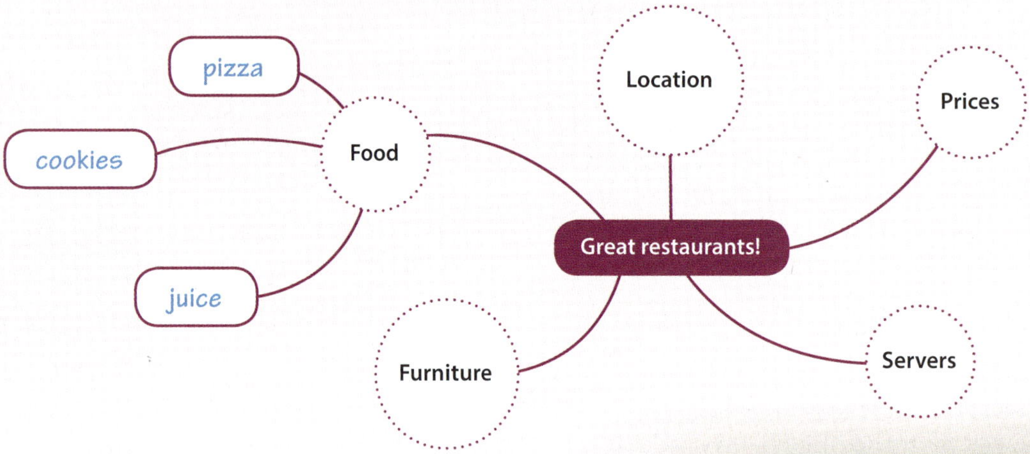


FIND IT

**C** **DECIDE** Work with a partner. Imagine you're opening a new restaurant. Choose a name for your restaurant and talk about the food and drink it has. Then create a great menu. You can go online to find ideas.

**D** **ROLE PLAY** Work with another pair. Welcome them to your restaurant. They choose a meal from your menu. Then change roles. Continue with other pairs.

**E** **PRESENT** Tell the class about some of the menus in exercise D. Were they good? What did you choose? What's your favorite menu?

*To check your progress, go to page 155.*

## USEFUL PHRASES

**DECIDE**

OK. First, what's the name of our restaurant?

What kind of food do we have?

Let's plan a great menu. We can have …

**ROLE PLAY**

Welcome to our restaurant!

What would you like to eat/drink?

Do you have … ?

So, you would like …

**PRESENT**

We went to a great restaurant. Its name was …

We liked / didn't like …

Our favorite menu is … because …

# REVIEW 4 (UNITS 10–12)

## 1 VOCABULARY

**A** **Look at the groups of words (1–6). For each group, circle the word that does not belong. Then match the groups with the categories (a–d). Some groups match the same category.**

| | | | | | | | |
|---|---|---|---|---|---|---|---|
| 1 | cheese | fish | potato | chicken | coat | ___ | |
| 2 | white | winter | rainy season | summer | dry season | ___ | **a** colors |
| 3 | red | green | brown | fall | yellow | ___ | **b** clothes |
| 4 | shirt | dress | skirt | pants | rice | ___ | **c** food |
| 5 | purple | blue | shorts | gray | black | ___ | **d** seasons |
| 6 | banana | tomato | apple | pink | cake | ___ | |

**B** **Match each word you circled in 1–6 to a different category (a–d). Then add one extra word to the categories.**

## 2 GRAMMAR

**A** **Make questions and answers in the simple past. Use the words in parentheses ( ).**

1 **A** ________________ you ________________ a good weekend? (have)
**B** Yes, it ________________ great, thanks. (be)

2 **A** What ________________ you ________________? (eat)
**B** We ________________ some Japanese food. (try)

3 **A** Where ________________ you on Saturday? (be)
**B** I ________________ at home in the morning, but not in the afternoon. (be)

4 **A** What ________________ you ________________ on TV last night? (watch)
**B** A movie, but it ________________ very good. (not be)

5 **A** ________________ you ________________ to the supermarket? (go)
**B** Yes, but we ________________ a lot. (not buy)

6 **A** ________________ you busy yesterday? (be)
**B** Yes, I ________________ all day. (work)

**B** PAIR WORK **Talk to a partner. Ask and answer five questions about things you did this month. Use the questions above, or your own ideas.**

**C** **Complete the paragraph. Use simple past forms of the verbs in parentheses ( ).**

At the airport, I [1] ____________ (go) to a store, and I [2] ____________ (buy) a cup of coffee and a sandwich. I [3] ____________ (drink) the coffee, but I didn't have time to eat the sandwich. So I [4] ____________ (take) it on the plane, and I [5] ____________ (eat) it on the flight. I [6] ____________ (have) lunch over the Atlantic Ocean. It was cool!

**D** **Write about a meal you had this month. Say when and where you had it, and what you ate.**

## 3 SPEAKING

**A** PAIR WORK **Talk about a day out or trip you went on.**

**B** **Write three sentences about your day out or trip. Compare with a partner. Were your days the same or different?**

On Saturday, I went out with some friends. We took a walk.

Where did you go?

## 4 FUNCTIONAL LANGUAGE

A **Complete the conversation with the words in the box.**

| can't | don't | have | idea | Let | Let's | maybe | sorry | sure | think |
|---|---|---|---|---|---|---|---|---|---|

**Min-jun** Why [1] ________ we go out on Friday night?

**Jamie** Um … I'm [2] ________, but I [3] ________. I [4] ________ to help my father on Friday.

**Min-jun** What about Saturday night?

**Jamie** [5] ________ me think. Yes, sure. Saturday's fine.

**Min-jun** OK. [6] ________ meet at Calendar Café. Do you know it?

**Jamie** I'm not [7] ________. Is it on Fourth Avenue?

**Min-jun** Yes. Near the movie theater.

**Jamie** OK, great. What time?

**Min-jun** The café is busy on Saturday night, I [8] ________. Let's get there early. How about 6 o'clock?

**Jamie** Good [9] ________. Then [10] ________ we can go to a movie after dinner.

B **Read the conversation and circle the correct words.**

**Yuri** I [1] *really* / *so* like this lamb.

**Susan** Thanks. Would you [2] *want* / *like* some more?

**Yuri** [3] *Yes,* / *No,* please. [4] *Can* / *Would* I have some more green beans, too?

**Susan** [5] *A* / *Of* course. [6] *Here* / *Have* you are. Oh, please [7] *pass* / *give* the potatoes, Yuri.

**Yuri** All [8] *course* / *right*. Here.

## 5 SPEAKING

A PAIR WORK **Choose one of the situations below. Talk to a partner. Have a conversation.**

1 You and your friend want to go out this weekend. Make suggestions about what you can do and where / what time you can meet. Look at page 102 for useful language.

> Let's go out on Saturday night.

2 A friend asks you about a movie. He/She wants to know the names of the actors in the movie, their nationalities, and other movies they are in. You are not 100% sure. Look at page 112 for useful language.

> Who was in *The Matrix*?

> The first Matrix movie? I'm not sure. He's American, I think. Um …

3 A friend is at your home for dinner. Offer him/her things to eat and drink. Look at page 122 for useful language.

> Would you like some chicken?

B PAIR WORK **Change roles and have another conversation.**

# GRAMMAR REFERENCE AND PRACTICE

## 1.1 *I AM, YOU ARE* (page 3)

| ***I am** (= **I'm**), **you are** (= **you're**)* | | | | |
|---|---|---|---|---|
| | **Affirmative (+)** | **Negative (-)** | **Question** | **Short answers** |
| I | **I'm** from Lima. | **I'm not** from Mexico City. | **Am I** in room 6B? | Yes, **you are.** / No, **you're not.** |
| You | **You're** from Paris. | **You're not** from Bogotá. | **Are you** from Tokyo? | Yes, **I am.** / No, **I'm not.** |

A **Match 1–6 to a–f to make sentences.**

1 I'm
2 I'm from
3 No, I'm

a not.
b Mexican.
c Honduras.

4 Are you
5 Yes, I
6 Are you from

d am.
e Brazil?
f Chinese?

## 1.2 *WHAT'S … ?, IT'S …* (page 5)

| ***What's … ?** (= **What is**)* | ***It's …** (= **It is**)* |
|---|---|
| **What's** your first name? | **It's** Juana. |
| **What's** the name of your college? | **It's** Garcia College. |
| **What's** your email address? | **It's** juanagarcia@bestmail.com. |

> **!** **Don't repeat the subject of the question:**
> ~~*The name of my company is*~~
> *It's Dallas Sales.*

A **Put the words in order to make sentences.**

1 first / is / My / Ruby. / name ______
2 is / address / My / dfox@kmail.com. / email ______
3 Green College. / my college / of / The name / is ______
4 my company / Dallas Sales. / The name / is / of ______

## 2.1 *IS / ARE* IN STATEMENTS AND *YES/NO* QUESTIONS (page 13)

| ***is / are** in statements and **yes/no** questions* | | | |
|---|---|---|---|
| | **Affirmative** | **Question** | **Short answers** |
| He / She / It | **'s** ten. (*'s = is*) | **Is** he your husband?<br>**Is** she your friend? | Yes, he **is**. / No, he**'s not**.<br>Yes, she **is**. / No, she**'s not**. |
| You / We / They | **'re** cousins. (*'re = are*) | **Are** you brothers?<br>**Are** they your children? | Yes, we **are**. / No, we**'re not**.<br>Yes, they **are**. / No, they**'re not**. |

A **Write sentences and questions with *is* and *are*.**

1 she / 22 She's 22.
2 they / your cousins ______?
3 he / 18 ______?
4 my grandparents / Brazilian ______.
5 we / in Room 5B ______?
6 no, you / not ______.

## 2.2 *IS NOT / ARE NOT* (page 15)

| ***is not*** **(=** ***'s not*****)** ***/ are not*** **(=** ***'re not*****)** | |
|---|---|
| He / She / It | **'s not** in Rio de Janeiro. |
| You / We / They | **'re not** shy. |

| ***isn't (= is not) / aren't (= are not)*** | | |
|---|---|---|
| Jack | **isn't** | boring. |
| The students | **aren't** | in the class room. |

> **!** After singular nouns (= 1 thing), use ***isn't***.
> After plural nouns (= 2+ things), use ***aren't***.

A **Circle the correct words to complete the sentences.**

1 Jan *is / isn't* from New York City. He's from Miami.
2 *She's / She's not* 18. She's not 20.
3 Daniel is in Moscow. *He's / He's not* in St. Petersburg.
4 You're not shy. *You're / You're not* really friendly!
5 My cousins are in Japan. *They're / They're not* in the U.S.
6 *We're / We're not* sisters. We're friends.

## 3.1 POSSESSIVE ADJECTIVES; POSSESSIVE *'S* AND *S'* (page 23)

| **Possessive adjectives** | |
|---|---|
| I → **my** | *This is* ***my*** *apartment.* |
| he → **his** | ***His*** *name is Sergei.* |
| she → **her** | *It's* ***her*** *favorite picture.w* |
| it → **its** | *Nice cat! What's* ***its*** *name?* |
| you → **your** | *Is this* ***your*** *room?* |
| we → **our** | ***Our*** *home is in La Paz.* |
| they → **their** | *Rita is* ***their*** *daughter.* |

| **Possessive *'s* and *s'*** |
|---|
| Add possessive *'s* to a singular noun. (= 1 thing)<br>*This is Sergei**'s** room.*<br>*My mother**'s** name is Kate.* |
| Add possessive *'* after the *s* of a plural noun. (= 2+ things)<br>*This is his parents**'** house.*<br>*My cousins**'** house is in Rio.* |

> **!** **Do not add another *s*:**
> ~~His parents's home~~ →
> His parents' home

A **Circle the correct words to complete the sentences.**

1 *My / I* email address is sky121@bestmail.com.
2 My *friends / friend's* name is Ramona.
3 This is *his / he's* hotel room.
4 Excuse me. What's *you / your* name?
5 This is my *parents's / parents'* new car.
6 David is *our / we* son.
7 The name of *Ann's / Anns'* company is Mason Sales.
8 What's *they're / their* telephone number?

## 3.2 *IT IS* (page 25)

> **!** *It* is a pronoun. *It* is always singular. Use *it* for things. For example, *the house* = *it*.
> Use *isn't* after nouns. Use *'s not* after pronouns.

**It is in statements and yes/no questions**

| | Affirmative | Negative | Question | Short answers |
|---|---|---|---|---|
| The house | **is** small. | **isn't** small. (*isn't* = *is not*) | **Is it** small? | Yes, **it is.** |
| **It's** (= *it is*) | small. | **not** small. | | No, **it's not.** |

A **Answer the questions so they're true for you. Write statements. Use *It's* and *It's not* to give more information.**

1 Is your home an apartment? My home isn't an apartment. It's a house.
2 Is your bedroom cool? ______
3 Is your kitchen big? ______
4 Is your parents' house old? ______
5 Is your friend's TV new? ______
6 Is your refrigerator tall? ______

## 3.4 INFORMATION QUESTIONS WITH *BE* (page 28)

| Question word | | *be* | |
|---|---|---|---|
| **What** | | **is** | your name? |
| **Where** | | **is** | the house? |
| **How old** | | **are** | they? |
| **Who** | | **are** | they? |
| **How many** | people | **are** | in the house? |
| **How many** | rooms | **are** | in it? |

> **!** Information questions ask for information about, for example, people, places, age, time, and quantity. Don't answer information questions with *yes/no* answers.
> Use *is* to talk about 1 thing. Use *are* to talk about 2+ things. Use a noun after *How many … ?*

A **Put the words in the correct order to make questions.**

1 is / Who / brother? / your Who is your brother?
2 you? / How / are / old ______
3 her / is / college? / Where ______
4 email / is / What / address? / your ______
5 many / are / people / How / the house? / in ______
6 apartment? / is / his / Where ______

## 4.1 SIMPLE PRESENT STATEMENTS WITH *I, YOU, WE* (page 35)

**Simple present statements with *I, you, we***

| | Affirmative | Negative |
|---|---|---|
| I / You / We | **have** a smartwatch. | **don't have** a smartwatch. |
| | **like** my phone. | **don't like** my phone. |
| | **love** games. | **don't love** games. |
| | **want** a tablet. | **don't want** a tablet. |

A **Put the words in order to make sentences.**

1 games. / like / I ______
2 your / I / smartwatch. / love ______
3 don't / I / a / laptop. / have ______
4 a / tablet. / want / We ______
5 like / don't / laptops. / You ______
6 camera. / want / I / don't / a ______

## 4.2 SIMPLE PRESENT *YES/NO* QUESTIONS WITH *I*, *YOU*, *WE* (page 37)

| Simple present *yes/no* questions with *I, you, we* | |
|---|---|
| *yes/no* **questions** | **Short answers** |
| **Do** I **send** nice emails? | Yes, you **do.** / No, you **don't.** |
| **Do** we **post** good photos? | Yes, you **do.** / No, you **don't.** |
| **Do** you **use** social media? | Yes, I **do.** / No, I **don't.** |
| **Do** you **and your friends play** games? | Yes, we **do.** / No, we **don't.** |

A **Write questions. Then answer the questions so they're true for you.**

1 you / call your family / on the weekends Do you call your family on the weekends? Yes, I do.
2 you / post comments / on Twitter ______? ______.
3 you / send text messages / to your parents ______? ______.
4 you and your friends / watch movies / on TV ______? ______.

## 4.4 *A/AN*; ADJECTIVES BEFORE NOUNS (page 40)

| *a/an* | **adjectives before nouns** |
|---|---|
| Use *a/an* with singular nouns. It means "one."<br>*Do you have **a** laptop?* (= 1 laptop)<br>*This is **an** app for photos.* (= 1 app)<br>Use ***a*** before consonant sounds (for example, *b, c, d, f, …*): ***a** tablet, **a** cookie*<br>Use ***an*** before vowel sounds (*a, e, i, o, u*): ***an** app, **an** apartment* | **Adjectives go before a noun:**<br>*You have a **nice** home.* ✓<br>*You have **a** ~~**home nice**~~.* ✗<br>*It's an **expensive** laptop. This is a **new** apartment.*<br>*I post **interesting** photos.*<br>The ending of an adjective is the same for singular and plural nouns. Do not add *s* to an adjective.<br>*I like **small** TVs.* ✓<br>*I like ~~**smalls**~~ TVs.* ✗ |
| **Don't use *a/an* with:** | |
| 1 plural nouns: *I like **photos**.*<br>2 *this* + noun: ***This tablet** is nice.* | 3 numbers + noun: *I have **one son** and **two daughters**.*<br>4 possessive adjectives + noun: ***My phone** is really old.* |

A **Circle the correct words to complete the sentences.**

1 Do you have *a camera / an camera?*
2 We don't want *a new TV / new a TV.*
3 *Your an apartment / Your apartment* is very nice.
4 I want coffee and *a cookie / a one cookie.*
5 *A game / This game* is really boring.
6 We have *a children / three children.*
7 I don't like *computers / computer.*
8 Do you live in *a apartment / an apartment?*

## 5.1 SIMPLE PRESENT STATEMENTS WITH *HE, SHE, THEY* (page 45)

**Simple present statements with *he, she, they***

| | Affirmative | Negative |
|---|---|---|
| He / She | **plays** basketball.<br>**goes out** every evening.<br>**watches** TV a lot.<br>**studies** on the weekend.<br>**has** a big house. | **doesn't play** basketball.<br>**doesn't go out** every evening.<br>**doesn't watch** TV a lot.<br>**doesn't study** on weekends.<br>**doesn't have** a big house. |
| They | **play** soccer.<br>**have** a big house. | **don't play** soccer.<br>**don't have** a big house. |

**!** Use *in* to talk about times of day: *I run in the morning.*
Use *on* to talk about days: *I play soccer on Saturdays.*

**!** Use adverbs of frequency say *how often* you do things.

100% **always** **usually** **often** **sometimes** **hardly ever** **never** 0%

Put adverbs of frequency before the verb: *She **sometimes** works on Saturday.*

With pronouns + *be*, adverbs of frequency go after the verb: *I'm **usually** at home in the evening.*

A **Circle the correct words to complete the sentences.**

1 My sister often *watch / watches* basketball on TV.
2 I don't like coffee, so I *usually / never* drink it.
3 My laptop is old and slow. I *always / hardly ever* use it.
4 My grandma *don't / doesn't* have a cell phone. She *always / hardly ever* calls me from home.
5 My friends are usually at work on Saturday and Sunday. They *have / don't have* free time on the weekend.

## 5.2 QUESTIONS IN THE SIMPLE PRESENT (page 47)

**Simple present: *yes/no* questions**

| *Yes/no* questions | | | Short answers |
|---|---|---|---|
| **Do** | I/we | **work** on the weekend? | Yes, I **do** / No, we **don't**. |
| **Do** | you | **eat** breakfast? | Yes, I **do**. / No, I **don't**. |
| **Does** | she/he | **study** in the evening? | Yes, she **does**. / No, he **doesn't**. |
| **Does** | it | **have** two bedrooms? | Yes, it **does**. / No, it **doesn't**. |
| **Do** | they | **go** to class on Monday? | Yes, they **do**. / No, they **don't**. |

**Simple present: information questions**

| | | | | |
|---|---|---|---|---|
| I / You / We / They | **Where**<br>**What time**<br>**What** | **do**<br>**do**<br>**do** | I / we<br>you<br>they | **go** every day?<br>**get up**?<br>**do** on Saturday? |
| He / She / It | **Where**<br>**When**<br>**What time** | **does**<br>**does**<br>**does** | he<br>she<br>it | **live**?<br>**meet** her friends?<br>**open**? |

**!** ***What time … ?* and *When … ?***

**A** *What time is it?*
**B** *It's 1.30.*
**A** *When does he study?*
**B** *He studies in the evening.*

A **Put the words in the correct order to make questions.**

1 lunch? / eat / does / he / Where ______
2 to / she / go / Does / this school? ______
3 their / do / meet / friends? / When / they ______
4 do / work? / you / What / go / to / time ______
5 soccer / your friends / after work? / play / Do ______

## 6.1 *THERE'S, THERE ARE; A LOT OF, SOME, NO* (page 55)

| ***There's** (= there is), **there are; a lot, some, no*** | | | |
|---|---|---|---|
| **Singular (= 1 thing)** | | **Plural (= 2+ things)** | |
| | | **There are no** stores on our street. | = zero |
| **There's a** restaurant near the hotel. | = one | **There are three** bedrooms in the house. | = an exact number |
| **There's no** shower in the bathroom. | = zero | **There are some** chairs in the kitchen. | = a small number |
| | | **There are a lot of** apps on my phone. | = a big number |

A **Look at the words in parentheses ( ). Then complete the sentences with the words in the box.**

| There's a | There's no | There are no | There are a lot of | There are some |
|---|---|---|---|---|

1 ______________________ parks in the city. (zero)
2 ______________________ people in the café. (a big number)
3 ______________________ great stores on Pacific Street. (a small number)
4 ______________________ park next to the hospital. (one)
5 ______________________ restaurant in this museum. (zero)

## 6.2 COUNT AND NON-COUNT NOUNS (page 57)

| **Count nouns (nouns with a singular and plural form)** | |
|---|---|
| **Singular** | **Plural** |
| Use *There is* with *a* or *an*. | Use *There are* with *no*, *some*, *a lot of*, or a number. |
| There's **a plant.** | There are **no plants.** There are **some plants.** |
| | There are **a lot of plants.** There are **two plants.** |
| **Non-count nouns (nouns with no singular or plural form)** | |
| Use *There is* with *no*, *some*, or *a lot of*. Do not use *a*, *an*, or a number. | |
| There's **no grass.** There's **some grass.** There's **a lot of grass.** ~~There's three grass.~~ | |

A **Write sentences with *There's* or *There are*. Make some nouns plural.**

1 no / milk / in the refrigerator *There's no milk in the refrigerator.*
2 a lot of / plant / in my house ______________________
3 a / restaurant / in the museum ______________________
4 some / sugar / on the table ______________________
5 some / small hotel / near here ______________________

## 7.1 PRESENT CONTINUOUS STATEMENTS (page 67)

| **Present continuous statements** | | |
|---|---|---|
| | **Affirmative** | **Negative** |
| I | **'m cooking** breakfast right now. | **'m not cooking** breakfast right now. |
| He / She / It | **'s helping** the children.<br>**'s taking** a shower.<br>**'s drinking** milk. | **'s not helping** the children.<br>**'s not taking** a shower.<br>**'s not drinking** milk. (the cat) |
| You / We / They | **'re eating** breakfast.<br>**'re cleaning** the kitchen.<br>**'re learning** a lot at school. | **'re not eating** breakfast.<br>**'re not cleaning** the kitchen.<br>**'re not learning** a lot at school. |

A Put the words in the correct order to make sentences.

1 My / aren't / TV. / parents / watching ______
2 coffee. / cup / drinking / a / I'm / of ______
3 a / She's / now. / bath / taking / right ______
4 TV / in / room. / Jack / his / watching / is ______
5 eating / the moment. / They're / breakfast / at ______
6 isn't / homework. / her / Maria / doing ______
7 our / helping / We're / now. / grandparents ______

## 7.2 PRESENT CONTINUOUS QUESTIONS (page 69)

| Present continuous: *yes/no* questions and short answers | | |
|---|---|---|
| I | **Am** I **talking** to John? | Yes, you **are**. / No, you**'re not**. |
| He / She / It | **Is** she **cleaning** the house? | Yes, she **is**. / No, she**'s not**. |
| | **Is** he **riding** his bike right now? | Yes, he **is**. / No, he**'s not**. |
| | **Is** it **working** at the moment? | Yes, it **is**. / No, it**'s not**. |
| You / They | **Are** you and your sister **sending** text messages? | Yes, we **are**. / No, we**'re not**. |
| | **Are** they **waiting** at the bus stop? | Yes, they **are**. / No, they**'re not**. |

| Present continuous: information questions | | | | |
|---|---|---|---|---|
| I | **Who** | **am** | I | **talking** to? |
| He / She / It | **Why** | **is** | he / she | **carrying** a bag? |
| | **Where** | **is** | he / she | **working** today? |
| | **How** | **is** | it | **going**? |
| You / We / They | **What** | **are** | we / you / they | **doing** right now? |
| | **Who** | **are** | | **waiting** for? |

> **!** You can answer *Why* questions with *because*.
> ***Why** is he carrying a bag?*
> *He's carrying a bag **because** he has a lot of books.* (= a complete sentence)
> ***Because** he has a lot of books.* (= an incomplete sentence in informal speech)

A Write questions for the answers. Use the words in parentheses ( ).

1 **A** ______ (you / send / a text to Carol)
**B** No, I'm not. I'm calling her.

2 **A** ______ (why / we / wait / for Paul)
**B** Because he's driving us home.

3 **A** ______ (Denny and Pam / do / the dishes)
**B** Yes, they are.

4 **A** ______ (Sandra / wash / the dog)
**B** No, she isn't. She's watching TV.

5 **A** ______ (who / your sister / help / right now)
**B** My brother.

## 8.1 *CAN* AND *CAN'T* FOR ABILITY; *WELL* (page 77)

| *can* and *can't* for ability; *well* | | | | |
|---|---|---|---|---|
| | **Affirmative** | **Negative** | **Questions** | **Short answers** |
| I | **can** paint. | **can't** paint well. | **Can** I dance? | Yes, I **can**<br>No, I **can't.** |
| He / She / It | **can** paint. | **can't** paint. | **Can** she dance well? | Yes, she **can.**<br>No, she **can't.** |
| You / We / They | **can** paint well. | **can't** paint. | **Can** they dance? | Yes, they **can.**<br>No, they **can't**. |

A **Put the words in order to make sentences.**

1 can / well. / swim / Cathy ______
2 a / you / car? / drive / Can ______
3 play / I / guitar. / can't / the ______
4 and paint? / you / Can / draw ______
5 well. / can't / I / very / skateboard ______
6 fix / My / table. / brother / your / can ______
7 surf / can't / or snowboard. / I ______
8 well. / son / can / Their / sing ______

## 8.2 *CAN* AND *CAN'T* FOR POSSIBILITY (page 79)

| *can* and *can't* for possibility | | |
|---|---|---|
| Information questions with *can* | | |
| I | **What can** I eat? | **How can** I pay for the food? |
| He / She /It | **Where can** he eat? | **How can** he get to the restaurant? |
| You / We / They | **When can** we eat? | **Who can** we have lunch with today? |

A **Read the answers. Then write questions.**

1 A Where can we work?
B We can work in the meeting room.

2 A ______?
B We can watch a movie.

3 A ______?
B We can get to the mall by bus.

4 A ______?
B We can have a meeting on Friday.

5 A ______?
B We can call my cousin.

6 A ______?
B We can play basketball.

7 A ______?
B We can meet at the hotel.

8 A ______?
B We can take a picture with my phone.

## 9.1 *THIS* AND *THESE* (page 87)

| *This* and *these* | |
|---|---|
| **This** is my ticket. | **These** are new boats. |
| **This** hotel is cheap. | **These** birds are funny. |
| Ryan loves **this** farm. | I don't like **these** pictures. |

A **Put the words in order to make sentences.**

1 a / is / tour / This / boring. ____________

2 these / I / birds. / like ____________

3 sisters. / are / These / my ____________

4 video. / watching / I'm / this ____________

5 really / animals are / funny. / These ____________

6 isn't / expensive. / This / vacation ____________

## 9.2 *LIKE TO, WANT TO, NEED TO, HAVE TO* (page 89)

| ***like to, want to*** | | ***need to, have to*** | |
|---|---|---|---|
| I | **like to play** soccer.<br>**want to play** soccer. | I | **need to work** on Saturday.<br>**have to work** on Saturday. |
| He / She / It | **likes to play** soccer.<br>**wants to play** soccer. | He / She / It | **needs to work** on Saturday<br>**has to work** on Saturday. |
| You / We / They | **want to play** soccer.<br>**like to play** soccer. | You / We / They | **need to work** on Saturday.<br>**have to work** on Saturday. |

A **Complete the sentences with *like to, want to,* or *have to/need to* and the verbs in parentheses ( ).**

> **!** You can use ***need to*** + a verb OR ***have to*** + a verb to talk about things that are necessary.

1 I ____________ (swim) in the ocean, but only in July and August.

2 One day, I ____________ (go) to Japan on vacation.

3 My son can't do his homework. I ____________ (help) him.

4 I'm late for work, so I ____________ (leave) now.

5 This is a great song. I ____________ (buy) it.

6 In Japan, you ____________ (drive) on the left side of the road.

7 At a movie theater, you ____________ (pay) before you watch the movie.

## 10.1 STATEMENTS WITH *BE GOING TO* (page 99)

| **Statements with *be going to*** | | |
|---|---|---|
| | **Affirmative** | **Negative** |
| I | **'m going to be** home tomorrow. | **'m not going to be** home tomorrow. |
| He / She / It | **'s going to take** a walk in the park.<br>**'s going to be** warm tomorrow. | **'s not going to go** shopping next week.<br>**isn't going to be** warm tomorrow. |
| You / We / They | **'re going to be** here next weekend. | **'re not going to be** here next weekend. |
| **Future time expressions** | | |
| this evening, tonight, tomorrow | on/next/this Monday | |
| this week/weekend/month/year | next week/weekend/month/year | |

A **Write sentences with the correct form of *be going to*.**

1 We / not play / soccer this weekend
We're not going to play soccer this weekend.

2 Vicky / meet / her friends tomorrow
______.

3 You / have / a party for your birthday
______.

4 They / not go / surf / next Saturday
______.

5 I / go / dancing this evening
______.

6 He / not do / the dishes after dinner
______.

## 10.2 QUESTIONS WITH *BE GOING TO* (page 101)

***be going to: yes/no* questions**

| | ***yes/no* questions** | **Short answers** |
|---|---|---|
| I | **Am** I **going to meet** him at 4:00? | Yes, you **are**.<br>No, you'**re not**. |
| He / She / It | **Is** she **going to see** a friend? | Yes, she **is**.<br>No, she'**s not**. |
| You / We / They | **Are** you **going to take** a hat? | Yes, I **am**. / Yes, we **are**.<br>No, I'**m not**. / No, we'**re not**. |

***be going to*: information questions**

| |
|---|
| **When are** you **going to leave**? |
| **Where is** Sofia **going to go**? |
| **What are** we **going to do** today? |
| **What time is** he **going to have** lunch? |
| **Who are** they **going to meet**? |
| **How are** you **going to get** to the airport? |

A **Circle the correct words to complete the sentences.**

1 Are you going *buying* / *to buy* some new jeans?
2 Who is he going to *go* / *going* shopping with?
3 Is she going to *cook* / *cooks* dinner for four people tonight?
4 *What* / *What time* are we going to drive to the airport?
5 Are *your parents* / *Mariana* going to send him an email?
6 What *they are* / *are they* going to wear to the party?

## 11.1 STATEMENTS WITH *WAS* AND *WERE* (page 109)

**Statements with *was* and *were***

| | **Affirmative** | **Negative** |
|---|---|---|
| I / He / She / It | **was** in the house. | **wasn't** noisy. |
| You / We / They | **were** at work. | **weren't** there. |

A **Complete the posts with the affirmative or negative form of *was* or *were*.**

**Carlene Rauss** I remember a great vacation. It [1] ______ January 2010, and we [2] ______ in Argentina. It [3] ______ summer, so the weather [4] ______ great! Buenos Aires is an exciting city, so we [5] ______ really happy there. #flashbackfriday #2010 #vacation

**Paulo Soto** I remember my twentieth birthday. My friends and I [6] ______ at the beach, but the weather [7] ______ awful! It [8] ______ really rainy. The café on the beach [9] ______ open, so there was no food. It's not a good memory because we [10] ______ very happy. I mean, it [11] ______ a happy birthday. 🙁

9 4

## 11.2 QUESTIONS WITH *WAS* AND *WERE* (page 111)

| Questions with *was* and *were* | | |
|---|---|---|
| | *yes/no* questions | Short answers |
| I / He / She | **Was** she at home on Saturday? | Yes, she **was.** / No, she **wasn't.** |
| You / We / They | **Were** you at home on Saturday? | Yes, I **was.** / No, I **wasn't.** |
| **Information questions with *was* and *were*** | | |
| I / He / She | **Where was** he? | |
| You / We / They | **How old were** you in this photo? | |

A **Write questions in the simple past to match the answers.**

1 ______________________________ ? The walls in my bedroom were blue.
2 ______________________________ ? My last vacation was in Brazil.
3 ______________________________ ? My brother's birthday party was on Friday.
4 ______________________________ ? Yes, my parents were at the party.
5 ______________________________ ? No, my house was small.
6 ______________________________ ? I was at work on Saturday because I was really busy.

## 12.1 SIMPLE PAST STATEMENTS (page 119)

| Simple past statements |
|---|
| Use the simple past to talk about events that are in the past and finished. |
| I **ate** a big lunch yesterday. We **played** soccer last weekend. We **went** to La Paz last year. |
| Simple past verbs can be regular or irregular. Simple past regular verbs end in *-ed*. |

| Some regular verbs | | | | |
|---|---|---|---|---|
| | *-ed* | *-d* | double consonant + *ed* | change *-y* to *-ied* |
| I / You / He / She / We / They | work**ed**<br>play**ed**<br>watch**ed**<br>want**ed**<br>walk**ed** | like**d**<br>love**d**<br>arrive**d**<br>use**d**<br>dance**d** | stop → sto**pped**<br>chat → cha**tted** | try → tr**ied**<br>carry → carr**ied**<br>study → stud**ied** |

| Some irregular verbs | | | | | |
|---|---|---|---|---|---|
| Base form | Simple past | Base form | Simple past | Base form | Simple past |
| have | had | write | wrote | ride | rode |
| go | went | send | sent | fly | flew |
| eat | ate | buy | bought | get up | got up |
| drink | drank | think | thought | leave | left |
| do | did | run | ran | meet | met |
| take | took | swim | swam | sing | sang |
| read | read | drive | drove | | |

A **Complete the chart with the words in the box.**

| ~~arrive~~ | buy | drink | eat | go | have |
|---|---|---|---|---|---|
| like | need | stay | stop | take | try |

| Base form | Rule | Simple past |
|---|---|---|
| *arrive* | Add *-d.* | *arrived* |
| | Add *-ed.* | |
| | Double *p* and add *-ed.* | |
| | Change *-y* to *-ied.* | |

| Base form | Irregular simple past form |
|---|---|
| | |
| | |
| | |
| | |
| | |

## 12.2 SIMPLE PAST QUESTIONS; *ANY* (page 121)

**Simple past questions**

| *yes/no* questions | Short answers | |
|---|---|---|
| **Did** you **have** apple juice? | Yes, I/we **did**. | No, I/we **didn't**. |
| **Did** we **arrive** on time? | Yes, we/you **did**. | No, we/you **didn't** |
| **Did** she/he **like** the fish? | Yes, she/he **did**. | No, she/he **didn't**. |
| **Did** they **go out** for dinner? | Yes, they **did**. | No, they **didn't**. |

**Information questions**

| | | |
|---|---|---|
| **How did** | I / you | **hear** about the restaurant? |
| **What did** | you / he / she | **have** for dinner last night? |
| **Who did** | we / they | **see** at the party? |

***any***

You can use *any* in *yes/no* questions and negative statements. *Any* = one, some, or all of something. *Not* + *any* = none.

Use *some* in affirmative statements. You can use *any* and *some* with count and non-count nouns.

**Simple past questions and statements with *any***

| *yes/no* questions | Negative statements |
|---|---|
| Did you have **any** vegetables? | I didn't have **any** juice. |
| Did Mary buy **any** milk? | Joel didn't eat **any** eggs. |
| Did they have **any** dessert? | We didn't drink **any** soda. |

A **Put the words in the correct order to make sentences.**

1 for dinner? / chicken / Did / make / you

2 they / did / for lunch? / have / What

3 eat / Did / any / vegetables? / Tonya

4 last night? / Where / she / go / did

5 coffee / buy / We / at the store. / didn't / any

6 at Pete's Pizza / last year? / you / Did / work

# VOCABULARY PRACTICE

## 1.1 COUNTRIES AND NATIONALITIES (page 2)

A **Write the country or the nationality.**

1 Are you Russian ? (Russia)
2 I'm from ______ . (Mexican)
3 I'm ______ . (Ecuador)
4 You're from ______ . (Chilean)
5 Are you ______ ? (Japan)
6 Are you from ______ ? (Brazilian)
7 I'm not ______ . (South Korea)
8 I'm from Madrid. I'm ______ . (Spain)

B **Underline two correct answers for each sentence.**

1 Are you from *Russia / Chilean / South Korea*?
2 I'm from *American / Mexico / Japan*.
3 You're not *French / Peru / Colombian*.
4 Are you from *New York / Chicago / American*?
5 I'm not *Mexico / Brazilian / Chinese*.
6 You are *Peruvian / French / Chile*.
7 Are you *Peruvian / Japan / South Korean*?
8 I'm from *Ecuadorian / Lima / Germany*.

## 1.2 THE ALPHABET; PERSONAL INFORMATION (page 5)

A **Add five missing letters to the alphabet, in order.**

1 A B C D E F G H I J L M O P Q R T U V W X Z
2 a c d e g h j k l m n o q r s t v w x y z

B **Complete the sentences with the words in the box.**

| College | company | email address | first name | last name |
|---|---|---|---|---|

1 The name of my ______ is Home Sales, Inc.
2 **A** What's your ______ ? **B** It's jenatkins@abc.net.
3 **A** Hey, Ana. What's your ______ ? **B** It's Gomez. Ana Gomez.
4 I'm a student at Hunter ______ in New York City.
5 **A** Hi, Susie Ball. How do you spell your ______ ? **B** S-U-S-I-E.

## 2.1 FAMILY; NUMBERS (page 13)

A **Write the words in the chart.**

| ~~aunt~~ | child | daughter | grandfather | husband | parent | son | wife |
|---|---|---|---|---|---|---|---|
| brother | cousin | father | grandmother | mother | sister | uncle | |

| Men and women | Women | Men |
|---|---|---|
| | aunt | |
| | | |
| | | |
| | | |
| | | |
| | | |

B **Write the numbers.**

1 twenty-two 22
2 fifty-one ______
3 thirty-nine ______
4 eighty-three ______
5 forty-six ______
6 sixty-seven ______
7 thirty-eight ______
8 seventy-four ______
9 ninety-five ______
10 twenty-six ______

## 2.2 DESCRIBING PEOPLE; *REALLY / VERY* (page 14)

A **Complete the sentences with the words in the box. You won't use all the words.**

| friendly | interesting | old | really | short |
|---|---|---|---|---|
| shy | smart | boring | tall | young |

1 Carrie is two. She's really ______.
2 He's a college student. He's ______.
3 My father is 190 cm. He's very ______.
4 He's not interesting. He's ______.
5 My friend Georgio is ______ funny!
6 Ariana is 95. She's very ______.

B **Unscramble the letters in parentheses ( ). Write the adjectives.**

1 Susana is interesting and really ______. (nteisreignt) / (tlal)
2 My son is ______ and ______. (mtras) / (ynufn)
3 My grandfather is ______ and ______. (dlo) / (rosth)
4 The child is very ______ and ______. (ynugo) / (ysh)
5 They're ______ and not ______. (fienrdyl) / (bgrion)

## 3.1 ROOMS IN A HOME (page 22)

A **Read the sentences and complete the words.**

1 This is our **d** ______ **a** ______, with a **p** ______ on the **w** ______.
2 This is my sister's **b** ______. It's next to the **b** ______.
3 This is our dog, Jack. He's on the **f** ______.
4 This is the **d** ______ of our house.
5 This is the **l** ______ **r** ______, with one big **w** ______.
6 And this is the **k** ______. It's my favorite room.

B **Circle the correct word to complete the sentences.**

1 My sister is in her *bedroom / floor.*
2 This is the bathroom, with one *wall / window.*
3 This is the *dining area / door* to the kitchen.
4 My family is in the *living room / bathroom* now.
5 The *picture / kitchen* on the wall is interesting.
6 Our cats are on the *door / floor.*

## 3.2 FURNITURE (page 24)

**A Match the words to the things in the picture.**

chair ~~couch~~ refrigerator rug sink table television

1 couch 2 ______ 3 ______ 4 ______

5 ______ 6 ______ 7 ______

**B Circle the correct words to complete the sentences. Check (✓) the sentences that are true for you.**

1 A big *bed / shower* is in the bedroom. ☐
2 My *rug / bookcase* is really tall. ☐
3 A small *shower / couch* is in the bathroom. ☐
4 My *TV / desk* is really old. It's from the year 1800. ☐
5 I have a small *lamp / chair* on a table in my bedroom. ☐

## 4.1 TECHNOLOGY (page 34)

**A Complete the sentences with the words in the box. You won't use all the words.**

app camera cell phone earphones games laptop smartwatch tablet

1 Is that a really big phone, or is it a ______ ?
2 I have a computer. It's a ______ .
3 Yes, I have a ______ . The number is (593) 555-2194.
4 I don't have a ______ , but I have the time on my cell phone.
5 This picture is great! The ______ on your cell phone is really good.
6 My emails are on my phone. I have an email ______ .
7 My computer isn't for work. It's for fun. I have my ______ on it.

**B Circle the correct words to complete the sentences.**

1 On my phone, I have a good *laptop / camera*.
2 I have a social media *app / smartwatch* on my tablet.
3 On my laptop, I have a *game / cell phone*.

## 4.2 USING TECHNOLOGY (page 36)

A **Cross out the word that doesn't belong with each verb.**

| | | | |
|---|---|---|---|
| 1 **call** | friends | social media | family |
| 2 **watch** | movies | videos | text messages |
| 3 **use** | music | technology | apps |
| 4 **post** | cell phone | comments | photos |
| 5 **send** | text messages | email | with friends |

B **Complete the sentences with the words in the box.**

chat listen play read watch

1 I ______________________ to music with earphones on my tablet.
2 We don't ______________________ movies on TV.
3 My brother and I ______________________ games on our tablets.
4 I don't ______________________ work emails at home.
5 Do you ______________________ with friends on the internet?

## 5.1 DAYS AND TIMES OF DAY; EVERYDAY ACTIVITIES (page 44)

A **Read the days and times of day (a–j). Then put them in the correct order (1–10).**

| | | | | | |
|---|---|---|---|---|---|
| **a** | on Thursday, in the morning | ___ | **f** | on Saturday, in the evening | ___ |
| **b** | on Tuesday, in the afternoon | ___ | **g** | on Wednesday, in the morning | ___ |
| **c** | on Thursday, in the evening | ___ | **h** | on Friday, in the afternoon | ___ |
| **d** | on Monday, at night | 1 | **i** | on Tuesday, in the evening | ___ |
| **e** | on Sunday, in the morning | ___ | **j** | on Saturday, in the afternoon | ___ |

B **Use phrases from exercise A to complete the sentences so they're true for you. Write an X if you never do the activity.**

1 I go out with friends ______________________.
2 I watch TV ______________________.
3 I study ______________________.
4 I run ______________________.
5 I play soccer ______________________.
6 I read ______________________.
7 I work ______________________.
8 I'm in bed ______________________.

## 5.2 TELLING THE TIME (page 46)

A **Look at the times (1–8). Then circle the correct sentence.**

| | | | |
|---|---|---|---|
| 1 3:40 | a It's twenty to four. | b It's forty to three. |
| 2 12:30 | a It's twenty thirty. | b It's twelve thirty. |
| 3 6:15 | a It's a quarter after six. | b It's a quarter to six. |
| 4 12:00 a.m. | a It's midnight. | b It's noon. |
| 5 1:45 | a It's a quarter to one. | b It's one forty-five. |
| 6 8:07 | a It's seven to eight. | b It's eight-oh-seven. |
| 7 9:15 | a It's nine fifteen. | b It's nine fifty. |
| 8 4:52 | a It's five forty-two. | b It's four fifty-two. |

B **Underline the correct words to complete the paragraph.**

Carmen *gets up / goes to* bed at 7:15 a.m. She eats *lunch / breakfast* at 7:45. Then she *goes to work / gets up*. She usually has *dinner / lunch* at 12:30 p.m. She drinks *coffee / class* in the afternoon. On Tuesday, she goes to *class / lunch* after work – she studies English. She usually eats *dinner / coffee* at 7:00. She goes to *bed / class* at 11 p.m.

## 6.1 PLACES IN CITIES (page 54)

A **Complete the sentences with the words in the box.**

| café | college | hotel | museum | park | school | mall | zoo |
|---|---|---|---|---|---|---|---|

1 We often eat breakfast in a __________ .
2 I sometimes run in the __________ .
3 The __________ has hundreds of old pictures and a lot of art.
4 The __________ in my neighborhood has 160 children.
5 The students at the __________ are 18 to 22 years old.
6 This is a great __________ . It has a lot of my favorite stores.
7 The rooms in the __________ have bathrooms with showers.
8 The __________ in my city has 20 elephants.

B **Cross out one word that does not complete each sentence.**

| | | | |
|---|---|---|---|
| 1 We have lunch in a __________ on Saturdays. | *restaurant* | *store* | *park* |
| 2 We learn about things at a __________ . | *school* | *restaurant* | *museum* |
| 3 We shop at the __________ every weekend. | *mall* | *hospital* | *supermarket* |
| 4 The __________ has a big TV. | *park* | *hotel* | *restaurant* |
| 5 She studies English in __________ . | *school* | *college* | *a movie theater* |

## 6.2 NATURE (page 56)

A **Complete the email with the words in the box.**

| flowers | lake | mountain | snow | trees |
|---|---|---|---|---|

Reply Forward

Hi Julia,

How are you? I'm great! My new town is *really* cool. I like nature, and there's a lot of nature here! There's a big, tall [1] ________ near my house. There's a forest on the mountain, with a lot of [2] ________. There's [3] ________ on top of the mountain in January and February. There's a small [4] ________ in my neighborhood, and I run next to the water in the morning. There are no [5] ________ now because it's January.

I love this town. Please visit soon!

Your friend,

Marisa

B **Circle the correct word to complete the sentences.**

1 My house is on the *beach / forest* next to the ocean.

2 There is a lot of *ocean / grass* in the park.

3 There are a lot of plants and flowers in the *forest / lake*.

4 There's a lot of water in the *river / desert*.

5 My grandma and grandpa live near the *ocean / flowers*.

6 A lot of animals eat *plants / mountains*.

7 Donna lives on a small *island / desert* in the Atlantic Ocean.

8 There are a lot of small *grass / hills* here, but there are no mountains.

## 7.1 ACTIVITIES AROUND THE HOUSE (page 66)

A **Match 1–6 with a–f to complete the sentences.**

1 Do they cook ___
2 Karen usually washes ___
3 I do a lot of ___
4 They're nice. They help ___
5 He takes ___
6 Do you clean ___

a her daughter's hair.
b your room on the weekend?
c breakfast every morning?
d me with my English.
e homework every day.
f a shower in the evening.

B **Add the words in parentheses ( ) to the correct place in each sentence. Then write the sentences.**

1 Do you the dishes after lunch? (do) *Do you do the dishes after lunch?*
2 Rudy his car on the weekend. (drives) ________
3 Does he his teeth every day? (brush) ________
4 My mother usually cooks at 6:30. (dinner) ________
5 She takes a every evening. (bath) ________
6 I often my grandmother. (help) ________

## 7.2 TRANSPORTATION (page 68)

**A Complete the sentences with the correct verbs in the box.**

| driving | going | riding | taking | waiting | walking |
|---|---|---|---|---|---|

1 I'm not ________________ to work because my son has my car today.
2 Where are you? Mike is ________________ for you at the train station.
3 Carolina is ________________ with her dog in the park right now.
4 We're ________________ to the mall because we need new shoes.
5 Tonya is ________________ her bike to the store.
6 Mark isn't ________________ the bus to class because it's late.

**B Circle the correct words to complete the sentences.**

1 Vic is at *the bus stop / his bike.*
2 Why are you carrying *a plant / the train*?
3 I usually take *the train station / the subway* to work.
4 When are you going to your *parents' house / mall*?
5 I'm sorry. I'm busy. I'm on *the bus stop / the train.*

## 8.1 VERBS TO DESCRIBE SKILLS (page 76)

**A Complete the sentences with the verbs in the box. You won't use all the verbs.**

| dance | fix | play | skateboard | speak |
|---|---|---|---|---|
| draw | paint | sing | snowboard | swim |

1 I don't ________________. There's a mountain near me but it doesn't have snow on it.
2 My friends usually ________________ the guitar and ________________ songs after dinner.
3 In my art class, we ________________ and ________________ a lot of different things.
4 I ________________ two languages – English and Korean.
5 In February and March, I ________________ in the ocean.
6 Do you have a problem with your laptop? My brothers ________________ computers.

**B Complete the words with vowels (*a, e, i, o, u*).**

1 d *a* nc *e*
2 f __ x th __ ngs
3 sn __ wb __ __ rd
4 sw __ m
5 pl __ y the g __ __ t __ r
6 sp __ __ k tw __ l __ ng __ __ g __ s
7 r __ __ d m __ s __ c
8 dr __ w
9 sk __ t __ b __ __ rd
10 p __ __ nt
11 s __ ng
12 s __ rf

## 8.2 WORK (page 78)

**A Complete the sentences with the words in the box.**

| break | coworkers | have | think |
|---|---|---|---|
| company | hard | office | worker |

1 I work for a big American ________________.
2 I have a new desk and a chair in my ________________.
3 She's doing a great job. She's a very good ________________.
4 It's time to take a ________________ and have a cup of coffee.
5 I work in a team with six ________________.
6 We're always busy. We work ________________.
7 Can we talk about this? Can we ________________ a meeting?
8 I don't know the answer. Can I ________________ about it for five minutes?

**B Circle the word that doesn't belong in each group.**

1 living room office kitchen bedroom
2 have a meeting play games call a coworker work hard
3 drink coffee have lunch take a break have a meeting
4 company couch chair desk
5 worker brother teacher coworker

## 9.1 TRAVEL (page 86)

**A Circle the correct words to complete the sentences.**

1 I have a *ticket / tour* for the bus.
2 This *city / ranch* is in the country.
3 I'm on *vacation / country* with my family.
4 My seat on the *plane / ticket* is by the window.
5 My house is in a small *town / boat*, but I work in the city.
6 This *tour / ticket* is expensive, but it's really interesting.

**B Circle the word that doesn't belong in each group.**

1 vacation tour work
2 ranch farm ticket country
3 boat hotel plane bus
4 ticket tour plane friend
5 country town city

## 9.2 TRAVEL ARRANGEMENTS (page 88)

A **Match 1–6 with a–f to complete the sentences.**

1 You can buy tickets ___
2 We can check in for our ___
3 I don't usually travel on ___
4 We're arriving at our ___
5 I'm staying at a really nice ___
6 We're flying from the new ___

a destination.
b airport.
c online.
d trains.
e flight.
f hotel.

B **David is traveling from Chicago to London. Put his trip in the correct order.**

g → ___ → ___ → ___ → ___ → ___ → ___ → ___

a Stay in the hotel.
b Drive to the airport.
c Arrive at the hotel.
d Leave home.
e Take a bus from the airport to the hotel.
f Check in for the flight at the airport.
g Buy a plane ticket online.
h Fly to the destination.

## 10.1 GOING OUT (page 98)

A **Circle the correct word to complete the sentences.**

1 Can you *meet* / *go* me at the airport on Friday?
2 Jennifer wants to *take* / *look* her brother to lunch for his birthday.
3 We're *doing* / *having* a picnic right now.
4 I like to *get* / *meet* together with friends on the weekends.
5 Do you usually *make* / *go* shopping at the mall?
6 I never *take* / *eat* outside.

B **Complete the sentences with the words in the box.**

| art | coffee | family | hotel | shopping | walk |
|---|---|---|---|---|---|

1 Do you want to take a ______________ in the park?
2 I like to look at interesting ______________ in museums.
3 I want to take you out for ______________ to my favorite café.
4 We often get together with ______________ on the weekends.
5 I have to meet my coworker at his ______________ on Friday.
6 Maria never goes ______________ with us. She doesn't like it.

## 10.2 CLOTHES; SEASONS (page 100)

A **Complete the clothes words with vowels (*a*, *e*, *i*, *o*, *u*).**

1 I want to buy some j__ __ns and a sw__ __t__r.
2 I'm going to wear a T-sh__rt and sh__rts to the beach.
3 This store sells sh__ __s and b__ __ts.
4 I'm going to buy a winter c__ __t and h__t.
5 We usually wear p__nts and a sh__rt at work.
6 Is she going to wear a dr__ss or a sk__rt?

**B Complete the paragraph with the words in the box.**

| dry season | fall | rainy season | spring | summer | winter |
|---|---|---|---|---|---|

In Japan, we have four seasons. I love [1] ___ and [2] ___ because there are a lot of flowers then. After summer, it's [3] ___, and this is usually from September to November. Then it's [4] ___, and you can do a lot of fun activities, for example, snowboard in the mountains. We have a short [5] ___, too. It usually starts in June and ends in July, and it is *very* rainy. We don't have a [6] ___ in Japan. It's not a desert country.

## 11.1 DESCRIBING PEOPLE, PLACES, AND THINGS (page 108)

**A Match the sentences with the correct responses.**

1 This new restaurant isn't good. ___
2 Your daughter is quiet. ___
3 This is a beautiful picture. ___
4 I love beach parties. ___
5 The train was very slow today. ___
6 These children are really noisy. ___

**a** Thanks. I think the artist is wonderful.
**b** Really? It's usually fast.
**c** Yes, but they're really cute.
**d** That's true. She's really shy.
**e** I know. The food is awful.
**f** Me, too. They're exciting, and the ocean is beautiful.

**B Read the sentences and complete the words.**

1 My cousin is **b** ___, and her children are really **c** ___.
2 It's a nice, **q** ___ restaurant, and it has **w** ___ food!
3 This movie is **a** ___. It's **s** ___ and boring.
4 I love soccer games. They're always **n** ___ and **e** ___.
5 My brother's happy because he has a **n** ___ car. It's really **f** ___.

## 11.2 COLORS (page 110)

**A Unscramble the color words (1–10.) Then match the words to the colors (a–j).**

1 dre ___
2 nreeg ___
3 leub ___
4 tiwhe ___
5 weyoll ___
6 nbwor ___
7 knip ___
8 ragnoe ___
9 ygre ___
10 klacb ___

a ___
b ___
c ___
d ___
e ___
f ___
g ___
h ___
i ___
j ___

**B Match five of the colors in exercise A to the things below.**

1 some milk ___
2 a coffee with milk ___
3 some grass ___
4 the ocean ___
5 an elephant ___

## 12.1 SNACKS AND SMALL MEALS (page 118)

**A Look at the pictures. Write the words in the chart.**

| Fruit and vegetables | Meat | Dairy products | Grains | Small meals |
|---|---|---|---|---|
| | | | | |

**B Circle the correct words to complete the sentences.**

1 **A** What do you want with your crackers?
  **B** I want cheese and *tomatoes* / *coconut*, please.

2 For a small meal, I like soup and *bread* / *potato*.

3 My favorite sandwich has bread, *butter* / *orange*, and chicken.

4 Beef is very good with *bananas* / *tomatoes*.

5 My brother really likes fruit. He eats bananas and *apples* / *lamb* every day.

## 12.2 MORE FOOD, DRINKS, AND DESSERTS (page 120)

**A Complete the menu with the words in the box.**

| beans | chocolate cake | cookies | ice cream |
|---|---|---|---|
| juice | pizza | soda | |

*Meals*

Fish with rice and black
1 ______
Cheese and tomato
2 ______

*Drinks*

3 ______
Apple, orange, or pineapple
4 ______

*Desserts*

5 ______
6 ______
7 ______

**B Circle the correct words to complete the sentences.**

1 *Steak* / *Rice* is my favorite meat.

2 *Cookies* / *Green beans* are good for you because they are vegetables.

3 Do you want some *pizza* / *ice cream* for dessert?

4 I like to eat *eggs* / *water* for breakfast.

5 Did you drink any *rice* / *juice* with your meal?

6 *Chocolate cake* / *soda* is my favorite dessert.

# PROGRESS CHECK

**Can you do these things? Check (✓) what you can do. Then write your answers in your notebook.**

| UNIT 1 | Now I can ... | Prove it |
|---|---|---|
| | ☐ say countries and nationalities. | Write your country and your nationality. |
| | ☐ use *I am.* | Write two sentences about you. Use *I'm* and *I'm from.* |
| | ☐ use the alphabet to spell words. | Spell your first name and your last name. Spell your email address. |
| | ☐ ask and answer questions with *What's ... ?* and *It's ....* | Write a question and answer about personal information. Use *What's* and *It's.* |
| | ☐ check into a hotel. | Write two questions you hear at a hotel. Write answers to the questions. |
| | ☐ write a profile. | Read your profile from lesson 1.4. Find a way to improve it. Use the Accuracy check, Register check, and the new language from this unit. |

| UNIT 2 | Now I can ... | Prove it |
|---|---|---|
| | ☐ say family names and numbers. | Write the names and ages of four members of your family. Write the numbers in words. |
| | ☐ use *is* and *are.* | Write four sentences with *is* and *are*. Write about you or your family and friends. |
| | ☐ use adjectives to describe people. | Complete the sentences with adjectives. *My parents are ... My best friend is ...* |
| | ☐ use *is not* and *are not.* | Make the three sentences negative. *She's tall. We're from Seoul. They're funny.* |
| | ☐ talk about ages and birthdays. | When's your birthday? How old is your best friend? Write answers in full sentences. |
| | ☐ write a post about friends in a photo. | Read your post about friends from lesson 2.4. Find a way to improve it. Use the Accuracy check, Register check, and the new language from this unit. |

| UNIT 3 | Now I can ... | Prove it |
|---|---|---|
| | ☐ talk about rooms in my home. | Write five rooms and five things in rooms. |
| | ☐ use possessive adjectives, *'s* and *s'.* | Change the words in parentheses ( ) to possessives. *This is my* (*brother*) *bedroom.* (*He*) *bedroom is between* (*I*) *bedroom and* (*we*) (*parents*) *bedroom.* |
| | ☐ talk about furniture. | Write five or more words for furniture. |
| | ☐ use *it is.* | Complete the questions. Then answer with your own information. ________ *your home big?* ________ *near your school?* |
| | ☐ offer and accept a drink and snack. | Someone says, "Coffee?" Write two different answers. |
| | ☐ write an email about a home-share. | Read your email from lesson 3.4. Find a way to improve it. Use the Accuracy check, Register check, and the new language from this unit. |

# PROGRESS CHECK

**Can you do these things? Check (✓) what you can do. Then write your answers in your notebook.**

## UNIT 4

| Now I can … | Prove it |
|---|---|
| ☐ talk about my favorite things. | Write about five things you like, love, or want. |
| ☐ use the simple present. | Write about a thing you have and a thing you don't have. |
| ☐ say how you use technology. | Write about three ways you use your phone. |
| ☐ use *yes/no* questions in the simple present. | Complete the questions. Then write the answers with your own information. ______ *you use apps on your phone?* ______ *you and your parents chat online?* |
| ☐ ask questions to develop a conversation. | Complete the conversation. ***A*** ______ *social media?* ***B*** *Yes, I do.* ______ *?* |
| ☐ write product reviews. | Read your product reviews from lesson 4.4. Find a way to improve them. Use the Accuracy check, Register check, and the new language from this unit. |

## UNIT 5

| Now I can … | Prove it |
|---|---|
| ☐ use days and times of days with everyday activities. | Write two things you do on weekdays in the morning. Write two things you do on Saturday. |
| ☐ use the simple present and adverbs of frequency. | Complete the sentences. Write about your friends. ______ *always* ______ *on the weekend.* ______ *and* ______ *never* ______ *in the evening.* |
| ☐ tell the time and talk about routines. | What time is it now? When do you get up on weekdays? What time do you usually have dinner? Write answers in full sentences. |
| ☐ ask *yes/no* and information questions in the simple present. | Complete the questions with *do* or *does*. Then write your answers. *What time* ______ *you get up on Saturday? Where* ______ *you and your friends eat lunch on Monday?* ______ *your teacher have lunch at school?* |
| ☐ show you agree or have things in common. | Read the statements. Write responses that are true for you. *Soccer is fun.* *I never run.* |
| ☐ write a report. | Read your WRAP report from lesson 5.4. Find a way to improve it. Use the Accuracy check, Register check, and the new language from this unit. |

## UNIT 6

| Now I can … | Prove it |
|---|---|
| ☐ use words for places in a city. | Write about six places in a city. |
| ☐ use *there's / there are* with *a/an, some, a lot of, no.* | Write four true sentences for your city. Use the sentences below. *There are* ______ *in my city. / There's* ______ *in my neighborhood.* |
| ☐ use words for places in nature. | Write about six places in nature. |
| ☐ use count and non-count nouns. | Write about the plants, trees, and grass in your neighborhood. |
| ☐ ask for and give simple directions. | Write one way to ask for directions and one way to give directions. |
| ☐ write a fact sheet. | Read your fact sheet from lesson 6.4. Find a way to improve it. Use the Accuracy check, Register check, and the new language from this unit. |

# PROGRESS CHECK

**Can you do these things? Check (✓) what you can do. Then write your answers in your notebook.**

| UNIT 7 | Now I can … | Prove it |
|---|---|---|
| | ☐ use words about activities around the house. | Write three things you do around the house. |
| | ☐ use the present continuous. | Write a sentence about what you are doing right now. Write a sentence about what your teacher is doing. |
| | ☐ use transportation words. | Complete the sentences with transportation words. *I'm on the* ______ *right now. Are you* ______ *to work? We're riding our* ______ *to the park.* |
| | ☐ ask *yes/no* and information questions in the present continuous. | Write one *yes/no* question and two information questions. Use the present continuous. |
| | ☐ start a phone call. | Write a way to answer the phone. Write a question to ask people how they are. |
| | ☐ write a blog about things happening now. | Read your blog from lesson 7.4. Find a way to improve it. Use the Accuracy check, Register check, and the new language from this unit. |

| UNIT 8 | Now I can … | Prove it |
|---|---|---|
| | ☐ talk about skills. | Write five skills that your friends or people in your family have. Use *can*. |
| | ☐ use *can* to talk about ability. | Write a sentence about something you can do well and a sentence about something you can't do well. |
| | ☐ talk about work. | Write three things that people do at work. |
| | ☐ use *can* to talk about possibility. | Write two questions. Use *What … ?* and *Where … ? + can*. |
| | ☐ give opinions. | Do you think technology is good for the world? Write a short answer. |
| | ☐ write an online comment. | Read your online comment from lesson 8.4. Find a way to improve it. Use the Accuracy check, Register check, and the new language from this unit. |

| UNIT 9 | Now I can … | Prove it |
|---|---|---|
| | ☐ use travel words. | Where can you take a tour? What do you need a ticket for? Answer the questions about your city or country. |
| | ☐ use *this* and *these*. | Complete these sentences with your own ideas. *I* ______ *this* ______. *I* ______ *these* ______. |
| | ☐ talk about travel arrangements. | Think of a city in your country, or in another country. Describe the trip from your home to the city. |
| | ☐ use *like to, want to, have to, need to*. | Write four sentences about things you like to do, want to do, have to do, and need to do. |
| | ☐ ask for information in a store. | Write three questions to ask for missing information. Begin your questions with *Where … ?, How much … ?,* and *What time does … ?* Then write the answers to your questions. |
| | ☐ write a description of a place. | Read your description of a place from lesson 9.4. Find a way to improve it. Use the Accuracy check, Register check, and the new language from this unit. |

# PROGRESS CHECK

**Can you do these things? Check (✓) what you can do. Then write your answers in your notebook.**

## UNIT 10

| Now I can … | Prove it |
|---|---|
| ☐ use words for going out activities. | How many going out activities can you remember? Make a list. |
| ☐ use *be going to* in statements. | Write two sentences about what you're going to do next month. Write two sentences about what you're not going to do next year. |
| ☐ use words for clothes and seasons. | What's your favorite season? What do you usually wear to class? What do you wear when you go out with your friends? |
| ☐ ask *yes/no* and information questions with *be going to.* | Complete these questions. Then write answers for you. *Are* ______ *(you, work) this summer? What* ______ *(you, do) for your next birthday?* |
| ☐ make and respond to suggestions. | Complete the suggestions with *Why don't we* or *Let's*. Then write answers to the suggestions. ______ *meet at a café tomorrow.* ______ *go shopping after class?* |
| ☐ write an online invitation. | Read your online invitation from lesson 10.4. Find a way to improve it. Use the Accuracy check, Register check, and the new language from this unit. |

## UNIT 11

| Now I can … | Prove it |
|---|---|
| ☐ use adjectives to describe people, places, and things. | Write three sentences. Use adjectives to describe a person, a place, and a thing. |
| ☐ use *was* and *were* in statements. | Write four sentences about the past. Use *was*, *were*, *wasn't*, and *weren't*. |
| ☐ talk about colors. | Look around you. What things can you see? What color are they? Write five sentences. |
| ☐ ask questions with *was* and *were.* | Write two questions with *was* and two questions with *were.* |
| ☐ express uncertainty. | Write the capital city of these countries: Australia, Germany, India, Indonesia. In your answer, write that you're not sure. |
| ☐ write an email about things you keep from the past. | Read your email from lesson 11.4. Find a way to improve it. Use the Accuracy check, Register check, and the new language from this unit. |

## UNIT 12

| Now I can … | Prove it |
|---|---|
| ☐ talk about snacks and small meals. | Write about food you like and don't like. Write about five things. |
| ☐ use simple past statements. | Write four sentences about things you did yesterday. |
| ☐ talk about food, drinks, and desserts. | Write something you ate yesterday, or last week, for dessert. Write something you drank. |
| ☐ use simple past questions. | Write three questions to ask a partner about what he or she did last week. |
| ☐ offer and request food and drink. | Imagine you're in a restaurant. Write a question the server asks, and write your answer. |
| ☐ write a restaurant review. | Read your restaurant review from lesson 12.4. Find a way to improve it. Use the Accuracy check, Register check, and the new language from this unit. |

# PAIR WORK PRACTICE (STUDENT A)

## 1.3 EXERCISE 5C STUDENT A

1 You are Sandra, the visitor. Give your information to your partner.

2 You are the hotel clerk. Ask for your partner's information. Complete the hotel card.

**HOTEL INFORMATION CARD:**
City Bed & Breakfast

| | |
|---|---|
| **First name:** | Sandra |
| **Last name:** | Mills |
| **Number of nights:** | Three |
| **Email:** | sandra85@listmail.net |
| **Phone number:** | 367 555 0219 |
| **Company/School:** | Big City Travel |

**HOTEL INFORMATION CARD:**
Tree House Hotel

| | |
|---|---|
| **First name:** | |
| **Last name:** | |
| **Number of nights:** | |
| **Email:** | |
| **Phone number:** | |
| **Company/School:** | |

## 2.3 EXERCISE 3D STUDENT A

1 Say a person from the table. Say the incorrect birthday. Then correct yourself.

*Anna. Her birthday is August 15. No, sorry, August 13.*

| Person | Anna | Martin | Paulo | Rosa | Jacob |
|---|---|---|---|---|---|
| Incorrect birthday | August 15 | December 2 | June 5 | October 21 | April 12 |
| Correct birthday | August **13** | December **3** | **July** 5 | October **31** | April **20** |

2 Listen to your partner. Write the correct birthday. Circle the correction (the number or the month).

| Person | Gloria | Larry | Helena | Susan | Bruno |
|---|---|---|---|---|---|
| Incorrect birthday | September 13 | November 6 | May 9 | February 30 | January 25 |
| Correct birthday | | | | | |

## 4.3 EXERCISE 2D STUDENT A

1 Follow the flow chart. Use the topics in the box or your own ideas. Talk about two or three topics.

| | |
|---|---|
| laptops | music videos |
| social media | video chat |

2 Follow the flow chart. Talk about the topics your partner chooses.

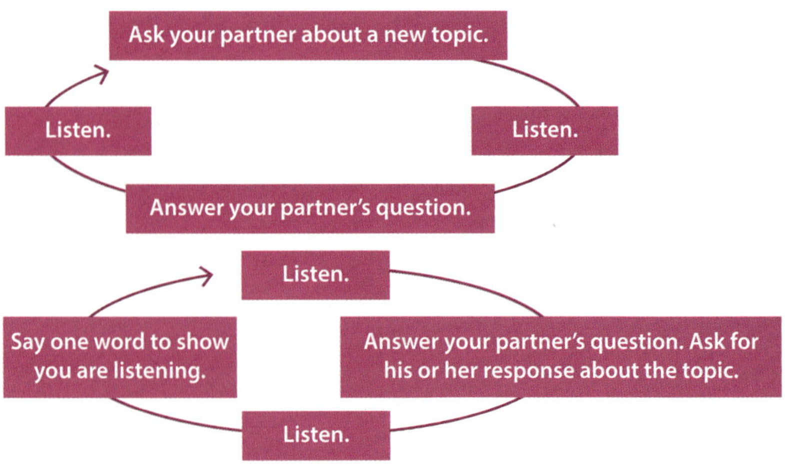

## 5.3 EXERCISE 2D STUDENT A

1 **Choose one of the jobs in the box. Don't tell your partner. Then complete the sentences about the job with *always, usually, often, sometimes, hardly ever,* or *never.***

doctor hotel clerk server student

1 I ________ get up early.
2 I ________ eat at home.
3 I ________ have free time.
4 I ________ work with friends.
5 I ________ read books.
6 I ________ send emails for work.
7 I ________ go to bed late.
8 I ________ work on the weekend.

2 **Your partner is a teacher, salesperson, chef, or artist. Ask questions and guess the job.**

Do you get up early?

Always.

Do you eat at home?

Never.

Are you a … ?

3 **Your partner asks you questions. Answer with one or two words. Your partner guesses your job.**

## 6.3 EXERCISE 2D STUDENT A

**Give the directions below to Student B. Student B repeats and you listen. Is it correct?**

1 Turn left here. Then go straight. It's on the left.
2 It's over there. Go two blocks. Turn right. Then turn right again.
3 Turn left here. Then turn left again. It's on the right.

## 7.3 EXERCISE 2D STUDENT A

**Imagine you're talking to your partner on the phone. Say the news below, and your partner reacts. Then your partner says some news to you, and you react. Take turns.**

1 My new job is really boring.
2 I'm having a cup of coffee.
3 It's my birthday today.
4 My dog is eating my lunch.
5 The people at my new college are friendly.
6 I'm on the subway.

## 8.3 EXERCISE 2D STUDENT A

1 **Say the sentences below to your partner. Add information to explain or say more. Then your partner gives his or her opinion.**

- Basketball is/isn't my favorite sport. I mean, …
- I can/can't read music. It's difficult/easy. I mean, …
- I like / don't like art. I mean, …
- I think computer skills are important. I mean, …

Basketball is my favorite sport. I mean, I can play really well, and it's fun.

I don't like basketball. I think soccer is the best sport.

2 **Listen to your partner. Then give your opinion.**

## 10.3 EXERCISE 2D STUDENT A

**Your partner makes a suggestion. You say you can't and give a reason. Take turns.**

| Suggestion | Reason |
|---|---|
| have coffee now | (Your partner) |
| (Your partner) | go home at lunchtime |
| have a meeting on Monday | (Your partner) |
| (Your partner) | go to the supermarket |
| go shopping on Saturday | (Your partner) |
| (Your partner) | work late |

Let's have coffee now.

I'm sorry, but I can't. I have to go to a meeting.

## 11.3 EXERCISE 2D STUDENT A

1 **Ask your partner these questions. Listen to their answers. Then tell your partner the correct answers.**

| Question | Answer |
|---|---|
| What was Leonardo DiCaprio's name in *Titanic*? | Jack Dawson |
| Where is the singer Carol Konka from? | Brazil |
| What country is *Crouching Tiger Hidden Dragon* from? | China |
| What was Elvis's last name? | Presley |
| What band is Chris Martin in? | Coldplay |
| What was the dog's name in *The Wizard of Oz*? | Toto |

What was Leonardo DiCaprio's name in *Titanic*?

Uh, I think it was Jack. / Um, I have no idea.

It was Jack Dawson.

2 **Answer your partner's questions. Use expressions of uncertainty for answers you don't know or are unsure about.**

# PAIR WORK PRACTICE (STUDENT B)

## 1.3 EXERCISE 5C STUDENT B

1 **You are the hotel clerk. Ask for your partner's information. Complete the hotel card.**

2 **You are Tom, the visitor. Give your information to your partner.**

**HOTEL INFORMATION CARD:**
City Bed & Breakfast

| | |
|---|---|
| **First name:** | |
| **Last name:** | |
| **Number of nights:** | |
| **Email:** | |
| **Phone number:** | |
| **Company/School:** | |

**HOTEL INFORMATION CARD:**
Tree House Hotel

| | |
|---|---|
| **First name:** | Tom |
| **Last name:** | Delaney |
| **Number of nights:** | four |
| **Email:** | delaneyt@techmail.com |
| **Phone number:** | 437 555 8812 |
| **Company/School:** | Warton Homes |

## 2.3 EXERCISE 3D STUDENT B

1 **Listen to your partner say the incorrect birthdays, and then the correct birthdays. Write the correct birthday. Underline the correction (the number or the month).**

| Person | Anna | Martin | Paulo | Rosa | Jacob |
|---|---|---|---|---|---|
| Incorrect birthday | August 15 | December 2 | June 5 | October 21 | April 12 |
| Correct birthday | | | | | |

2 **Say a person from the table. Say the incorrect birthday. Then correct yourself.**

*Gloria. Her birthday is September 13. No, sorry, September 30.*

| Person | Gloria | Larry | Helena | Susan | Bruno |
|---|---|---|---|---|---|
| Incorrect birthday | September 13 | November 6 | May 9 | February 30 | January 25 |
| Correct birthday | September **30** | November **16** | **March** 9 | February **20** | January 2**4** |

## 4.3 EXERCISE 2D STUDENT B

1 **Follow the flow chart. Talk about the topics your partner chooses.**

2 **Follow the flow chart. Use the topics in the box or your own ideas. Talk about two or three topics.**

| | |
|---|---|
| laptops | music videos |
| social media | video chat |

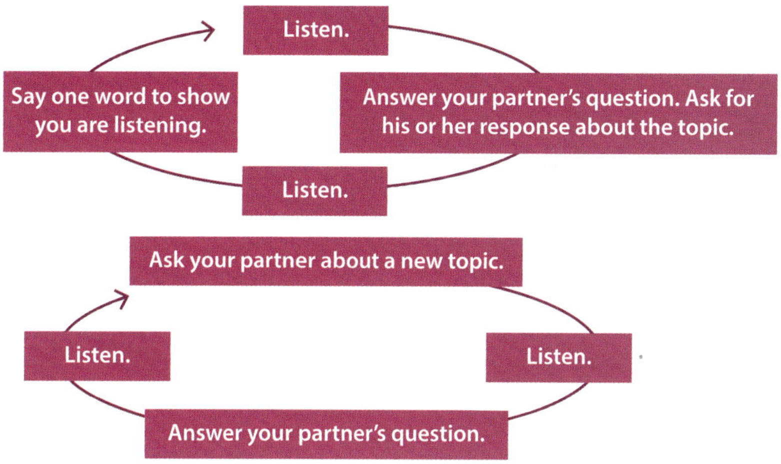


## 5.3 EXERCISE 2D STUDENT B

1 **Choose one of the jobs in the box. Don't tell your partner. Then complete the sentences about the job with *always*, *usually*, *often*, *sometimes*, *hardly ever*, or *never*.**

artist chef salesperson teacher

**1** I ________ get up early.
**2** I ________ eat at home.
**3** I ________ have free time.
**4** I ________ work with friends.
**5** I ________ read books.
**6** I ________ send emails for work.
**7** I ________ go to bed late.
**8** I ________ work on the weekend.

2 **Your partner asks you questions. Answer with one or two words. Your partner guesses your job.**

*Do you get up early?* *Always.* *Do you eat at home?* *Never.* *Are you a … ?*

3 **Your partner is a student, doctor, server, or hotel clerk. Ask questions and guess the job.**

## 6.3 EXERCISE 2D STUDENT B

**Give the directions below to Student A. Student A repeats and you listen. Is it correct?**

**1** Turn left. Go straight. That's San Gabriel Street.
**2** Go straight. Then turn right. It's on the right.
**3** Turn right here. Turn right again. Then turn left. It's on the right.

## 7.3 EXERCISE 2D STUDENT B

**Imagine you're talking to your partner on the phone. Your partner says some news to you, and you react. Then you say the news below, and your partner reacts. Take turns.**

1 I'm cooking dinner.
2 I'm at a party on the beach.
3 I'm watching TV.
4 I'm working on Saturday and Sunday.
5 I have a new plane.
6 My train is three hours late.

## 8.3 EXERCISE 2D STUDENT B

1 **Listen to your partner. Then give your opinion.**

Basketball is my favorite sport. I mean, I can play really well, and it's fun.

I don't like basketball. I think soccer is the best sport.

2 **Say the sentences to your partner. Add information to explain or say more. Then your partner gives his or her opinion.**

- Friday is/isn't my favorite day. I mean, …
- I like / don't like music. I mean, …
- I can/can't snowboard. It's difficult/easy. I mean, …
- I think good food is important. I mean, …

## 10.3 EXERCISE 2D STUDENT B

**You make a suggestion. Your partner says he/she can't and gives a reason. Take turns.**

| Suggestion | Reason for refusal |
|---|---|
| (Your partner) | go to a meeting |
| have lunch | (Your partner) |
| (Your partner) | go out |
| take a walk after work | (Your partner) |
| (Your partner) | study this weekend |
| watch a movie tonight | (Your partner) |

Let's have coffee now.

I'm sorry, but I can't. I have to go to a meeting.

## 11.3 EXERCISE 2D STUDENT B

1 **Answer your partner's questions. Use expressions of uncertainty for answers you don't know or are unsure.**

2 **Ask your partner these questions. Listen to their answers. Then tell your partner the correct answers.**

| Question | Answer |
|---|---|
| What was Kate Winslet's name in *Titanic*? | Rose |
| Where is the band *Awesome City Club* from? | Japan |
| How many *Pirates of the Caribbean* movies was Johnny Depp in? | five |
| What is Shakira's last name? | Mebarak Ripoll |
| What band was John Lennon in? | The Beatles |
| What animals are in *101 Dalmatians*? | dogs |

What was Leonardo DiCaprio's name in *Titanic*?

Uh, I think it was Jack. / Um, I have no idea.

It was Jack Dawson.